Study Guide

Criminal Justice in America

SIXTH EDITION

George F. Cole
The University of Connecticut

Christopher E. Smith
Michigan State University

Prepared by

Sameer Hinduja
Florida Atlantic University

 WADSWORTH
CENGAGE Learning

Australia • Brazil • Japan • Korea • Mexico • Singapore • Spain • United Kingdom • United States

For product information and technology assistance, contact us at **Cengage Learning Customer & Sales Support, 1-800-354-9706**

For permission to use material from this text or product, submit all requests online at **www.cengage.com/permissions** Further permissions questions can be emailed to **permissionrequest@cengage.com**

ISBN-13: 978-0-495-81087-2
ISBN-10: 0-495-81087-8

Wadsworth
20 Davis Drive
Belmont, CA 94002-3098
USA

Cengage Learning is a leading provider of customized learning solutions with office locations around the globe, including Singapore, the United Kingdom, Australia, Mexico, Brazil, and Japan. Locate your local office at: **www.cengage.com/global**

Cengage Learning products are represented in Canada by Nelson Education, Ltd.

To learn more about Wadsworth, visit **www.cengage.com/wadsworth**

Purchase any of our products at your local college store or at our preferred online store **www.CengageBrain.com**

Printed in the United States of America
1 2 3 4 5 6 7 13 12 11 10 09

TABLE OF CONTENTS

CRIMINAL JUSTICE IN AMERICA, 6TH EDITION

STUDY GUIDE

PART V: CONTEMPORARY ISSUES IN CRIMINAL JUSTICE

THE CRIMINAL JUSTICE SYSTEM

OUTLINE

- The Goals of Criminal Justice
- Criminal Justice in a Federal System
- Criminal Justice as a Social System
- Characteristics of the Criminal Justice System
- Operations of Criminal Justice Agencies
- The Flow of Decision Making in the Criminal Justice System
- Crime and Justice in a Multicultural Society

CHAPTER 1
THE CRIMINAL JUSTICE SYSTEM

LEARNING OBJECTIVES

After reading the material in this chapter, students should be able to:

1. Understand the goals of the criminal justice system

2. Recognize the different responsibilities of federal and state criminal justice operations

3. Analyze criminal justice from a system perspective

4. Identify the authority and relationships of the main criminal justice agencies, and understand the steps in the decision-making process for criminal cases

5. Understand the criminal justice "wedding cake" concept as well as the Due Process Model and Crime Control Model

6. Recognize the possible causes of racial disparities in criminal justice

CHAPTER SUMMARY

The three goals of criminal justice are doing justice, controlling crime, and preventing crime. The dual court system in the U.S. provides for both a national system and state systems of criminal justice that enforce laws, try cases, and punish offenders. Criminal justice is a system made up of a number of parts or subsystems—police, courts, and corrections. Exchange is a key concept for the analysis of criminal justice processes. The four major characteristics of the criminal justice system are discretion, resource dependence, sequential tasks, and filtering. The processing of cases in the criminal justice system involves a series of decisions by police officers, prosecutors, judges, probation officers, wardens, and parole board members, and can be divided into thirteen steps spread throughout the stages of law enforcement, adjudication, and corrections. As the four-layered criminal justice "wedding cake" model proposed by Walker indicates, not all cases are treated equally.

Herbert Packer provides two competing models of the criminal justice system: the more idealistic due process model, with its emphasis on freedom and the rights of individuals, and the more pragmatic crime control model, with its emphasis on efficiency and order. Fairness and equal treatment are key American values, but because the U.S. is a highly diverse society, discrimination and disparities often occur, and the criminal justice system is no exception.

Theorists generally offer one of three explanations for racial disparities in criminal justice: minorities commit more crime, the criminal justice system is racist, or the criminal justice system expresses the racism of society.

CHAPTER OUTLINE

I. THE GOALS OF CRIMINAL JUSTICE

A. Doing Justice
Without a system founded on justice there would be little difference between criminal justice in the United States and that in authoritarian countries. Elements of the goal of justice include: offenders will be held fully accountable for their actions; the rights of persons who have contact with the system will be protected; like offenses will be treated alike; officials will take into account relevant differences among offenders and offenses.

B. Controlling Crime
The criminal justice system is designed to control crime by apprehending, prosecuting, convicting, and punishing those members of the community who do not live according to the law. There is a constraint on that goal: efforts to control crime must be carried out within the framework of law.

C. Preventing Crime
The criminal justice system may exert a deterrent effect on future criminal activity. Citizens can also take an active role in crime prevention through simple precautions. Unfortunately many people leave homes and cars unlocked, and take other actions that facilitate crime.

II. CRIMINAL JUSTICE IN A FEDERAL SYSTEM

A. Two Justice Systems
The U.S. criminal justice system is based on the concept of federalism, in which power is divided between the national and regional (state) levels. The federal and state systems of government are sometimes in conflict.

B. Expansion of Federal Government
The United States government has greatly expanded its role in law enforcement in recent years, especially after September 11th. With the development of the Department of Homeland Security, many more crimes are now defined as federal offenses.

III. CRIMINAL JUSTICE AS A SOCIAL SYSTEM

Since criminal justice is a system—a complex whole made up of interdependent parts—the agencies and processes of criminal justice are linked. The actions of the police, for example, have an impact on the other parts of the system, such as prosecution, courts, and corrections.

Key to any system is *exchange*, the mutual transfer of resources among individual actors, each of whom has goals that he or she cannot accomplish alone. Plea bargaining is an obvious example of exchange. The prosecutor and defense attorney reach agreement on the plea and sentence. Each actor, including the defendant and the judge, gains a benefit as a result. The concept of exchange reminds us that decisions are the products of interactions among individuals in the system and that the subsystems of criminal justice are linked together by the actions of individual decision makers.

IV. CHARACTERISTICS OF THE CRIMINAL JUSTICE SYSTEM

A. Discretion
At all levels of the justice process, officials have significant ability to act according to their own judgment and conscience. Police officers, prosecutors, judges, and correctional officials may consider a wide variety of circumstances and exercise many options as they dispose of a case. The need for discretionary power has been justified primarily on two counts: resources and justice.

B. Resource Dependence:
Criminal justice does not produce its own resources, but is dependent on others for them. It must therefore develop special links with people responsible for the allocation of resources—that is, the political decision makers. Criminal justice actors must be responsive to the legislators, mayors, and city council members who control their funding. Justice officials seek to maintain a positive image in news reports and to keep voters happy.

C. Sequential Tasks:
Every part of the criminal justice system has distinct tasks that are carried out sequentially.

D. Filtering:
The criminal justice process may be viewed as a filtering process through which cases are screened: some advance to the next level of decision making, others are either rejected, or the conditions under which they are processed are changed.

V. OPERATIONS OF CRIMINAL JUSTICE AGENCIES

A. Police
The many public organizations in the United States engaged in law enforcement activities are characterized by complexity and fragmentation. Only fifty are federal law enforcement agencies; the rest are state and local.

4

The responsibilities of police organizations include keeping the peace, apprehending law violators and fighting crime, engaging in crime prevention, and providing social services.

B. Courts

The dual court system is used in the United States. Each state has its own separate judicial structures in addition to the national structure. Interpretation of the law can vary from state to state. Judges have discretion to apply the law as they feel it should be applied until they are overruled by a higher court. Courts are responsible for adjudication, which involves determining whether defendants are guilty according to fair procedures.

C. Corrections

On any given day, nearly 7 million Americans are under the supervision of the corrections system. Only about a third of convicted offenders are actually incarcerated; the remainder are under supervision in the community through probation, parole, community-based halfway houses, work release programs, and supervised activities. The federal government, all the states, most counties, and all but the smallest cities are engaged in the corrections enterprise. Increasingly, nonprofit private organizations such as the YMCA have contracted with governments to perform correctional services. For-profit businesses have undertaken the construction and administration of institutions through contracts with governments.

VI. THE FLOW OF DECISION MAKING IN THE SYSTEM

A. Steps in the Decision-Making Process

Remember that formal procedures outlined may not always depict reality. The system as depicted appears to be an assembly line for making decisions about defendants. The actual process is shaped by variables such as discretion, filtering, and exchange.

1. **Investigation**: Police are normally dependent on a member of the community to report the offense.
2. **Arrest**: Taking a person into custody when police determine there is enough evidence indicating a particular person has committed a crime. Arrests are sometimes based on a warrant, but most times are not.
3. **Booking**: Procedure by which an administrative record is made of the arrest; a suspect may be fingerprinted, photographed, interrogated, and placed in a lineup for identification by the victim or witnesses. All suspects must be warned that they have the right to counsel, that they may remain silent, and that any statement they make may later be used against them.
4. **Charging**: Prosecuting attorneys determine whether there is reasonable cause to believe that an offense was committed and that the suspect committed it.
5. **Initial Appearance**: Suspects must be brought before a judge to be given formal notice of the charge for which they are being held, to be advised of their rights, and to be given the opportunity to post bail. The judge determines if there is sufficient evidence to hold the suspect for further criminal processing.

6. **Preliminary Hearing/Grand Jury**: The preliminary hearing, used in about half the states, allows a judge to determine whether probable cause exists to believe that the accused committed a known crime within the jurisdiction of the court.

7. **Indictment/Information**: The prosecutor prepares the formal charging document and enters it before the court.

8. **Arraignment**: The accused person is next taken before a judge to hear the indictment or information read and is asked to enter a plea. The judge must determine if a guilty plea is made voluntarily, and whether the person has full knowledge of the possible consequences of the plea.

9. **Trial**: For the relatively small percentage of defendants who plead not guilty, the right to a trial by an impartial jury is guaranteed by the Sixth Amendment for defendants facing charges which carry six months or more of imprisonment. Most trials are summary or bench trials conducted by a judge without a jury. It is estimated that only about 10-15% of cases go to trial and only about 5% are heard by juries.

10. **Sentencing**: The judge's intent is to make the sentence suitable to the particular offender within the requirements of the law and in accordance with the retribution (punishment) and rehabilitation goals of the system.

11. **Appeal**: Defendants found guilty may appeal their convictions to a higher court based on claims that the rules of procedure were not properly followed or that the law forbidding the behavior is unconstitutional. Defendants lose about 80 percent of appeals. A successful appeal typically leads to a new trial rather than release.

12. **Corrections**: Probation, intermediate sanctions, and incarceration are the sanctions most generally imposed and supervised by the corrections subsystem.

13. **Release**: Release may be accomplished through serving the full sentence imposed by the court or by returning to the community under supervision of a parole officer with restrictive conditions.

B. The Criminal Justice Wedding Cake

Cases can be differentiated according to the way in which criminal justice officials and the public react to them.

Layer 1: The few "celebrated" cases that are exceptional, get great public attention, result in a jury trial, and often have extended appeals.

Layer 2: Felonies that are deemed to be serious by officials, e.g., crimes of violence committed by persons with long criminal records against victims unknown to them.

Layer 3: Felonies by offenders who are seen as of lesser concern than those in Layer 2; many cases are filtered out of the system, and plea bargaining is encouraged.

Layer 4: Misdemeanors encompassing 90% of all cases handled in the criminal justice system; processes are speedy and informal, and fines, probation, or short jail sentences result. Assembly-line justice reigns.

C. Crime Control versus Due Process

Herbert Packer's two competing models describe two methods of how justice is dispensed. Packer recognizes that the administration of criminal justice operates within contemporary American society and is therefore influenced by cultural forces that, in turn, determine the models' usefulness.

1. **Crime Control Model: Order as a Value**
   The goal of crime control is the repression of criminal conduct. This model stresses efficiency, and the process can be described as administrative and filtering. The main decision point is completed by on police and prosecutors, and they use discretion as the basis for decision making. The best analogy for this model is the "assembly line."

2. **Due Process Model: Law as a Value**
   The goal of the due process model is to preserve individual liberties. This model stresses reliability (i.e., accurate decisions about guilt and innocence), and the process can best be described as adversarial. The main decision point is in the courtroom (i.e., trial), and they use law as the basis for decision making. The best analogy for this model is the "obstacle course."

VII. CRIME AND JUSTICE IN A MULTI-CULTURAL SOCIETY

A. **Disparity and Discrimination**
   African-Americans, Hispanics, and other racial and ethnic minorities are drawn into the criminal justice system at much higher rates than the white majority. The term *disparity* refers to a difference between groups, which may or may not be attributable to legitimate factors. *Discrimination* occurs when groups are differentially treated without regard to their behavior or qualifications.

B. **Explaining Disparities**
   Most attempts to explain the disparities in the criminal justice system fall into one of three categories:

   1. **People of Color Commit More Crimes**: There is no evidence of an ethnic link to criminal behavior. There is a link between crime and economic disadvantages which disproportionately affect these minority groups. Unemployment rates are higher and average family income is lower among these minority groups. Because most crime is interracial rather than interracial, minority group members in poor neighborhoods also suffer from more significant victimization rates. On average, African-Americans and Hispanics are arrested more often and for more serious crimes than whites. Analysts question whether crime control efforts should shift to an emphasis on reducing social problems that may contribute to crime.

   2. **The Criminal Justice System Is Racist**: Research indicates that people of color are arrested more often for drug offenses even though they do not engage in drug use more often than whites. Also, unfounded arrests of African-Americans occur at four times the rate of unfounded arrests of whites. The rate of incarceration for poor and minority citizens is greater than even their higher offense rates would justify. Disparities need not be the result of overt racism. For example, if police patrols concentrate on poor neighborhoods, more arrests will be made there than elsewhere. Poor people are less likely to make bail or hire their own attorneys, two factors that may contribute to a higher imprisonment rate.

3. **America Is A Racist Society**. There is some evidence of racism in the way that society asks the criminal justice system to operate. For example, federal sentencing guidelines punish users of crack cocaine about one hundred times more harshly than users of powder cocaine, even though the drugs are nearly identical. The only difference is that whites tend to use the powder form while people of color tend to use crack. Sentencing studies find a stronger link between unemployment and sentencing than between crime rates and sentencing. This suggests that prisons are being used to confine people who cannot find jobs. Drug law enforcement is aimed primarily at low-level dealers in minority neighborhoods. There are numerous examples of African-American and Hispanic professionals who have been falsely arrested when police saw a person of color whom they believed was "out of place."

REVIEW OF KEY TERMS

Define each of the following:

Adjudication

Arrest

Crime control model

Discretion

Discrimination

Disparity

Dual court system

Due process model

Exchange

Federalism

Felonies

Filtering process

Indictment

Information

Misdemeanors

Plea bargain

System

Warrant

9

SELF-TEST SECTION

KEY TERMS

Fill in the appropriate term for each statement:

1. _____ is the authority to make decisions using one's own judgment and conscience, which provides the basis of adapting the administration of justice to individuals and circumstances.

2. _____ occur when the defense attorney and prosecuting attorney reach an agreement regarding the sentence of an accused in exchange for a "guilty" plea.

3. _____ is the physical taking of a person into custody.

4. _____ is a document charging an individual with a specific crime prepared by a prosecuting attorney and presented to a court at a preliminary hearing.

5. A _____ has a separate state and national court system. Each case is tried in the jurisdiction in which the law was broken.

6. _____ consists of separate judicial structures for states and for the national government.

7. _____ is the unequal treatment of one group by the criminal justice system.

8. _____ is a complex whole consisting of interdependent parts whose operations are directed toward goals and are influenced by the environment within which they function.

9. _____ is a characteristic of the criminal justice system that describes how one subsystem must complete its responsibilities before a case is passed to the authority of another subsystem.

10. _____ depicts the criminal justice system as emphasizing reliable decisions that protect individuals' liberty through an adversarial process based on law.

11. _____ is a court order authorizing law enforcement officials to take certain actions, for example, to arrest suspects or to search premises.

12. _____ occurs when differential treatment of individuals occurs based on race, ethnicity, gender, sexual orientation or economic status rather than behavior or qualifications.

13. _____ are serious crimes carrying penalties of one year or more imprisonment.

14. _____ is the process of determining whether or not a defendant is guilty.

15. _____ is a mutual transfer of resources or information that underlies the motivations and decisions of actors within the criminal justice system.

16. _____ is a document returned by a grand jury as a "true bill" charging an individual with a specific crime.

17. _____ are less serious offenses carrying penalties of no more than one year of incarceration.

18. _____ depicts the criminal justice system as one that emphasizes efficient repression of crime through the exercise of discretion in administrative processing of cases.

FILL-IN-THE-BLANK EXERCISE

Prosecutors exercise **1.** _____ in making decisions about which cases will leave the criminal justice system through the **2.** _____ and which cases will be discussed with criminal defense attorneys in the **3.** _____ process that obtains convictions without taking cases to trial.

In states that do not initiate formal charges by having a prosecutor file an **4.** _____, a group of citizens, known as the **5.** _____, decides whether or not there is sufficient evidence to pursue a case. If they find the existence of sufficient evidence, they issue an **6.** _____.

Although it does not accurately characterize the processing of most cases in the criminal justice system, **7.** _____ was developed by **8.** _____ to illustrate how the system's primary goal in some cases could be to preserve individual liberty through careful, reliable determinations of guilt or innocence.

MULTIPLE CHOICE

1.1. Which of the following is a goal of the American criminal justice system?
a) consolidating power at the local level
b) preventing crime
c) consolidating power at the federal level
d) dramatizing crime
e) all of the above are goals of the criminal justice system

1.2. Which of the following statements about the American criminal justice system is TRUE?
a) Citizens have authority to enforce the law.
b) Most people take steps to protect themselves against crime.
c) There is little difference between the U.S. criminal justice system and the criminal justice systems found in authoritarian countries.
d) Criminal justice officials are limited by the constitutional rights of individuals.
e) Criminal justice officials never fall short of doing justice.

1.3. Which of the following statements about discretion within the American system of criminal justice is TRUE?
a) Discretion does not exist within the American system of criminal justice.
b) Discretion exists but for only a few participants.
c) Discretion exists for all participants, but it does not limit the values of the American system.
d) Discretion exists, and its use limits the values of the American system.
e) Discretion in the American system, but only for judges.

1.4. Which of the following statements about the American system of criminal justice is TRUE?
a) Very few suspects who are arrested are then prosecuted, tried, and convicted.
b) All suspects who are arrested are then prosecuted, tried, and convicted.
c) No suspects who are arrested are then prosecuted, tried, and convicted.
d) A large percentage of suspects who are arrested are then prosecuted, tried, and convicted.
e) None of the above statements are true.

1.5. Which of the following is an attribute of the American system of criminal justice?
a) mandatory actions
b) resource dependence
c) independence of actors
d) rigidity of institutions
e) independent subsystems

1.6. How many state and local law enforcement agencies exist within the American system of criminal justice?
   a) roughly 5,000
   b) roughly 7,000
   c) roughly 10,000
   d) roughly 18,000
   e) roughly 35,000

1.7. In which layer of the "criminal justice wedding cake" (see below) would the O.J. Simpson murder case belong?

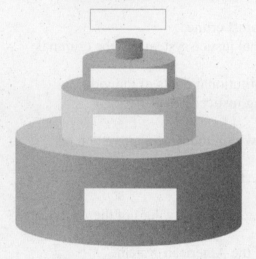

   a) Layer 1
   b) Layer 2
   c) Layer 3
   d) Layer 4
   e) Layer 5

1.8. Which state does NOT have a state law enforcement agency?
   a) California
   b) Ohio
   c) New York
   d) South Dakota
   e) Hawaii

1.9. Which of the following is most likely to be a federal crime?
   a) assault
   b) larceny
   c) arson
   d) espionage
   e) auto theft

1.10. Which of the following are major duties of police agencies?
a) keeping the peace
b) apprehending criminals
c) providing social services
d) preventing crime
e) all of the above

1.11. Which of the following functions of the police is being performed by a police officer who is directing traffic?
a) solving crime
b) apprehending criminals
c) providing social services
d) preventing crime
e) all of the above

1.12. Which of the following functions of the police is being performed by a police officer who provides emergency aid?
a) solving crime
b) apprehending criminals
c) providing social services
d) preventing crime
e) all of the above

1.13. Which of the following activities accounts for the smallest amount of an officer's time?
a) keeping the peace
b) apprehending criminals
c) providing social services
d) preventing crime
e) completing paperwork

1.14. Which of the following engage in corrections?
a) federal government
b) state government
c) most counties
d) most cities
e) all of the above

1.15. Which of the following issues has increasingly occupied the resources of the Federal Bureau of Investigations, diminishing its role in other criminal investigations?
a) domestic violence
b) drug enforcement
c) homeland security
d) immigration
e) homicide

1.16. The right to a trial by an impartial jury is guaranteed by which of the following amendments to the Constitution??
a) First Amendment
b) Fifth Amendment
c) Sixth Amendment
d) Eighth Amendment
e) Tenth Amendment

1.17. The Department of Homeland Security oversees which of the following agencies?
a) the Federal Bureau of Investigation
b) the Central Intelligence Agency
c) the Bureau of Alcohol, Tobacco, and Firearms
d) the Immigration and Naturalization Service
e) the Government Accounting Office

1.18. Which of the following does the crime control model stress?
a) freedom
b) order
c) law
d) socialism
e) all of these

1.19. Where are accused offenders typically placed while awaiting arraignment?
a) a holding cell
b) a prison
c) a county jail
d) a community facility
e) a squad car

1.20. According to the chart below, which level of government is most likely to run correctional institutions?

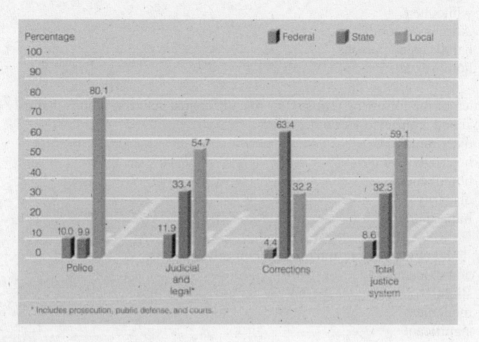

a) Federal
b) State
c) Local
d) State and local have about the same probability
e) Federal and local have about the same probability

1.21. What layer of the criminal justice wedding cake contains ninety percent of all cases?
a) Layer 1 (celebrated cases)
b) Layer 2 (serious felony cases)
c) Layer 3 (less important felony cases)
d) Layer 4 (misdemeanor cases)
e) Layer 5 (federal cases)

1.22. Which of the following is NOT a layer of the criminal justice wedding cake?
a) Layer 1 (celebrated cases)
b) Layer 2 (serious felony cases)
c) Layer 3 (less important felony cases)
d) Layer 4 (misdemeanor cases)
e) Layer 5 (federal cases)

1.23. Which of the following group was on the minds of those who framed the Fourteenth Amendment's equal protection clause?
   a) women
   b) white men
   c) African-Americans
   d) handicapped persons
   e) homosexuals

1.24. Which of the following terms refers to a difference between groups that may be explained legitimately or otherwise?
   a) discrimination
   b) heterogeneity
   c) homogeneity
   d) disparity
   e) impartiality

1.25. The link between crime and economic disadvantage is...
   a) non-existent
   b) slight
   c) moderate
   d) significant
   e) a universal law of causal and effect

TRUE/FALSE

1.1. _____ All laws are applied fairly in the United States.

1.2. _____ The easiest goal of the American system of criminal justice is to do justice.

1.3. _____ The U.S. Constitution does not provide for a national police force.

1.4. _____ There are no federal law enforcement agencies in the U.S.

1.5. _____ Under the National Stolen Property Act, the FBI may investigate thefts of more than $5,000 in value.

1.6. _____ Even though white women are more likely than African American women to be carrying contraband through customs, African American women are nine times more likely to be stopped than white women.

1.7. _____ Discretion means that all actors in the criminal justice system enforce laws equally every time.

1.8. _____ The subsystems of the American system of criminal justice are interdependent.

1.9. _____ Eighty percent of American police operate at the federal level.

1.10. _____ African Americans are treated fairly within the American system of criminal justice.

1.11. _____ All fifty states in the U. S. have state law enforcement agencies.

1.12. _____ The U. S. criminal justice system processes most of its cases at the federal level.

1.13. _____ State courts are required by the U. S. Supreme Court to decide all cases in a similar fashion.

1.14. _____ The crime control model emphasizes individual rights.

1.15. _____ U.S. citizens have the authority to arrest other citizens.

1.16. _____ The due process model emphasizes law as a value.

1.17. _____ The drafters of the Fourteenth Amendment's equal protection clause were concerned solely with women's rights.

1.18. _____ There is a large disparity between the sentences imposed upon those convicted for possession of crack cocaine and those convicted for possession of powder cocaine.

1.19. _____ Some have argued that the "War on Drugs" was designed to disadvantage black youths.

1.20. _____ The link between crime and economic disadvantage is not really significant.

ANSWER KEY

Key Terms

1. discretion [p. 12, LO4]
2. plea bargains [p.11, LO4]
3. arrest [p.18, LO2]
4. information [p.19, LO4]
5. dual court system [p.15, LO3]
6. federalism [p.6, LO3]
7. disparity [p.24, LO4]
8. system [p.11, LO3]
9. filtering process [p.13, LO3]
10. due process [p.22, LO5]
11. warrant [p.18, LO4]
12. discrimination [p.24, LO6]
13. felonies [p.21, LO5]
14. adjudication [p.15, LO4]
15. exchange [p.11, LO4]
16. indictment [p. 19, LO4]
17. misdemeanors [p. 22, LO5]
18. crime control [p. 22, LO6]

Fill-in-the-Blank

1. discretion [p.12, LO4]
2. filtering process [p.13, LO4]
3. plea bargaining [p.11, LO4]
4. information [p. 19, LO4]
5. grand jury [p.19, LO4]
6. indictment [p.19, LO4]
7. due process [p. 22, LO5]
8. Herbert Packer [p. 22, LO5]

Multiple Choice

1.1. B [p. 6, LO1]
1.2. D [p. 7, LO2]
1.3. D [p. 12, LO4]
1.4. A [p. 13, LO3]
1.5. B [p. 13, LO3]
1.6. D [p. 15, LO2]
1.7. A [p. 21, LO5]
1.8. E [p. 15, LO2]
1.9. D [p. 7, LO2]
1.10. E [p. 5, LO1]
1.11. C [p. 15, LO3]
1.12. C [p. 15, LO3]
1.13. B [p. 15, LO3]
1.14. E [p. 15-16, LO3]
1.15. C [p. 9, LO2]
1.16. C [p. 19, LO5]
1.17. D [p. 9, LO2]
1.18. B [p. 22, LO5]
1.19. A [p. 18, LO5]
1.20. B [p. 10, LO2]
1.21. D [p. 22, LO5]
1.22. E [p. 22, LO5]
1.23. C [p. 24, LO5]
1.24. D [p. 24, LO6]
1.25. D [p. 26, LO6]

True/False

1.1. F [p. 5, LO1]
1.2. F [p. 5, LO1]
1.3. T [p. 7, LO2]
1.4. F [p. 7, LO2]
1.5. T [p. 8, LO2]
1.6. T [p. 24, LO6]
1.7. F [p. 12, LO3]
1.8. T [p. 14, LO3]
1.9. F [p. 14-15, LO3]
1.10. F [p. 26, LO6]
1.11. F [p. 15, LO2]
1.12. F [p. 21, LO5]
1.13. F [p. 15, LO4]
1.14. F [p. 22, LO5]
1.15. F [p. 6, LO1]
1.16. T [p. 23, LO5]
1.17. F [p. 24, LO6]
1.18. T [p. 27-28, LO6]
1.19. T [p. 7, LO6]
1.20. F [p. 26, LO6]

WORKSHEET 1.1: SYSTEM ATTRIBUTES

Imagine that you are a county prosecutor. Briefly describe how the attributes of the criminal justice system (discretion, resource dependence, sequential tasks, and filtering) would affect your relationships, decisions, and actions with respect to each of the following.

Police: _____

_____

_____

_____

Defense Attorneys: _____

_____

_____

_____

Trial Judges: _____

_____

_____

_____

News Media: _____

_____

_____

_____

County Commissioners: _____

_____

_____

_____

WORKSHEET 1.2: STEPS IN THE PROCESS

Briefly describe what happens at each of the following steps in the justice process.

Booking: _____

_____

_____

Preliminary
Hearing: _____

_____

_____

Grand Jury Proceeding: _____

_____

_____

Arraignment: _____

_____

_____

Trial: _____

_____

_____

Sentencing
: _____

_____

_____

Appeal: _____

_____

_____

WORKSHEET 1.3: EXPLAINING THE AMERICAN SYSTEM

A group of visiting police cadets from the Ukraine is touring your university. They are from a country that is attempting to create new governing institutions and processes after gaining independence from the old Soviet Union. While having lunch with the cadets, they ask you to tell them about the characteristics of the American criminal justice system. How would you explain to them the impact of the following characteristics? Use examples to enhance your explanation.

Discretion _____

_____

_____

_____

Filtering: _____

_____

_____

_____

Exchange Relations: _____

_____

_____

_____

Sequential Operations: _____

_____

_____

_____

WORKSHEET 1.4: CRIME CONTROL VERSUS DUE PROCESS

The two models of the American criminal justice process—Crime Control and Due Process—present stark contrasts in many ways. To test your understanding of these models, identify two advantages (or benefits) and two disadvantages (or costs) of each model. Then consider what would happen if all cases went through one model or the other.

Pros-Cons of Due Process Model: _____
_____
_____
_____

Pros-Cons of Crime Control Model: _____
_____
_____
_____

Consequences of a Due Process Model for all cases: _____
_____
_____
_____

Consequences of a Crime Control Model for all cases: _____
_____
_____
_____

CRIME AND JUSTICE IN AMERICA

OUTLINE

- Defining Crime
- Types of Crime
- How Much Crime is There?
- Crime Victimization
- Causes of Crime

CHAPTER 2
CRIME AND JUSTICE IN AMERICA

LEARNING OBJECTIVES

After reading the material in this chapter, students should be able to:

1. Understand the legal definitions of crime

2. Categorize crimes by their type

3. Recognize the different methods of measuring crime

4. Understand why some are at higher risk of victimization than others

5. Recognize the negative consequences of victimization

6. Understand the theories put forward to explain criminal behavior

7. Analyze crime causation theories and women offenders

CHAPTER SUMMARY

Defining crime can be a difficult task for the researcher interested in studying criminal behavior. While some acts (such as murder) are easily defined as criminal, others (such as assisted suicide or drug use) are not so easily categorized. Crimes that are *mala in se* are acts that are wrong in and of themselves. For *mala in se* offenses, the public generally agrees that the offenses should be illegal. However, crimes that are *mala prohibita* are defined by the government as criminal, while the American public might not agree that they should be crimes. Examples of *mala prohibita* crimes include smoking marijuana or public drunkenness. Many scholars argue that the government uses the law to impose values upon the public.

There are many different types of crime, such as occupational, organized, visible, political, crimes without victims, hate crimes, and cybercrime. Law enforcement authorities focus largely on visible crime, which involves street crimes such as burglary or homicide, because people fear this type of crime more than any other. However, occupational and political crime can impose great financial costs upon society.

Crime is a complicated issue to research, because the data on crime are not always reliable. The FBI's Uniform Crime Reports provide data reported to police, but do not track the dark figure of crime, which is crime not reported to the police. The National Crime Victimization Survey reports information gathered from residents of the United States about their victimization experiences, but respondents may not report accurately due to embarrassment, memory problems, or other issues.

Victimology surfaced in the 1950s as a field of criminology that studied the role of the victim in the criminal act. Researchers have found that young male residents of lower-income communities are the most likely to be victimized by crime. Because of the connection between race and social status in the United States, African Americans are more frequently victimized by crime than whites. Most crime is intraracial. A significant percentage of crimes are committed by acquaintances and relatives of victims, especially crimes committed against women. The financial and emotional costs incurred by crime have a significant impact on our entire society. In recent years, there has been a growing trend for government agencies to be more sensitive to the needs of crime victims, often in response to demands made by victims' rights movements. Thus, there are now programs in many places that provide services and compensation to the victims of crime.

The classical school of criminology emphasized reform of the criminal law, procedures, and punishments. The rise of the scientific method led to the positivist school, which viewed behavior as stemming from social, biological, and psychological factors. Positivist criminology has dominated the study of criminal behavior in the twentieth century. The criminality of women has only recently been studied. It is argued by some that as women become more equal with men in society, crimes committed by females will increase in number. Recent data indicate this theory may not hold true.

CHAPTER OUTLINE

I. DEFINING CRIME

We can categorize crimes as either *mala in se* or *mala prohibita*. *Mala in se* crimes are crimes such as murder, rape, or assault that are considered wrong in themselves, based on shared values or consensus. *Mala prohibita* crimes are not wrongs in themselves but are punished because they are prohibited by the government. There is often a lack of consensus about whether such actions (e.g., use of marijuana, gambling, prostitution) should be illegal. People's views of the seriousness of various crimes depend on their race, sex, class, and victimization experience.

II. TYPES OF CRIME

In addition to categorizing crime as *mala in se* or *mala prohibita*, we may also categorize them as felonies or misdemeanors. Crime can be described using other categories, such as their level of risk and profitability, the degree of public disapproval, or the cultural characteristics of offenders.

29

A. Visible Crime

Street crime or "ordinary crime," from shoplifting to homicide, committed primarily by members of the lower classes. Visible crimes make up the FBI's Uniform Crime Reports.

1. Violent Crime

Crimes against individuals in which either physical injury or death occurs. These offenses are usually considered the most serious.

2. Property Crime

Crimes involving theft, damage, or destruction of property. Some professional criminals earn their livelihood through property crime.

3. Public Order Crimes

Crimes that threaten public "peace," such as disorderly conduct, vagrancy, and vandalism. These crimes increase citizen fear of crime, and some view them as contributing to an overall feeling of disorder that encourages more serious crime.

B. Occupational Crime:

A violation of law committed through opportunities created in the course of a legal business or profession.

C. Organized Crime

Social framework for the perpetration of criminal acts, rather than specific acts themselves. Organized criminals provide goods and services to people, and will engage in any illegal activity as long as it is low risk and high profit (e.g., pornography, money laundering, illegal disposal of toxic waste).

Organized crime has been associated with many different ethnic and immigrant groups who have struggled to gain access to the legitimate economic opportunities typically monopolized by more established groups. In recent years, organized crime has expanded increasingly beyond national borders.

D. Crimes Without Victims

These are mainly offenses that are *mala prohibita*. Some argue there is such thing as a truly "victimless" crime, because all crimes harm society. The "war on drugs" is one example of law enforcement's pursuit of a victimless crime.

E. Political Crime

Crimes carried out for ideological or political reasons. They can be committed against the government or by the government.

F. Cybercrime

Crime committed using technology, usually computers and the Internet. Possible victims include individuals, corporations/organizations, or the government.

III. HOW MUCH CRIME IS THERE?

The term "dark figure of crime" refers to the amount of crime that is not reported to the police. Many people do not report criminal victimizations due to fear, embarrassment, retaliation or other reasons.

A. Uniform Crime Reports:
Use official crime data collected by police departments. **The National Incident-Based Reporting System (NIBRS)** uses incident-based crime data that identifies individual offenses and offenders.

B. National Crime Victimization Surveys
Collect information from residents who have been surveyed regarding household and individual victimization

C. Trends in Crime
Analysis of crime trends indicates that crime is not on the increase. Both the UCR and NCVS reflect decreases in crime since the early 1980s. Several factors affect crime rates:

1. **Age:** The proportion of people aged 16-24 (statistically the most crime-prone group) in a community may greatly affect its crime rates, so changes in this distribution over time must be analyzed.

2. **Crack Cocaine:** The increased use of this illegal drug had significant effects on the crime rate in the late 1980s and early 1990s

3. **Crime Trends: What Do We Really Know?:** The causes of crime are extremely complex, and there are rarely simple answers for analyzing the crime rate.

IV. CRIME VICTIMIZATION

The field of victimology emerged in the 1950s and 1960s, exploring what types of people are victimized, the impact of victimization, and the role of victims in preventing and/or precipitating attacks.

A. Who Is Victimized?

1. **Men, Youths, Nonwhites**
While African-Americans are more likely than whites to be victims, most violent crime is intraracial (i.e., the offender and the victim are same race). Young people are more likely than old people to be victims. Men, city dwellers, and those with low incomes are more likely to be victims than women and those living in wealthier or more rural areas.

31

2. **Low-Income City Dwellers**
   Lifestyle-exposure theory: Violent crime is primarily an urban phenomenon, in areas with high incidence of physical deterioration, economic insecurity, poor housing, family disintegration, and transience.

B. **Acquaintances and Strangers**
   People are more likely to be victimized by people they know, especially in the cases of sexual crimes. Women are more likely to experience violent victimization by an acquaintance or intimate.

C. **The Impact of Crime**
   Costs of crime range from tangible losses (such as those caused by theft, destruction, or vandalism of property) to those losses that are intangible (like pain, trauma, loss of quality of life). Fear of crime is also a cost on which a dollar value cannot be placed.

   1. **Costs of Crime**: Estimates of losses from crime include those that are tangible ($105 billion), intangible ($450 billion) and must also include the costs of operating the criminal justice system (over $167 billion per year).

   2. **Fear of Crime**: Ironically, those who are least likely to be victims (women and the elderly) sometimes experience the most fear of crime. Americans tend to fear crime more than their individual victimization risk would suggest. This may be due to the large amount of attention given to criminal victimization by the media.

D. **The Experience of Victims within the Criminal Justice System**
   Traditionally, the victims of crime have been overlooked and forgotten, and their interactions with the criminal justice system have sometimes had the effect of making their victimization even more traumatic. Over the past two decades, justice agencies have taken new interest in the treatment and welfare of crime victims. While the proposed "Victim's Rights" constitutional amendment was not passed, the "Justice for All Act" of 2004 has helped to place additional emphasis on victims' rights. There may be instances in which victims' and offenders' rights are contrary to one another, based on new legislation.

E. **The Role of Victims in Crime**
   Victims may increase their risk of victimization through negligence, precipitation, or provocation.

V. CAUSES OF CRIME

These theoretical explanations of crime can help to identify factors that increase individual propensity for crime. They may also help to create policy designed to reduce criminal behavior. Early explanations for crime were mostly supernatural in nature, characterizing it as the "work of the devil," committed by people who had been lured by evil forces. Starting in the eighteenth century, newer, more rational perspectives on criminal behavior began to emerge.

A. Classical and Positivist Theories

1. **The Classical School** Classical theories of crime focus on the rational nature of crime (i.e., the idea that criminals make conscious decisions about whether to engage in criminal behavior by weighing its costs and benefits). Classical theorists also argued that punishment should fit the crime, and that those who commit the same crime should receive similar punishments.

2. **Neoclassical Criminology** refers to the recent revival of interest in ideas such as rational choice theory that have been associated with classical criminology, often in the context of political conservatism.

3. **Positivist Criminology** views criminal behavior as stemming from biological, social, and psychological factors rather than as a result of free will. These theorists argue that punishment should be tailored to individuals.

B. Biological Explanations

Biological explanations of criminal behavior focus on the individual, genetically inherited differences between criminals and non-criminals. Biological theories fell out of favor after World War II, when they were displaced by sociological theories. However, there has been a renewed interest in biological theories of crime since the mid-1980s. Some genetic factors may increase an individual's propensity (risk) for exhibiting criminal behavior. These factors are known as criminogenic factors.

C. Psychological Explanations

Psychological explanations for crime conceptualize criminal behavior as caused by mental illness or limited intelligence. Psychiatrists have linked criminal behavior to such concepts as innate impulses, psychic conflict, and the repression of personality.

D. Sociological Explanations

Sociological explanations of crime assume that the offender's actions are molded by contact with the social environment and factors such as race, age, gender, and income. In the 1920s, researchers at the University of Chicago looked closely at the ecological factors that gave rise to crime: poverty, inadequate housing, broken families, and the problems of new immigrants.

1. **Social Structure Theories** attribute criminal behavior to the stratified nature of Western societies, giving particular prominence to the fact that different social classes

33

control very different amounts of wealth, status, and power. Thus deprivations and inequality lead the lower classes to crime. Structural factors can permit *anomie* to develop, in which rules or norms that regulate behavior weaken or disappear.

2. **Social Process Theories** assume that criminality results from the interactions of people with the institutions, organizations, and processes of society. Thus everyone has the possibility of being a criminal, regardless of social status or education.

   There are three types of social process theories. *Learning theories* hypothesize that criminal activity is normal learned behavior, and this behavior is learned from family and peers who are involved in crime. *Control theories* assume that all members of society have the potential to commit crimes, but most people are restrained by their ties to such conventional institutions and individuals as family, church, school, and peer groups. Criminality results when these primary bonds are weakened and the person no longer follows the expected norms for behavior. *Labeling theories* state that certain individuals come to be labeled as deviant by society after committing a crime. The stigmatized individuals then come to believe that the label is true and they assume a criminal identity and career. By arguing, in effect, that the criminal justice system creates criminals by labeling individuals as such, this approach advocates the decriminalization of certain offenses to avoid needlessly placing labels on people.

3. **Social conflict theories** argue that criminal law and criminal justice are mainly the means of controlling society's poor and its have-nots. The rich commit crimes but are much less likely to be punished since they have more power (socially, politically, and economically) than the poor.

   Critical, radical, or Marxist criminologists argue that the class structure of society results in certain powerless groups in society being labeled as deviant. When the status quo is threatened, criminal laws are altered to label and punish threatening groups and deviant criminals.

E. Life Course Explanations
These theories examine criminal offending across an individual's life course, and hypothesize that crime is caused by a number of factors discussed in biological, psychological, and sociological theories of crime. Some theorists discuss pathways to crime, in which young offenders begin with minor crimes and then move into more serious offenses.

Policy implications of these theories include the decreased use of incarceration for first-time offenders, and supporting life transitions that serve as turning points away from criminal careers.

F. Women and Crime

Most theories about the causes of crime are based almost entirely on observations of men. Except with respect to prostitution and shoplifting, little crime research focused on women prior to the 1970s. It was assumed that women did not commit serious crimes because of their nurturing, dependent nature. Women offenders were viewed as moral offenders: "fallen women."

Freda Adler believed the social equality promoted by the women's movement led to an increasing similarity between male and female criminal behavior beginning in the 1970s.

Rita Simon emphasized greater freedom and opportunities in the job market as the source of changes in women's criminality. The number of women being arrested seems to be growing faster than the number of men. However, the number of women arrested is still relatively small. Some researchers believe that women will become more involved in economic and occupational crimes as more women pursue careers in business and industry. In general, like male offenders, women arrested for crimes tend to come from poor families in which physical and substance abuse are present.

G. Assessing Theories of Criminality

The body of existing criminological theories addresses distinct aspects of criminal behavior, and some focus on specific types of offenders. Criminological theory would be improved by the development of an integrated theory which merges these disparate theories into a single theory of criminal behavior.

REVIEW OF KEY TERMS

Define each of the following:

anomie

biological explanations

classical criminology

control theories

crimes without victims

criminogenic

cyber crimes

dark figure of crime

labeling theories

learning theories

life course theories

mala in se

mala prohibita

money laundering

National Crime Victimization Survey (NCVS)

National Incident-Based Reporting System (NIBRS)

occupational crime

organized crime

political crime

positivist criminology

psychological explanations

social conflict theories

social process theories

social structure theories

sociological explanations

theory of differential association

Uniform Crime Reports (UCR)

victimology

visible crime

SELF-TEST SECTION

Fill in the appropriate term for each statement:

1. _____ is the term used for the amount of crime that goes unreported to the police.

2. _____ is generated from a compilation of reports from law enforcement agencies throughout the country.

3. _____ is also known as "street crime" or "ordinary crime".

4. The process of making illegally obtained funds appear legitimate is called _____.

5. _____ involve the willing and private exchange of illegal goods and services.

6. _____ are offenses that are wrong by their very nature.

7. _____ measures the amount of crime from the perspective of victims.

8. _____ measures crime by police officers recording and reporting each offense in a crime incident instead of merely describing the most serious crime in the incident.

9. _____ is conduct committed through opportunities created through professional or employment activities.

10. _____ are acts, such as treason and sedition, which constitute threats against the state.

11. _____ are offenses that are banned by statute but are not inherently wrong.

12. _____ is a social framework for the perpetration of criminal acts, often on a basis that crosses state and national boundaries.

13. Offense committed through the use of computers are called _____.

14. _____ assert that crime is normal behavior which may be undertaken by anyone depending on the social forces and groups that influence their behavior.

15. _____ asserts that criminal behavior stems from free will, and therefore the system should demand accountability from offenders through deterrence-oriented punishments.

16. _____ assert that certain individuals are treated as criminals by the system, and thus these individuals receive a message from the system that leads them to act as lawbreakers.

17. _____ assert that criminal law and the criminal justice system are primarily means of controlling the poor.

18. _____ is a state of normlessness caused by a breakdown in the rules of social behavior.

19. _____ assert that is crime learned behavior.

20. _____ assert that criminal behavior is caused by physiological and neurological factors.

21. _____ assert that crime is the creation of a lower-class culture as poor people respond to poverty and deprivation.

22. _____ assert that criminal behavior results when the bonds that tie an individual to others in society are broken.

23. _____ includes the study of how victims cope with crime and the social costs of crime.

24. _____ asserts that criminal behavior is not based on free will, but stems from social, biological, and psychological factors.

25. _____ are influences that are thought to bring about criminal behavior in an individual.

26. _____ hypothesize that crime must be studied over time, and many factors must be examined that can affect criminal behavior at individual points in time.

27. _____ assert that mental processes and associated behaviors are the cause of criminal behavior.

28. _____ assert that people become criminals when they identify with family members and individuals who regard criminal activity as normal and usual.

29. _____ assert that social conditions are the causes of crime.

FILL-IN-THE-BLANK EXERCISE

Acts that are wrong by nature are called **1.** _____, while acts that are prohibited by law but not wrong in themselves are called **2.** _____.

Two sources of data on crime are a reporting system where police describe each offense, which is known as the **3.** _____, and interviews of samples of the U. S. population, called **4.** _____. The **5.** _____ cannot adequately measure **6.** _____ because reports from police departments are limited to crimes that are reported to or discovered by law enforcement officials.

7. _____ established the groundwork for **8.** _____ by arguing that people choose to commit crimes and that fear of punishment keeps people in check.

With the development of **9.** _____, science-based theories emerged about the causes of criminal behavior, including **10.** _____ drawing from **11.** _____'s assertions about the influence of mental processes over behavior.

Among the **12.** _____, **13.** _____ posits that criminals identify and emulate people who view crime as normal, acceptable activity and **14.** _____ asserts that criminal behavior stems from the deterioration of ties between an individual and conventional institutions and people that support and reinforce society's rules and values.

MULTIPLE CHOICE

2.1.   Which of the following refers to acts that are wrong by nature?
a) *mala in se*
b) the dark figure of crime
c) victimology
d) *mala prohibita*
e) *mala nocturnus*

2.2.   Which of the following refers to acts prohibited by government?
a) *mala in se*
b) the dark figure of crime
c) victimology
d) *mala prohibita*
e) *mala nocturnus*

2.3.   Which of the following refers to an organized crime syndicate usually associated with "families"?
a) occupational crime
b) victimless crime
c) visible crime
d) organized crime
e) cybercrime

2.4.   The "war on drugs" is associated with what type of crime?
a) occupational crime
b) crimes without victims
c) visible crime
d) organized crime
e) cybercrime

2.5.   If a doctor is murdered because he or she performs abortions, how might we best classify that crime?
a) occupational crime
b) victimless crime
c) visible crime
d) organized crime
e) political crime

2.6. What type of crime is using "insider" stock trading information for personal gain?
a) occupational crime
b) victimless crime
c) visible crime
d) organized crime
e) political crime

2.7. According to the chart below, which of the following statements is TRUE??

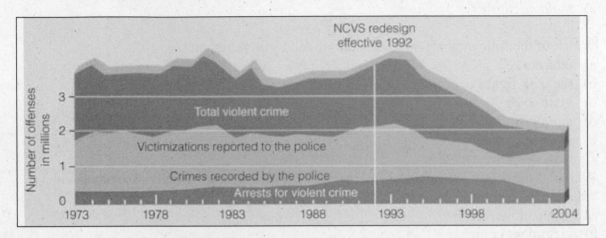

a) Total violent crime has increased dramatically since 1995.
b) Since 2000, the number of victimizations reported to police and crime recorded by the police have been the same.
c) Since 2000, crimes recorded by the police have decreased.
d) Since 1993, arrests for violent crime have increased overall.
e) The violent crime rate was very stable from 1973 to 2004.

2.8. What is the name for crime not reported to the police?
a) subtle crime
b) victimless crime
c) invisible crime
d) silent crime
e) dark figure of crime

2.9. What is the most accurate measure of crime in America?
a) Uniform Crime Reports
b) dark figure of crime
c) National Incident-Based Reporting System
d) National Crime Victimization Survey
e) there is no accurate measure

2.10. Which measure of crime relies upon more detailed reports of crime by police agencies?
a) NSA Statistics Data
b) dark figure of crime
c) National Incident-Based Reporting System
d) National Crime Victimization Survey
e) there is no such measure

2.11. Which of the following age groups commits the most crime?
a) 15 and under
b) 16-24
c) 25-34
d) 35-44
e) 45 and over

2.12. Why was there an increase in violent crime in the late 1980s and early 1990s?
a) spread of crack cocaine
b) greater use of semi-automatic handguns
c) fewer law enforcement personnel on the streets
d) a and b
e) none of these

2.13. According to your textbook, what factors might affect crime rates?
a) economic changes
b) law enforcement strategies
c) demographic changes
d) use of imprisonment
e) all of these

2.14. Women are most likely to be sexually victimized by:
a) someone they know
b) a stranger
c) a co-worker
d) a family member
e) none of the above

2.15. Which of the following factors is considered to be criminogenic?
a) being born into a middle- to upper-class household
b) experiencing hereditary traits such as alcoholism, epilepsy, or syphilis
c) attending college
d) being employed full-time
e) being raised in a two-parent household

2.16. Which of the following is the best definition of anomie?
   a) the breakdown of social norms that guide behavior
   b) the increase of women involved in crime
   c) increasing numbers of people in poverty committing crime
   d) a severe decrease in genetic predispositions to crime
   e) the effect of unemployment and poverty on crime

2.17. Which of the following statements about women and crime is TRUE?
   a) There has been more research about women as opposed to men.
   b) Women commit the same types of crime as men.
   c) The number of crimes committed by women has increased recently.
   d) Women now account for one-half of all U.S. arrests.
   e) All of the above are true.

2.18. Which two terms best describe life course criminology?
   a) anomie/dysfunction
   b) epilepsy/syphilis
   c) predisposition/precipitation
   d) poverty/economic inequality
   e) pathways/turning points

2.19. Which of the following people is most likely to be victimized?
   a) an elderly person watching television at home alone
   b) a white female shopping during the day
   c) a young black male at a nightclub
   d) a young Hispanic child at school
   e) a homosexual male prisoner in solitary confinement

2.20. According to the chart below, which of the following groups is most likely to be victimized?
   a) White females, aged 16-19
   b) White males, aged 50-64
   c) African American females, aged 50-64
   d) White males, aged 25-34
   e) African American males, aged 25-34

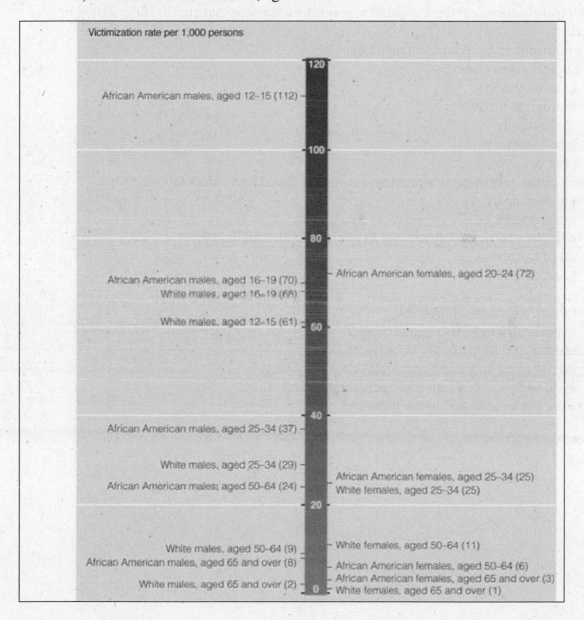

2.21. How did Adler suggest the women's movement would affect crime?
a) It would increase male crime, but female crime would remain the same.
b) It would decrease female crime, but male crime would remain the same.
c) Female crime would become more like male crime.
d) Male crime would become more like female crime.
e) The women's movement would have no discernible effect on crime.

2.22. Which criminological theory would support the argument that sterilization should be used
as a punishment to reduce criminal behavior?
a) social process theory
b) conflict theory
c) biological theory
d) strain theory
e) labeling theory

2.23. Which of the following is a problem commonly faced by victims of crime?
a) emotional stress
b) missed work
c) defense attorneys may attempt to question their credibility
d) all of the above
e) none of the above

2.24. Overall, criminological theories…
a) explain all kinds of crime very well
b) are focused too strongly on gender issues
c) do not explain crime using social class or poverty
d) need to be merged into more general theories
e) have not been tested in the literature

TRUE/FALSE

2.1. _____ Most hate crimes are committed by groups representing hate-based organizations.

2.2. _____ There have been significant decreases in every type of violent crime in the U. S. in recent years.

2.3. _____ Americans are not in agreement about which acts are criminal.

2.4. _____ *Mala prohibita* crimes are acts encouraged by government.

2.5. _____ *Mala in se* are acts considered to be wrong by nature.

2.6. _____ Law enforcement officials focus largely upon visible crime.

2.7. _____ Violent offenders are more likely to victimize strangers than acquaintances.

2.8. _____ Persons usually provide accurate information when interviewed about their experiences with crime.

2.9. _____ Cybercrime is currently a minor problem, because the majority of computer owners are middle- and upper-income persons, who usually do not commit crimes.

2.10. _____ Women commit less crime than men.

2.11. _____ A wealthy elderly women has a greater risk of becoming a victim of crime than the average citizen.

2.12. _____ Crime does not impose any costs on the operation of the criminal justice system.

2.13. _____ People cannot take precautions to protect themselves against crime.

2.14. _____ Classical criminology portrays the commission of crime as a rational choice.

2.15. _____ Neoclassical criminology is return to psychological theories of crime.

2.16. _____ Learning theory is a biological explanation for criminal behavior.

2.17. _____ Sigmund Freud is most often associated with psychological explanations for criminal behavior.

2.18. _____ Positivist criminologists argue that criminals are different from noncriminals.

2.19. _____ Demographic factors (such as age, gender and income) affect lifestyle, which in turn affects people's exposure to dangerous places.

ANSWER KEY

Key Terms

1. dark figure of crime [p. 43, LO 3]
2. Uniform Crime Reports [p. 43, LO3]
3. visible [p. 38 , LO1]
4. money laundering [p. 39, LO1]
5. crimes without victims [p. 40, LO1]
6. *mala in se [p.37, LO1]*
7. National Crime Victimization Survey [p. 45, LO3]
8. National Incident-Based Reporting System [p. 45 , LO3]
9. occupational crime [p. 39, LO1]
10. political crimes [p. 40 , LO1]
11. *mala prohibita [p. 37, LO1]*
12. organized crime [p. 39, LO1]
13. cybercrime [p. 41, LO1]
14. social process theories [p. 59, LO6]
15. classical criminology [p. 59, LO6]
16. labeling theories [p. 59, LO6]
17. social conflict theories [p. 60, LO6]
18. anomie [p. 58, LO6]
19. learning theories [p.59, LO6]
20. biological explanations [p. 57, LO6]
21. social structure theories [p. 58, LO6]
22. control theories [p. 59, LO6]
23. victimology [p. 54, LO5]
24. positivist criminology [p. 56, LO6]
25. criminogenic factors [p. 56, LO6]
26. life course theories [p. 60, LO6]
27. psychological explanations [p. 57, LO6]
28. differential association theories [p. 59, LO7]

Fill-in-the-Blank

1. mala in se [p.37, LO1]
2. mala prohibita [p.37, LO1]
3. National Incident-Based Reporting System [p. 45, LO3]
4. National Crime Victimization Survey [p. 45, LO3]
5. Uniform Crime Reports [p. 43, LO3]
6. dark figure of crime [p. 43, LO3]

7. Cesare Beccaria [p. 55, LO6]
8. classical criminology [p. 56, LO6]
9. positivist criminology [p. 56, LO6]
10. psychological explanations [p. 57, LO6]
11. Sigmund Freud [p. 57, LO6]
12. social process theories [p. 59, LO6]
13. differential association theory [p. 59, LO6]
14. control theory [p. 59, LO6]

Multiple Choice

2.1. A [p.37, LO1]
2.2. D [p.37, LO1]
2.3. D [p. 39, LO1]
2.4. B [p. 40, LO1]
2.5. E [p. 40, LO1]
2.6. A [p. 39, LO1]
2.7. B [p. 47, LO4]
2.8. E [p. 43, LO3]
2.9. E [p. 43, LO3]
2.10. C [p.45, LO3]
2.11. B [p. 47, LO4]
2.12. D [p. 48, LO5]
2.13. E [p. 42, LO2]
2.14. A [p. 52, LO4]
2.15. B [p. 56, LO2]
2.16. A [p. 58, LO6]
2.17. C [p. 62, LO6]
2.18. E [p.60,61, LO6]
2.19. C [p. 50, LO5]
2.20. A [p. 51, LO4]
2.21. C [p. 62, LO6]
2.22. C [p. 57, LO6]
2.23. D [p. 53, LO4]
2.24. D [p. 62, LO6]

True/False

2.1. F [p.42, LO2]
2.2. T [p.46,47, LO4]
2.3. T [p.37, LO1]
2.4. F [p.37, LO1]
2.5. T [p.37, LO1]
2.6. T [p. 38, LO1]
2.7. F [p. 52, LO2]
2.8. F [p. 54, LO5]
2.9. F [p. 41, LO1]
2.10. T [p.61,62, LO7]
2.11. F [p. 50, LO2]
2.12. F [p. 53, LO2]
2.13. F [p. 54, LO5]
2.14. T [p. 56, LO6]
2.15. F [p. 56, LO6]
2.16. F [p. 59, LO6]
2.17. T [p. 57, LO6]
2.18. T [p. 56, LO6]
2.19. T [p. 50, LO7]

WORKSHEET 2.1: DEFINING NEW TYPES OF CRIME

This chapter discusses the evolving nature of criminal justice not only in how we *define* crime but it our *responses* toward the problem of crime. The rapidly changing nature of technology over the past decade has posed significant challenges to traditional criminal justice practices. The issue of "peer-to-peer file sharing" has been of particular interest over the past few years. It is estimated that tens of millions of individuals have illegally shared copyrighted software, music, movies, and e-books over the Internet. In the face of billions of dollars of lost revenue caused by the sharing of music and movies over the internet, the recording industry and certain recording artists have bought thousands of lawsuits against individuals believed to be "serious violators" of copyright law.

Assignment: You are currently employed as a legislative aid to your State Senator who is considering introducing legislation intended to "crack down" on internet-based file sharing. You are instructed to write a position or policy paper stipulating whether the State should pursue such legislation. When writing such a paper, you should consider the following issues:

- Should internet-based file swapping be considered a crime? Why or why not?

- If a crime, what is the extent of harm associated with the behavior?'

- Should the government aggressively pursue violators of such a law if it existed? Why or why not?

- Given the current state of challenges facing the criminal justice system, are crimes such as file-swapping worthy of attention?

- What might some of the potential negative consequences of aggressive enforcement of such statutes?

WORKSHEET 2.2: CONSENSUS OR NOT?

For each of the following activities, consider the following criminal acts and explain whether you believe the law defining each as criminal is based on a consensus in American society.

Prostitution: _____

_____

_____

_____

_____

Smoking Marijuana: _____

_____

_____

_____

_____

Income Tax Evasion: _____

_____

_____

_____

_____

Underage Drinking: _____

_____

_____

_____

_____

51

WORKSHEET 2.3: CRIME SERIOUSNESS

For each of the following categories of crimes, give examples of two of the most serious crimes within the category. Then explain whether this category of crime should be a high priority for contemporary law enforcement officials. Explain your answer.

Visible Crime: _____

_____

_____

_____

_____

Occupational Crime: _____

_____

_____

_____

_____

Crime without Victims: _____

_____

_____

_____

_____

Cybercrime: _____

_____

_____

_____

_____

WORKSHEET 2.4: THEORY-BASED CRIME PREVENTION STRATEGIES

You are a police chief. Your town has been struck by a rash of burglaries. What strategies would you pursue to address this crime problem if it could be clearly attributed to one cause? In other words, for each of the following theories of crime causation, what strategies would you use to address burglaries caused under that theory?

Classical and Positivist Theories: _____

_____

_____

_____

Biological Theories: _____

_____

_____

_____

Psychological Theories: _____

_____

_____

_____

Social Process Theories: _____

_____

_____

_____

Social Structure Theories: _____

_____

_____

_____

CRIMINAL JUSTICE AND THE RULE OF LAW

OUTLINE

- Foundations of Criminal Law
- Substantive Criminal Law
- Responsibility for Criminal Acts
- Procedural Criminal Law
- Constitutional Rights and Criminal Justice Professionals

CHAPTER 3
CRIMINAL JUSTICE AND THE RULE OF LAW

LEARNING OBJECTIVES

After reading the material in this chapter, students should be able to:

1. Recognize the bases and sources of American Criminal Law

2. Understand how substantive criminal law defines a crime and the legal responsibility of the accused

3. Understand how procedural criminal law defines the rights of the accused and the processes for dealing with a case

4. Recognize the U.S. Supreme Court's role in interpreting the criminal justice amendments to the Constitution

CHAPTER SUMMARY

The area of criminal law focuses on the prosecution and punishment of people who violate specific laws enacted by legislatures, while the area of civil law concerns disputes between private citizens or businesses. Criminal law is divided into two parts: substantive law, which defines offenses and penalties, and procedural law, which defines the rights of accused individuals and the processes that criminal justice officials must follow in handling cases. Criminal law is found in written constitutions, statutes, judicial decisions, and administrative regulations.

Substantive criminal law involves seven important elements that must exist and be demonstrated by the prosecution in order to obtain a conviction: legality, *actus reus,* causation, harm, concurrence, *mens rea,* and punishment. The *mens rea* element, which concerns the defendant's intent or state of mind, can vary with different offenses, such as various degrees of murder or sexual assault. It may also be disregarded for strict liability offenses that punish actions without considering intent. Criminal law provides the accused opportunities to present several defenses based on lack of criminal intent: entrapment, self-defense, necessity, duress (coercion), immaturity, mistake, intoxication, and insanity. Standards for the insanity defense vary by jurisdiction, with various state and federal courts using several different tests.

The provisions of the Bill of Rights were not applicable to state and local officials until the mid-twentieth century, when the Court incorporated most of the Bill of Rights' specific provisions into the due process clause of the Fourteenth Amendment. The Fourth Amendment prohibition of unreasonable searches and seizures has produced many cases questioning the application of the exclusionary rule. Decisions by the Burger and Rehnquist Courts during the 1970s, 1980s, and 1990s have created several exceptions to the exclusionary rule and given greater flexibility to law enforcement officials. The Fifth Amendment provides protections against compelled self-incrimination and double jeopardy. As part of the right against compelled self-incrimination, the Supreme Court provided for the creation of *Miranda* warnings, which must be given to suspects before they are questioned in custody. The Sixth Amendment guarantees the accused the right to counsel, the right to a speedy and public trial, and the right to an impartial jury.

The Eighth Amendment includes protections against excessive bail, excessive fines, and cruel and unusual punishments. Many of the Supreme Court's most well known Eighth Amendment cases concern the death penalty, which the Court has endorsed, provided that states employ careful decision-making procedures that consider aggravating and mitigating factors.

CHAPTER OUTLINE

I. FOUNDATIONS OF THE CRIMINAL LAW

The law must proscribe an act before it can be regarded as a crime and carry accompanying punishment. Civil law concerns contracts, property, and personal injuries. Criminal law concerns conduct that is punished by the government.

Criminal law is divided into substantive and procedural law. Substantive law stipulates the types of conduct that are criminal and the punishments to be imposed. Procedural law sets forth the rules that govern the enforcement of the substantive law.

II. SUBSTANTIVE CRIMINAL LAW

A. Seven Principles of Criminal Law

1. **Legality**: existence of a law defining the crime. The U.S. Constitution prohibits *ex post facto* laws, or laws used to punish crimes that occurred before the law came into existence.
2. *Actus reus*: behavior of either commission or omission.
3. **Causation**: causal relationship between the act and the harm suffered.
4. **Harm**: damage inflicted on legally protected value (e.g., person, property, reputation). This also includes the potential for harm, as evidenced in inchoate offenses that are planned but not executed.
5. **Concurrence**: the simultaneous occurrence of the intention and the act.
6. *Mens rea* (a guilty state of mind): guilty mind requires intention to commit the act.
7. **Punishment**: the stipulation in the law of sanctions to be applied against persons found guilty of the forbidden behavior.

B. Elements of a Crime

A crime is composed of three elements: the act (*actus rea*), the intent to commit the act (*mens rea*), and the attendant circumstances.

C. Statutory Definitions of Crimes

Federal and state laws may define crimes differently. Aspects of individual crimes (such as malice aforethought) can help distinguish crimes, such as homicide and manslaughter.

D. Responsibility for Criminal Acts

Mens rea is a key element for establishing the perpetrator's responsibility. Guilt is decided based on whether a reasonable man in the defendant's situation and with his physical characteristics would have had a consciousness of guilt ("objective *mens rea*"). Accidents are not crimes, because of the absence of *mens rea*, although acts of extreme negligence or recklessness may be criminal. Occasionally, legislatures criminalize acts that do not require demonstration of intent, as in the case of pure food and drug laws, housing laws, and sanitation laws. However, such offenses usually do not lead to incarceration unless there is a refusal to comply after given notice of violation.

1. **Entrapment** is a defense based on the absence of intent, presenting the defendant as a law-abiding citizen who lacks predisposition but was induced by the government to commit a crime.

2. **Self-defense** occurs when a person who feels in immediate danger of being harmed by another's unlawful use of force wards off the attack using physical means. Generally, individuals must use only the force level necessary to defend themselves.

3. **Necessity** may be used as a defense when a crime is committed for one's own preservation or to avoid a greater evil.

4. **Duress (or coercion)** occurs when a person has committed a crime under the threat of force or other consequences.

5. **Immaturity**: traditionally, Anglo-American law has excused criminal behavior by children under the age of seven on the ground that they are immature and not responsible for their actions.

6. **Mistake of fact** can be claimed when someone unwittingly commits a crime (although this does not cover ignorance of the law).

7. **Intoxication** is usually not defense against criminal behavior unless the crime required specific rather than general intent. For example, a person tricked into consuming an intoxicating substance can use intoxication as a defense.

8. **Insanity** is a controversial and relatively rare defense, successful in only about 1% of cases. The insanity defense is usually accompanied by civil commitment statute permitting insane offenders to be hospitalized until their condition improves.

Important rulings on the use of the insanity defense include the M'Naghten Rule, the Irresistible Impulse Test, the *Durham* Rule, the Model Penal Code's Substantial Capacity Test, and the Comprehensive Crime Control Act.

III. PROCEDURAL CRIMINAL LAW

Procedural due process assures that accused offenders are accorded certain rights and protections in keeping with the Constitution of the United States. Procedures may be followed both to enhance truth seeking (e.g., trial by jury) and to prevent improper governmental actions (e.g., unreasonable searches and seizures).

A. Bill of Rights and the Fourteenth Amendment
These ten amendments added to the U.S. Constitution in 1789 include protections against self-incrimination and double jeopardy. The case of *Barron v. Baltimore* (1833) initially determined that Bill of Rights only provided protection for individuals against actions by the federal government, not actions by state governments. The constitutions of many states contained their own lists of protections for people within those states.

B. The Fourteenth Amendment and Due Process
During the twentieth century, the Supreme Court gradually made most of the provisions of the Bill of Rights applicable against the states (a process referred to as incorporation). The Court stated that individual rights had been incorporated into the Fourteenth Amendment right to due process. The concept of "fundamental fairness" was used to determine which specific rights were applicable against the states as a component of the Fourteenth Amendment right to due process.

C. The Due Process Revolution
The Warren Court (beginning in 1953) made decisions that required states to abide by the due process protections set forth in the Fourteenth Amendment. This continued with the Burger Court (1969-1986), and resulted in most criminal justice rights in the United States Constitution being applied to the states.

D. Fourth Amendment: Unreasonable Searches and Seizure
The Exclusionary Rule, contained in this amendment, holds that illegally obtained evidence could be excluded from a criminal trial. Conservatives argue that exclusion is not effective against police misconduct and that it exacts a high price from society. Liberals argue that it is better for a few guilty people to go free than to permit police to engage in misconduct. Recent Supreme Court decisions give greater flexibility to police for conducting searches.

E. Fifth Amendment: Self-Incrimination and Double Jeopardy
The Constitution guarantees criminal defendants the right to refuse to testify against themselves in court. This is the right against self-incrimination. In addition, criminal defendants are protected against double jeopardy, meaning an individual cannot be tried twice for the same offense. However, double jeopardy does not preclude the possibility of successive prosecutions in different (i.e., state or federal) jurisdictions.

F. <u>Sixth Amendment: Right to Counsel and Fair Trial</u>
  1. **The Right to Counsel**: *Gideon v. Wainwright* (1963) required appointed counsel for indigent state court defendants facing six months or more of incarceration.

  2. **The Right to a Speedy and Public Trial**: In some countries, even today, defendants may be incarcerated for years awaiting their trial, which is typically hidden from the public. In order to assure fairness, the Constitution requires a public trial.

  3. **The Right to an Impartial Jury**: Citizens have a guaranteed right to be judged by a jury of their peers.

G. <u>Eighth Amendment: Fines, Bail, and Punishment</u>
  1. **Release on bail**: The Supreme Court decided that release is not required, but that bail cannot be "excessive." Federal statutes permit holding defendants in jail after a finding that they may be dangerous to the community or that no conditions of release may prevent flight from the jurisdiction.

  2. **Excessive fines**, which can include the value of property seized by law enforcement under civil forfeiture, are prohibited by the United States Constitution.

  3. **Cruel and unusual punishment**: There has been significant debate about the use of the death penalty in the United States and whether it constitutes "cruel and unusual punishment." In 1972, the Court decided that the way in which the death penalty was being implemented amounted to cruel and unusual punishment (*Furman v. Georgia*). States changed their laws to create more extensive deliberative procedures, and the Supreme Court approved the use of the death penalty following those changes in 1976 (*Gregg v. Georgia*).

IV. CONSTITUTIONAL RIGHTS AND CRIMINAL JUSTICE PROFESSIONALS

With each new Supreme Court decision, criminal justice professionals must change their policies to adapt. Recent changes in the composition of the Supreme Court will likely mean a more conservative court, ruling more often on the side of the police than suspects.

REVIEW OF KEY TERMS

Define each of the following:

Bill of Rights

civil law

double jeopardy

entrapment

fundamental fairness

grand jury

inchoate offense

incorporation

legal responsibility

mens rea

procedural criminal law

self-incrimination

substantive criminal law

Barron v. Baltimore

Gideon v. Wainwright

Powell v. Alabama

61

SELF-TEST SECTION

KEY TERMS

Fill in the appropriate term for each statement:

1. _____ defines the undesirable behaviors that the government will punish.

2. The _____ defines the legal protections accorded to citizens under the Constitution.

3. _____ is the body of rules that regulate conduct between individuals in their private relationships.

4. _____ is the accountability of an individual for a crime.

5. _____ is the extension of due process to make the Bill of Rights binding on state governments.

6. _____ is the intent element of a crime.

7. _____ is the production of damaging testimony against one's self.

8. Court decisions that have the status of law and serve as precedents for later decisions are known as _____.

9. _____ provides a defense when law enforcement officers are too aggressive in seeking to induce a particular individual to commit a crime.

10. _____ occurs when one offender is tried twice for the same offense.

11. _____ are crimes that include conspiracies and attempts.

12. In _____, the Supreme Court found that the Bill of Rights did not apply to the states.

13. _____ supports the idea that the Constitution has not been violated so long as a state's conduct maintains basic standards of fairness.

14. _____ is the case that required states to provide attorneys for indigent defendants who faced serious criminal charges.

15. _____ is the case that required offenders charged with capital offenses to receive benefit of counsel.

16. A body of citizens known as a _____ is sometimes called to determine whether an individual should be charged with a crime.

FILL-IN-THE-BLANK EXERCISE

When a defendant wishes to claim that he or she is not guilty by reason of **1.** _____, the rule applied by the court for determining capacity of criminal responsibility will vary from state to state.

When a defendant wishes to claim that he or she is not guilty by reason of **2.** _____, the court will determine whether the level of force used was based on a reasonable fear and did not exceed the perceived threat.

Society has many rules for the behavior of its citizens. Under **3.** _____, the government defines rules that make violators subject to punishment by the government. By contrast, the rules known as **4.** _____, govern disputes between individuals.

Police behavior is controlled by a number of legal rules. For example, under the defense of **5.** _____ in substantive criminal law, a defendant may show that the police essentially initiated the commission of the crime.

Under the leadership of Chief Justice Earl Warren, the Supreme Court decided a variety of cases, such as **6.** _____, which provided a right to counsel for indigent defendants facing serious charges, through the process of **7.** _____ in which rights from the **8.** _____ were recognized as applying to the states through the **9.** _____ Amendment.

MULTIPLE CHOICE

3.1. What do some people fear about the powers of government in the wake of the September 11th terrorist attacks?
a) government will not be powerful enough to protect our national security
b) government will be too powerful and move away from traditional constitutional values
c) government will ignore the problem
d) people are not in fear of the government
e) none of the above

3.2. What type of law governs business deals, contracts, and real estate?
a) civil law
b) criminal law
c) authoritarian law
d) substantive law
e) common law

3.3. Procedural criminal law is defined by:
a) State legislatures through statutes
b) The federal government through Congress
c) The United Nations
d) Courts through judicial rulings
e) Defense attorneys, through the Bar Examination process

3.4. In countries using a system of Islamic law (such as Pakistan) how must a woman typically prove that she was raped?
a) her word that a crime occurred is usually sufficient
b) she must provide a DNA sample from the accused individual(s)
c) she must find four Muslim men to act as witnesses
d) rape is not a crime under Islamic law
e) a, b, and c are correct

3.5. A person who has legal responsibility for a crime is:
a) Not guilty of the crime
b) Defendable at trial
c) Not likely to be convicted
d) Innocent of the crime
e) Accountable for the crime

3.6. Which of the following is an example of a mitigating circumstance?
a) premeditation
b) waiving the right to remain silent
c) lying about the crime
d) a crime in the heat of passion
e) showing indifference to life

3.7. The level of force used in self-defense cannot exceed the...
a) police's reasonable perception of the threat
b) person's (using self-defense) reasonable perception of the threat
c) judge's reasonable perception of the threat
d) average person's reasonable perception of the threat
e) threat as perceived by the person who is the attacker (not the person exercising self-defense)

3.8. In the case of *The Queen v. Dudley and Stephens*, what was the defense's argument in the murder of a young sailor?
a) insanity
b) self-defense
c) necessity
d) entrapment
e) duress

3.9. Crimes that are attempted or planned (but not completed), are referred to as:
a) Crimes of necessity
b) Civil offenses
c) Misdemeanor crimes
d) Inchoate offenses
e) Legal offenses

3.10. The term "penal code" also refers to:
a) Substantive criminal law
b) Procedural criminal law
c) Civil law
d) The insanity defense
e) Necessity

3.11. In what case did the U. S. Supreme Court rule that the Bill of Rights did not apply to the states?
a) *Marbury v. Madison* (1803)
b) *Barron v. Baltimore* (1833)
c) *Durham v. United States* (1954)
d) *Mapp v. Ohio* (1961)
e) *Gibbons v. Ogden* (1824)

3.12. The amendments added to the U.S. Constitution immediately after the Civil War were designed to:

a) Protect individuals' rights against infringement by state and local government officials

b) Abolish slavery

c) Accord women the right to vote

d) Provide affirmative-action rights to former slaves

e) Formally state America's independence from Britain

3.13. Which of the following landmark U.S. Supreme Court cases stated that "cruel and unusual punishments" must be defined according to contemporary standards?

a) *Mapp v. Ohio* (1961)

b) *Weeks v. United States* (1914)

c) *Trop v. Dulles* (1958)

d) *Gideon v. Wainwright* (1963)

e) *Powell v. Alabama* (1932)

3.14. One cannot be charged with a crime unless this is present:

a) Mental instability

b) A criminal record

c) *Mens rea*

d) An alibi

e) A conspirator

3.15. In which of these circumstances might an offender claim he/she is not guilty due to intoxication?

a) A woman at a bar claims her drink was spiked with ecstasy, and thus she should not be charged with consuming an illegal drug

b) A man claims he should not be charged with Driving Under the Influence, since he was too drunk to make a reasonable decision about whether to drive his car

c) Several college students argue they should not be arrested for public intoxication, since they were unaware there was a law against being drunk in public

d) A woman charged with homicide claims she should not be responsible for the crime, since she is mentally unstable.

e) A man charged with beating his wife claims he is innocent, because she was drunk and tried to attack him.

3.16. Islamic law is concerned with:

a) The safety of the public from physical attack, insult, and humiliation

b) The stability of the family

c) The protection of property against theft, destruction, or unauthorized interference

d) The protection of the government and the Islamic faith against subversion

e) All of the above

3.17. The idea of fundamental fairness protects citizens against:
a) Leniency in the sentencing process
b) Police corruption
c) Abusive and unjust practices by the government
d) Federal prosecution for misdemeanor offenses
e) All of the above

3.18. Procedural criminal law dictates:
a) Which acts are crimes and which are not
b) How laws will be enforced by the criminal justice system
c) Which type of defense can be used for each different crime
d) Which constitutional amendments apply to the states
e) Whether certain individuals are entitled to a trial by jury

3.19. In 2005, President George W. Bush appointed which of the following two individuals to the Supreme Court?
a) Sandra Day O'Connor and Ruth Bader Ginsburg
b) Earl Warren and Warren Burger
c) Donald Rumsfeld and Alberto Gonzales
d) John Roberts and Samuel Alito
e) Stephen Colbert and John Stewart

3.20. Which of the following rights has not been nationalized upon the states?
a) right against double jeopardy
b) right against unreasonable seizure
c) right to an attorney
d) right to a grand jury
e) all of the above have been nationalized

3.21. *Gideon v. Waiwnright* (1963) made which right binding upon the states?
a) The right to a fair trial
b) The right to counsel
c) The right to face one's accuser
d) The right to an impartial jury
e) The right to act as one's own attorney

3.22. The M'Naghten Rule is also known as:
a) Clear and present danger
b) The immunity rule
c) The "right-from-wrong" test
d) The need for necessity
e) The due process clause

3.23. Which of the following terms describes the criminal act, either by commission or omission?
   a) *mens rea*
   b) *ex post facto*
   c) *e pluribus unum*
   d) *actus reus*
   e) *fac simile*

3.24. Which of the following is likely to be an element of the crime of fraud?
   a) The use of deception to obtain property or money from another person unjustly
   b) Causing physical harm to another person
   c) Knowingly damaging someone else's property or possessions
   d) Taking another person's life, whether intentionally or accidentally
   e) Taking another person's property without their permission

3.25. Accused individuals may use the defense of entrapment if:
   a) they committed the crime in self-defense
   b) they were not aware they were committing a crime
   c) they were coerced into committing the crime by the police
   d) they have no criminal record
   e) they are first-time offenders

TRUE/FALSE

3.1. _____ If you are being sued for damages after harming someone in a car accident, the action takes place under civil law.

3.2. _____ A person cannot be arrested for being addicted to drugs.

3.3. _____ The Bill of Rights was nationalized through the Fifteenth Amendment.

3.4. _____ Chief Justice Earl Warren was criticized for protecting criminals' rights.

3.5. _____ Self-defense is based on the defending person's perception of the threat.

3.6. _____ The criminal defendants' rights are found in the Fourth, Fifth, Sixth, Seventh, and Eighth Amendments.

3.7. _____ Only a few of the Bill of Rights have been nationalized upon the states.

3.8. _____ The Bill of Rights was ratified by the states at the same time as the U.S. Constitution.

3.9. _____ The Fourth Amendment contains the right against unreasonable search and seizure.

3.10. _____ The Supreme Court has decided that all methods used in the death penalty are constitutional (i.e., not cruel and unusual).

3.11. _____ A primary function of civil law is to define behaviors labeled as criminal.

3.12. _____ The Constitution contains several *ex post facto* laws.

3.13. _____ Federal and state penal codes do not always define crimes in the same way.

3.14. _____ Some American states still have laws against adultery and premarital cohabitation.

3.15. _____ Legality is one aspect of procedural law.

3.16. _____ Many countries throughout the world use Islamic law to define their crimes and punishments.

3.17. _____ The Durham Rule states than an offender is not criminally responsible if mental disease or defect is present.

3.18. _____ Drinking wine and other intoxicants is permitted under Islamic law.

3.19. _____ In the U.S., children are occasionally tried in criminal court as adults.

3.20. _____ According to federal law, someone found guilty by reason of insanity must be incarcerated in a psychiatric facility until they are deemed not to pose a danger to society.

ANSWER KEY

Key Terms

1. substantive criminal law [p. 69,LO1]
2. Bill of Rights [p. 81, LO3]
3. civil law [p. 69, LO1]
4. legal responsibility [p. 69, LO1]
5. incorporation [p. 85, LO4]
6. *mens rea* [p. 71, LO1]
7. self-incrimination [p. 82, LO3]
8. case law
9. entrapment [p. 75, LO1]
10. double jeopardy [p. 82, LO3]
11. inchoate offenses [p. 71, LO1]
12. *Barron v. Baltimore* [p. 84, LO4]
13. fundamental fairness [p. 85, LO4]
14. *Gideon v. Wainwright* [p. 87, LO4]
15. *Powell v. Alabama* [p. 85, LO54]
16. grand jury [p. 87, LO4]

Fill-in-the-Blank

1. insanity [p. 78, LO2]
2. self-defense [p. 77, LO2]
3. substantive criminal law [p.69, LO1]
4. civil law [p. 69, LO1]
5. entrapment [p. 75, LO1]
6. *Gideon v. Wainwright* [p. 87, LO4]
7. incorporation [p. 85, LO4]
8. Bill of Rights [p. 81, LO4]
9. Fourteenth [p. 84, LO4]

Multiple Choice

3.1. B [p. 69, LO1]
3.2. A [p. 69, LO1]
3.3. D [p. 69, LO1]
3.4. C [p. 74, LO2]
3.5. E [p. 69, LO1]
3.6. D [p. 72, LO1]
3.7. B [p. 77, LO2]
3.8. C [p. 77, LO2]
3.9. D [p. 71, LO1]
3.10. A [p. 69, LO1]
3.11. B [p. 84, LO4]
3.12. A [p. 84, LO4]
3.13. C [p.90, LO4]
3.14. C [p. 71, LO1]
3.15. A [p. 78, LO2]
3.16. E [p. 74, LO2]
3.17. C [p. 85, LO4]
3.18. B [p. 69, LO1]
3.19. D p. 92, LO4]
3.20. D [p. 87, LO4]
3.21. B [p. 87, LO4]
3.22. C [p.78,79 , LO3]
3.23. D [p. 70, LO3]
3.24. A [p. 72,73, LO3]
3.25. C [p. 75, LO1]

True/False

3.1. T [p. 69, LO1]
3.2. T [p. 70, LO1]
3.3. F [p. 81,82, LO3]
3.4. T [p. 85, LO4]
3.5. T [p. 77, LO2]
3.6. T [p. 83,84, LO4]
3.7. F [p. 81, LO4]
3.8. F [p. 81, LO4]
3.9. T [p. 83, LO4]
3.10. F [p. 91, LO4]
3.11. F [p. 69, LO1]
3.12. F [p.70, LO1]
3.13. T [p. 72, LO2]
3.14. T [p. 74, LO4]
3.15. F [p. 80,81, LO4]
3.16. F [p. 74, LO4]
3.17. T [p.78, LO4]
3.18. F [p. 75, LO4]
3.19. T [p. 77, LO4]
3.20. T [p. 78, LO4]

WORKSHEET 3.1: THE INSANITY DEFENSE

You are a defense attorney. You are representing a young man who is accused of hiding in the trunk of a car, pointing a rifle through a hole in the trunk, and randomly shooting strangers. You want to pursue an insanity defense. The standards for such defenses vary by jurisdiction. What arguments would you make to attempt to represent your client under each of the following standards?

M'Naghten Rule: _____

_____

_____

_____

_____

Durham Rule: _____

_____

_____

_____

_____

_____

Model Penal Code: _____

_____

_____

_____

_____

WORKSHEET 3.2: THE BILL OF RIGHTS

Describe how each of the following components of the Bill of Rights is relevant to the work of police and prosecutors.

Fourth Amendment: _____

_____

_____

_____

_____

Fifth Amendment: _____

_____

_____

_____

_____

Sixth Amendment: _____

_____

_____

_____

_____

Eighth Amendment: _____

_____

_____

_____

_____

POLICE

OUTLINE

CHAPTER 4
POLICE

After reading the material in this chapter, students should be able to:

1. Understand how policing evolved in the United States

2. Recognize the main types of law enforcement agencies

3. Identify why people become police officers and how they learn their job

4. Understand the elements of the police officer's "working personality"

5. Comprehend the functions and organization of the police

6. Analyze influences on police policy and styles of policing

CHAPTER SUMMARY

The police in the United States have their roots in the early nineteenth-century development of policing in England. Like their English counterparts, the American police have limited authority, are under local control, and are organizationally fragmented. American policing is divided into three major historical eras: the political era (1840-1920), the professional era (1920-1970), and the community policing era (1970-present). Under the U.S. federal system of government, police agencies are found at the national, state, county, and municipal levels. Improvements have been made during the past quarter-century in recruiting more officers who are female, who are members of racial and ethnic minority groups, and who have higher levels of education. The primary functions of the police are order maintenance, law enforcement, and service. Police agencies are organized in a hierarchical fashion, with division of labor and a strict chain of command. Agencies are divided into organization units that handle specific kinds of cases, such as patrol, investigation, traffic, vice and juvenile. Police officers have an enormous amount of discretion, and make difficult decisions every day about whether to arrest citizens for breaking the law or handle situations informally. Police-community relations are extremely important, since citizens can assist in maintaining order in communities. Policing in a multicultural society requires sensitivity to the diverse attitudes and cultures that officers encounter in the course of their work, in order to maintain a connection with the community and serve residents more effectively.

CHAPTER OUTLINE

I. THE DEVELOPMENT OF THE POLICE IN THE UNITED STATES

A. The English Roots of the American Police

Three major policing traditions passed from England to the United States: limited authority, local control, and organizational fragmentation. In early England, the frankpledge system required that groups of ten families, called tithings, agree to uphold the law, maintain order, and commit to court those who had violated the law. Every male above the age of twelve was required to be part of the system. The tithing was fined if members did not perform their duties.

The parish constable system was established in England in 1285 under the Statute of Winchester. All citizens were required to pursue criminals under the direction of constables. This traditional system of community law enforcement was maintained well into the eighteenth century.

The early English police mandate was to maintain order while keeping a low profile. Officers attempted to use nonviolent methods and minimize conflict between police and public. Leaders feared that if the police were too powerful or too visible, they might threaten civil liberties.

B. Policing in the United States

1. **The Colonial Era and the Early Republic**. Before the Revolution, Americans shared the English belief that community members had a basic responsibility to help maintain order. Over time, ethnic diversity, local political control, regional differences, the opening up of the West, and the violent traditions of American society caused policing to develop along different lines in the United States than it had in England.

2. **The Political Era: 1840-1920**. Increased urbanization and the growth of cities led to pressures to modernize law enforcement with the creation of full-time police forces. Police had close ties with and were mutually dependent on local political leaders. Styles of policing differed dramatically in different regions of the United States and often involved the police in multiple roles. In the urbanized Northeast, the police performed service functions, such as caring for the homeless and operating soup kitchens, in addition to foot patrol, while U.S. marshals operating in the western territories might serve as bailiffs and jailers as well as law enforcement officers.

3. **The Professional Model Era: 1920-1970**. Based on a progressive reform movement favored by upper- and middle-class educated Americans that sought to professionalize police and remove the connections between police and local politicians. The Progressives were primarily concerned with creating efficient government and using government services to improve services for the poor. Under

this model, the primary goal of policing shifted to disciplined crime fighting and equal enforcement of laws.

4. **The Community Policing Era: 1970-Present**. In response to concerns that the professional style isolated police from their communities and contributed to negative attitudes towards police, many forces have shifted their focus away from pure crime-fighting to incorporate both providing service and maintaining order. The latter is in keeping with Wilson and Kelling's "broken windows" theory that having police focus on controlling less serious crime problems improves quality of life in neighborhoods by preventing deterioration. Community policing also improves a department's public image by allowing police to interact more with their fellow citizens.

C. <u>Homeland Security: The Next Era for Policing?</u>
The terrorist attacks of September 11th, 2001, have increased the police focus on national security and antiterrorism. Increasing numbers of police departments are training their officers on these issues to provide an adequate response in the face of threats to security.

II. LAW ENFORCEMENT AGENCIES

Most law enforcement officers in the United States can be found working in local police agencies. Federal agencies make up the smallest percentage of officers in the United States, but the number of federal agents has been increasing since September 11th.

A. <u>Federal Agencies</u>
1. **FBI**. This agency has the power to investigate all federal crimes that are not already being investigated by other agencies. Their priorities have shifted to include threats from terrorism and foreign intelligence/espionage.

2. **Specialization in Federal Law Enforcement**. The remaining federal agencies are quite specialized and focus their enforcement activities on a smaller range of crimes. Agencies under the command of the Department of Justice include the Drug Enforcement Administration (DEA), the Bureau of Alcohol, Tobacco, and Firearms (ATF), and the U.S. Marshals Service. Several other federal law enforcement agencies are subsumed under the umbrella of the Department of Homeland Security, including Customs and Border Protection, the Secret Service, and the Transportation Security Administration (TSA). Many other agencies exist that help to enforce federal laws.

B. <u>Federal Agencies after September 11</u>
In the aftermath of September 11th, 2001, the President created the Department of Homeland Security to protect the United States from terrorist attacks. Agencies that operate as part of the DHS include the National Cyber Security Division of the Directorate for Preparedness, the Transportation Security Administration, Customs and Border Protection, the U.S. Secret Service, and the U.S. Coast Guard.

B. State Agencies

Every state except Hawaii has a state police force. In many states they fill the void for enforcement in rural areas, and may also administer the state crime lab available to all local law enforcement agencies.

C. County Agencies

Sheriffs are found in almost all of the 3,100 counties in the U.S. Traditionally, they have had responsibility for rural policing and maintain responsibility for the local jail. Sheriffs may be selected by election or by political appointment depending on the state.

D. Native American Tribal Police

Native American tribes have significant autonomy due to their official status as sovereign nations. Tribal law enforcement agencies may enforce laws on Native American reservations against non-Native Americans as well as residents.

E. Municipal Agencies

Most police officers in the United States are employed by local law enforcement agencies. These local agencies enforce the laws of their jurisdictions, but also work with other agencies at the county, state, and national level to combat crime.

III. POLICE FUNCTIONS

Police provide other services besides law enforcement. They protect constitutional guarantees of free speech and assembly, facilitate movement of people and vehicles, resolve conflicts, identify problems, create and maintain feeling of security in community, and assist those who cannot care for themselves.

A. Order Maintenance

Police officers frequently work to prevent disturbances and threats to public peace. Order Maintenance requires the exercise of significant discretion when officers decide how to handle situations as they arise.

B. Law Enforcement

The law enforcement mandate of the police is frequently the most visible to the public. In these situations, the law has been violated and police work to determine the identity of the guilty parties. Enforcement of the law can be especially difficult when victims delay calling the police, thereby reducing the likelihood of apprehending the offender.

C. Service

Police officers frequently provide assistance to the community by administering first aid, rescuing animals, and extending social welfare services, especially to lower class citizens. Many of these functions may assist crime control, such as checking the doors of buildings, dealing with runaways and drunks, and settling family disputes.

D. Implementing the Mandate
Police administrators have learned that they can gain greater support for their budgets by emphasizing the crime-fighting function. Some have argued the police do not prevent crime, however, because (a) there is no connection between number of officers and the crime rate, and (b) primary strategies adopted by the police have not been shown to affect crime.

IV. WHO ARE THE POLICE?

A strong and trustworthy police force is vitally important to a society's protection and safety. Unfortunately, many police officers receive low pay for their work and experience a great deal of stress while on the job. Individuals interested in becoming police officers are attracted to many aspects of police work, including the variety of daily tasks, the chance to serve the public, the opportunity to exercise significant responsibilities, and the high degree of job security.

A. Recruitment
Some departments pay officers quite well, but salaries are extremely variable. Departments are increasingly able to attract college-educated recruits. Due to the expansion of undergraduate criminal justice programs, it has become much easier for police departments to find candidates with college degrees.

B. The Changing Profile of the Police
Historically, police departments were composed mainly of white male officers. This has changed in recent decades due to the passage of equal employment opportunity laws, as well as an increasing perception that police who reflected the ethnic makeup of the community they served would be more culturally adept and less likely to provoke conflict.

1. **Minority Police Officers**: The percentage of minority police officers has increased dramatically in the past 30 years, reflecting the changing demographics of the United States.

2. **Women on the Force**: Traditional beliefs about police being "men's work" have kept women off of the force. This has changed in recent years, with more women serving than ever before. Most women have easily met performance requirements, but it is at the social level that they have met their greatest resistance, including doubt about their physical capabilities and sexual harassment by male colleagues. Studies show that female officers may have superior abilities in certain areas such as defusing violent situations and interviewing crime victims. However, the great majority of female officers remain at the bottom of the police hierarchy, and to date only a few have risen to the very top ranks of large departments.

C. Training

Police academies may be run by large departments for their own officers, or by the state for rural and town recruits. Community colleges also offer police academies for prospective officers. Recruits are often told that real learning will take place on the job. This process of *socialization* includes learning informal practices as well as formal rules. In addition, officers work in an organizational framework in which rank carries privileges and responsibilities. Performance is usually measured by an individual's contribution to the group's success.

V. THE POLICE SUBCULTURE

A subculture is a smaller part of a larger societal culture that has a shared system of beliefs, values and attitudes. The shared values of the police lead them to have shared expectations about human behavior. Subcultures can change over time, especially when the department changes in terms of ethnicity and gender composition.

A. The Working Personality

The working personality of the police shapes the way officers interpret events. There are two important elements that define the working personality: danger and authority.

1. **Danger**: Police are especially attentive to signs of potential violence because they work in dangerous situations. The socialization process teaches recruits to be cautious and suspicious. Their orientation toward watching and questioning citizens can contribute to tension and conflict in contacts with the public. Police officers are constantly on edge, watching for unexpected dangers whether on or off duty.

2. **Authority**: Police officers, a symbol of authority with a fairly low occupational status, must often be assertive in establishing authority with citizenry. This can lead to conflict, hostility, and perhaps overreaction and police brutality. Officers are expected to remain detached, neutral, and unemotional even in very tense, challenging situations.

B. Police Morality

There is a high sense of morality in the law enforcement subculture. The code of morality helps police determine their course of action in response to the dilemmas that they frequently encounter on the street.

C. Police Isolation

The public is generally supportive of the police, but police perceive the public to be hostile. Officers' contacts with the public are frequently during moments of conflict, crisis, and emotion, which isolates them from more normal interactions. In addition, officers tend to socialize primarily with other officers. Because police officers are closely identified with their jobs, members of the public frequently treat them as police, even when they are off-duty.

D. <u>Job Stress</u>
The police working environment and subculture take a toll on physical and mental health in the form of the higher rates of health problems, marital problems, alcoholism and suicide among officers. Police stress is caused by a variety of factors that include the emotional, organizational, personal, and operational. Because of the traditional "tough guy" image of the police, departments have been slow to address issue of stress, but many have developed counseling, liberal disability rules and other mechanisms.

VI. ORGANIZATION OF THE POLICE

A. The functions of the police can be classified into three groups: (1) order maintenance, (2) law enforcement, and (3) service. Police agencies divide their resources among these functions on the basis of community need, citizen requests, and departmental policy.

1. **Watchman style**: emphasizes order maintenance. These types of departments are most likely to be found in cities that are declining industrial towns, racially heterogeneous, and/or blue-collar.

2. **Legalistic style**: emphasize law enforcement. These departments tend to be found where the city government is focused on reform, and/or has a mixed socioeconomic composition.

3. **Service style**: emphasizes the balance between maintaining order and law enforcement. This model is typically found in middle-class suburban communities.

B. Most law enforcement agencies are organized using a military hierarchy, but they are also bureaucracies concerned with efficiency and meeting objectives.

<u>Bureaucratic Elements</u>
1. **Division of Labor**: Tasks are typically divided among units of the police department to increase efficiency. Units within each department can be very specialized (training and crime scene investigation, for example).

2. **Chain and Utility of Command**: The militaristic character of police departments results in a chain-of-command, which makes clear the powers and duties of officers at each level.

3. **Rules and Procedures**: More complex organizations required complex regulations and guidelines to maintain efficiency and order. While there cannot be a rule for every possible circumstance, agencies attempt to guide their officers' behavior through official rules.

C. <u>Operational Units</u>
These specialized units focus on their respective assignments. Units typically take the form of patrol, investigation (detectives), traffic, vice, and juvenile. Larger police

82

departments tend to have a larger number of specialized units (for example: robbery/homicide, domestic violence, and internal affairs).

D. <u>**The Police Bureaucracy and the Criminal Justice System**</u>
The discretion used by police officers affect the entire criminal justice system—police officers have enormous control over who is arrested, and the crime with which they are charged. However, after offenders enter the system the police have little control over the process. Officers are also expected to follow commands but also use discretion, and these two tasks are sometimes at odds with one another.

VII. POLICE POLICY

Police executives must develop policies regarding how the members of their department will use limited resources to meet organizational goals. For example, officers will need guidance to determine which neighborhoods to patrol and whether to patrol in cars or on foot, and policies provide direction towards this end.

<u>**REVIEW OF KEY TERMS**</u>

<u>**Define each of the following:**</u>

frankpledge

preventive patrol

socialization

subculture

working personality

order maintenance

law enforcement

service

bureaucracy

division of labor

SELF-TEST SECTION

KEY TERMS

Fill in the appropriate term for each statement:

1. _____ is the function that the public often believes is the primary focus of police resources.

2. _____ is the function provided by the police that provides assistance to the public, usually in matters unrelated to crime.

3. _____ provided the early English system of families committing themselves to protect each other and their communities.

4. _____ emphasizes the prevention of behavior that either disturbs or threatens to disturb the public peace.

5. An officer's _____ is developed through their experiences and interactions with citizens.

6. _____ is the process by which the rules, symbols, informal practices, and values of a group are learned by its members.

7. _____ is a group with a shared system of beliefs. It is a smaller part of the larger society.

FILL-IN-THE-BLANK EXERCISE

Although many Americans believe the police devote their primary efforts to the **1.** _____ function, in part because the police created this image with the emphasis they developed during the **2.** _____ era, most scholars recognize that officers devote more time and tasks to the **3.** _____ function.

Among the agencies concerned with law enforcement responsibilities, **4.** _____ agencies cover the largest jurisdictional areas. However, they do not have responsibilities for as many crimes as local officials, such as the county **5.** _____.

When police officers perform their **6.** _____ function, such as when they are called to **7.** _____ situations, they must use **8.** _____ to determine whether or not make arrests.

There are two elements in the **9.** _____ which affect police officers' views and interpretations of situation. One element, **10.** _____, leads officers to be suspicious and cautious, and the other element, **11.** _____, leads officers to feel isolated from a society in which people always see the officer as enforcer of the law, even in off-duty hours.

MULTIPLE CHOICE

4.1. A tithing was:
  a) monies paid to the government under the English system of law
  b) in the hands of the local sheriff
  c) an early form of a constitution
  d) derived from the Magna Carta
  e) a group of families that kept order in their communities

4.2. Why did an organized police force develop in England during the eighteenth century?
  a) growth of commerce and industry
  b) decline of farming
  c) social disorder in the large cities
  d) all of the above
  e) none of the above

4.3. This federal agency was created after September 11th, 2001:
  a) The Department of Human Service
  b) The Federal Bureau of Investigation
  c) The Central Intelligence Agency
  d) The Internal Revenue Service
  e) The Department of Homeland Security

4.4. Federal law enforcement agencies are part of what branch of government?
  a) judiciary
  b) executive
  c) legislative
  d) local
  e) state

4.5. In the Southern United States, _____ were an early form of law enforcement, sometimes responsible for looking for African-Americans who might disrupt society.
  a) Juvenile gangs
  b) Constable-watch groups
  c) Community policing
  d) Slave patrols
  e) Bobbies

4.6. The largest number of police officers work at the _____ level:
  a) Municipal
  b) County
  c) State
  d) Federal
  e) Tribal

86

4.7.   The public generally believes that this is the most important police function:
a) law enforcement
b) social service
c) crime prevention
d) crime investigation
e) order maintenance

4.8.   What community would you most likely find the service style of policing?
a) reform-minded city
b) middle class suburban
c) mixed racial/ethnic composition
d) blue collar
e) all of the above

4.9.   The book <u>Fixing Broken Windows</u> hypothesized that:
a) Focusing on vice-related crimes, such as prostitution and gambling, would reduce violent crime
b) Focusing on gang-related crimes would reduce violent crime
c) Focusing on minor offenses would reduce violent crime
d) Redistributing the police to high crime areas would reduce violent crime
e) Police have very little control over violent crime

4.10.   What are the three historical periods of policing?
a) political, professional, and community model
b) pre-colonial, colonial, and post-colonial
c) crime fighter, crime preventer, and service provider
d) watchman, legalistic, and service
e) crime control, crime and order, and order

4.11.   Where did the term "posse" originate?
a) Latin term for " police"
b) French term for "public"
c) Old English term for "possessing the convict"
d) Latin term for "power of the country"
e) German term for "capture of prisoners"

4.12.   During what policing era did fingerprinting develop?
a) political
b) professional
c) community
d) all of the above
e) none of the above

87

4.13. As Americans expanded into the West, communities typically relied on _____ to maintain law and order.
   a) Vigilante groups
   b) Slave patrols
   c) SWAT teams
   d) Shire reeves
   e) Bobbies

4.14. Problem-oriented policing is closely related to:
   a) The professional model of policing
   b) The watchman style of policing
   c) Order maintenance
   d) Community policing
   e) Service

4.15. The beating of Rodney King is an example of an abuse resulting from the:
   a) Watchman style
   b) Service style
   c) Legalistic style
   d) All of the above
   e) None of the above

4.16. Which of the following statements is <u>true</u> about state police officers in the U.S.?
   a) Not all state police agencies have law enforcement responsibilities
   b) State police agencies usually run the state's forensic science lab
   c) Alaska is the only state that does not have a state police force
   d) Most state police officers do not have the authority to regulate traffic on main highways
   e) State police officers have responsibilities very similar to that of municipal police officers

4.17. Which of the following is TRUE of police work?
   a) working personality and occupational environment are closely linked and have a major impact on police work
   b) working personality and occupational environment are closely linked and have a minor impact on police work
   c) working personality and occupational environment are not linked and have no impact on police work
   d) working personality and occupational environment are closely linked and have no impact on police work
   e) working personality and occupational environment are not linked and have a major impact on police work

4.18. What type of stress is produced by real threats and dangers?
   a) external stress
   b) organizational stress
   c) personal stress
   d) operational stress
   e) none of the above

4.19. What are the two elements that define a police officer's working personality?
   a) Danger and uncertainty
   b) Danger and authority
   c) Weapons and uniform
   d) Badge and gun
   e) Discretion and platitudes

4.20. When are police officers most likely to show disrespect to citizens?
   a) When the citizen commits a crime in their presence
   b) When the citizen strikes the officer physically
   c) When the citizen first shows disrespect to the officer
   d) When the citizen files a complaint
   e) When the citizen flees the scene

4.21. What activity do officers usually spend the most time doing in the course of a shift?
   a) Order maintenance
   b) Provide medical assistance
   c) Traffic enforcement
   d) Free patrol
   e) Administration

4.22. What is TRUE about the profile of the American police officer in the 21st century?
   a) there are fewer women than in the past
   b) there are fewer nonwhites than in the past
   c) officers are better educated than in the past
   d) all of the above are TRUE
   e) all of the above are FALSE

4.23. Which of the following is NOT a function of a well-organized police department?
   a) clear lines of authority
   b) division of labor
   c) each working separately to achieve goals
   d) unity of command
   e) link duties with appropriate authority

4.24. Urban police departments are divided into...
  a) units
  b) wards
  c) precincts
  d) classes
  e) categories

4.25. How can a police officer best handle stress?
  a) work harder
  b) keep to yourself
  c) seek counseling
  d) all of the above
  e) none of the above

4.26. Which of the following situations is the best example of the police engaging in order maintenance?
  a) Asking a loud party to quiet down
  b) Arresting college students for public intoxication
  c) Stopping a speeding driver
  d) Directing traffic when a stoplight fails
  e) Assisting injured citizens at the scene of a car accident

4.27. Which of the following is a characteristic of the bureaucracy of police departments?
  a) Autonomy in work assignments
  b) Discretion to arrest
  c) Authority over citizens
  d) Tenacity in crime control
  e) Unity of command

4.28. These units form the core of the modern police department:
  a) Media relations and training
  b) Vice and juvenile
  c) Patrol and investigation
  d) Forensic science and planning
  e) Investigation and traffic

4.29. Which of the following statements does NOT help define the police bureaucratic system?
  a) Lacking chain of command, police officers make decisions "on the street" with no input from supervisors
  b) Individuals enter the system through the police, and the early process is vital to obtaining a conviction later.
  c) Police officers are expected to follow rules
  d) Final outcomes of cases rely on the decisions of others
  e) Police officers are entitled to make independent, discretionary decisions

4.30. Police policies are defined by:
  a) Police executives
  b) Politics
  c) Public pressure
  d) Social context
  e) All of the above

TRUE/FALSE

4.1. _____ The structure of American policing derives largely from the English system.

4.2. _____ The professional era of policing involved staying out of politics.

4.3. _____ The professional era of policing was challenged by the attacks on September 11th, 2001.

4.4. _____ The early focus on community policing involved making greater contact with citizens.

4.5. _____ Police officers providing first aid is an example of a service function.

4.6. _____ British police are called "bobbies" after Sir Robert Peel.

4.7. _____ In the United States, police powers are centralized in the federal government.

4.8. _____ In some southern U.S. cities, fear of slave revolts was a major factor in creating police agencies.

4.9. _____ One aspect of American policing is unlimited authority.

4.10. _____ The Federal Bureau of Investigation was created to investigate crime committed by white-collar offenders.

4.11. _____ The frankpledge system involved bribing government officials to free incarcerated criminals.

4.12. _____ Police corruption was a major problem during the political era of policing.

4.13. _____ The watchman style of policing emphasizes law enforcement.

4.14. _____ Public confidence is important for police if they are to do their job well.

4.15. _____ Prior to the eighteenth century, British citizens were expected to pursue criminals and help control crime.

4.16. _____ All men were required to act as members of the watch in the early American settlements.

4.17. _____ The DEA is the federal government's general law enforcement agency.

4.18. _____ Policing is not a stressful job.

4.19. _____ Women are prohibited from being patrol officers "on the street."

4.20. _____ Police often feel isolated from the public.

4.21. _____ Before the 1970s, many police departments did not hire nonwhite officers.

4.22. _____ Police officers are generally well paid.

4.23. _____ One assumption of the "Broken Windows" theory is that citizens must help the police to reduce crime.

ANSWER KEY

Key Terms

1. law enforcement [p. 119, LO6]
2. service [p. 120, LO6]
3. frankpledge [p. 99, LO1]
4. order maintenance [p. 119, LO6]
5. working personality [p. 115, LO4]
6. socialization [p. 114, LO4]
7. subculture [p. 115, LO4]

Fill-in-the-Blank

1. law enforcement [p. 119, LO6]
2. Professional [p. 101, LO2]
3. service [p. 120, LO6]
4. federal [p. 106, LO2]
5. sheriff [p. 106, LO2]
6. order maintenance [p. 119, LO6]
7. domestic violence [p. 111, LO5]
8. discretion [p. 111, LO6]
9. working personality [p. 115, LO6]
10. danger [p. 116, LO6]
11. authority [p. 116, LO6]

Multiple Choice

4.1. E [p. 99, LO1]
4.2. D [p. 99, LO1]
4.3. E [p. 105, LO2]
4.4. B [p. 106, LO3]
4.5. D [p. 100, LO1]
4.6. A [p. 108, LO3]
4.7. A [p. 119, LO6]
4.8. B [p. 125, LO6]
4.9. C [p. 104, LO4]
4.10. A [p. 101,102,103, LO1]
4.11. D [p. 102, LO1]
4.12. B [p. 102, LO2]
4.13. A [p. 102, LO2]
4.14. D [p. 103,104, LO6]
4.15. C [p. 125, LO6]
4.16. B [p. 108, LO2]
4.17. A [p. 115, LO4]
4.18. A [p. 118, LO4]
4.19. B [p. 116, LO4]
4.20. C [p. 116, LO4]
4.21. A [p. 116, LO5]
4.22. C [p. 112, LO3]
4.23. C [p. 121, LO5]
4.24. C [p. 101, LO5]
4.25. C [p. 118, LO4]
4.26. A [p. 119, LO6]
4.27. E [p. 121, LO5]
4.28. C [p. 122, LO5]
4.29. A [p. 123, LO5]
4.30. E [p. 124,125, LO6]

True/False

4.1. T [p. 99, LO1]
4.2. T [p. 102,103, LO1]
4.3. F [p. 102,103, LO1]
4.4. T [p. 103,104, LO1]
4.5. T [p. 120, LO6]
4.6. T [p. 100, LO1]
4.7. F [p. 107, LO2]
4.8. T [p. 100, LO1]
4.9. F [p. 99, LO1]
4.10. T [p. 106,107, LO2]
4.11. F [p. 99, LO1]
4.12. T [p. 101,102, LO1]
4.13. F [p. 125, LO6]
4.14. T [p. 125, LO6]
4.15. T [p. 99, LO1]
4.16. T [p. 99, LO1]
4.17. F [p. 107, LO2]
4.18. F [p. 117, LO4]
4.19. F [p. 113,114, LO3]
4.20. T [p. 117, LO4]
4.21. T [p. 112, LO3]
4.22. F [p. 109, LO4]
4.23. T [p. 104, LO6]

WORKSHEET 4.1: ORGANIZATION OF THE POLICE

Imagine that you are a member of Congress. One of your staff assistants brings you a proposal to nationalize law enforcement throughout the United States. The proposal calls for abolishing state police agencies, county sheriffs, and local police departments. Instead, Congress would create a new U.S. Department of Law Enforcement. A Secretary of Law Enforcement would oversee a national police agency which would have units established in each state, county, city, and town. Your assistant argues that the new organization would save resources by coordinating the work of every law enforcement officer in the nation and creating a standard set of law enforcement policies and priorities. In addition, the plan would standardize training, salary, and benefits for police officers everywhere and thus raise the level of professionalism of police, especially in small towns and rural areas. Before you decide whether or not to present this proposal to Congress, respond to the following questions.

1. Are there any undesirable consequences that could result from putting this plan into action?

_____

_____

_____

2. As a politician, you are concerned about how others will react to the plan. How do you think each of the following groups will react, and why?

  a. Voters: _____

_____

_____

  b. State and local politicians: _____

_____

_____

  c. Police officers: _____

_____

_____

3. Will you support the proposal? Why or why not?

_____

_____

_____

WORKSHEET 4.2: POLICE POLICY

You are a retired police chief. A state government has hired you to provide advice on the appropriate police policy to implement in several jurisdictions. You advise them as to whether to choose the watchman, legalistic, or service style. Explain why.

A. A city of 100,000 that contains a diverse mixture of whites, African Americans, Asian Americans, and Hispanics. The unemployment rate is high. Few wealthy people live in the city. Most people are middle-class, but 25 percent of the citizens qualify for government assistance. The police department reflects the racial/ethnic mix of the city's population.

B. A small town of 2,000 residents. Most residents work in the town's one lumber mill or in businesses that serve loggers and farmers who live in the area. The town's population is almost entirely white, except when large numbers of people from various minority groups arrive in the summer and fall to work on local farms.

C. A suburb with 15,000 residents. Twenty percent of the residents are members of minority groups. Nearly all of the town's residents are white-collar or professional workers with high incomes. Most people commute to a big city to work.

A. _____

_____

_____

_____

_____

B. _____

_____

_____

_____

_____

C. _____

_____

_____

_____

_____

WORKSHEET 4.3: RECRUITMENT/TRAINING OF POLICE OFFICERS

1. What qualifications would you require for someone to be hired as a police officer? Why?

_____

_____

_____

2. What salary and benefits would you offer in order to attract such candidates?

_____

_____

_____

3. What are the three most important subjects that new police recruits should learn? Why?

_____

_____

_____

4. Could training be used to minimize any negative aspects of the police subculture and working personality? If so, how?

_____

_____

_____

WORKSHEET 4.4: POLICE OFFICER TRAINING

As a police chief, what sort of training would provide to prepare your offices to handle each of the following categories of activities? Be sure to identify specific skills and knowledge that officers need for each category.

Service: _____

_____

_____

_____

_____

_____

Order Maintenance: _____

_____

_____

_____

_____

_____

Law Enforcement: _____

_____

_____

_____

_____

_____

WORKSHEET 4.5: SOLVING JOB-RELATED POLICING PROBLEMS

If you were a police chief, what steps would you take in training, supervision, distribution of assignment responsibilities, and overall administration to address the following issues?

Police Morality: _____

_____

_____

_____

_____

Police Isolation: _____

_____

_____

_____

_____

Police Job Stress: _____

_____

_____

_____

_____

TWENTY-FIRST CENTURY CHALLENGES IN POLICING

OUTLINE

- Police Response and Action
- Delivery of Police Services
- Issues in Patrolling
- Police and the Community
- Homeland Security
- Security Management and Private Policing

CHAPTER 5
TWENTY-FIRST CENTURY
CHALLENGES IN POLICING

LEARNING OBJECTIVES

After reading the material in this chapter, students should be able to:

1. Understand the everyday actions of the police

2. Recognize the factors that affect police response

3. Understand the main functions of police patrol, investigation, and special operations units

4. Analyze patrol strategies that police departments employ

5. Recognize the importance of connections between the police and the community

6. Identify issues and problems that emerge from law enforcement agencies' increased attention to homeland security

7. Understand the policing and related activities undertaken by private sector security management

CHAPTER SUMMARY

The police are mainly reactive rather than proactive, which often leads to incident-driven policing. The organization of the police bureaucracy influences how the police respond to citizens' calls. The productivity of a force can be measured in various ways including clearance rate, however, measuring proactive approaches is more difficult. Police services are delivered through the work of the patrol, investigation, and specialized operations units. The investigative function is the responsibility of detectives in close cooperation with patrol officers. The felony apprehension process is a sequence of actions that includes crime detection, preliminary investigation, follow-up investigation, clearance, and arrest. Large departments usually have specialized units dealing with traffic, drugs, and vice. Police administrators make choices about possible patrol strategies, which include directed patrol, foot patrol, and aggressive patrol. Community policing seeks to involve citizens in identifying problems and working with police officers to prevent disorder and crime. Police face challenges in dealing with special populations such as the mentally ill and homeless, who need social services yet often disturb or offend other citizens as they walk the streets. Policing in a multicultural society requires an appreciation of the attitudes, customs, and languages of minority group members. To be effective, the police must maintain their connection with the community.

Homeland security has become an important priority for law enforcement agencies at all levels of government since September 11, 2001. Agencies need planning and coordination in order to gather intelligence and prepare for possible threats and public emergencies. The federal government provides funding for state and local fusion centers and emergency preparedness equipment. New laws, such as the USA Patriot Act, have caused controversy about the proper balance between government authority and citizens' rights. The expansion of security management and private policing reflects greater recognition of the need to protect private assets and plan for emergencies. Security management produces new issues and problems including concerns about the recruitment, training, and activities of lower-level private security personnel. Public-private interaction affects security through such means as joint planning for emergencies, hiring private firms to guard government facilities, and hiring police officers for off-duty private security work

CHAPTER OUTLINE

I. POLICE RESPONSE AND ACTION

Police officers' actions and effectiveness depend on the resources available to them, and are marked by discretion – in a variety of contexts and circumstances.

A. Encounters Between Police and Citizens

The probability that a citizen will be arrested is related to the degree of access police have to the citizen, the complainant's demeanor and characteristics, and the type of violation committed. Citizens exercise control over police work through their decisions about whether to call the police. Many people fail to call the police to report crimes because they believe that it is not worth the effort and cost of the citizens' time.

B. Police Discretion

Discretion is a characteristic of organizations: officials are given the authority to base decisions on their own judgment rather than on a formal set of rules. Formal rules cannot cover all situations; officers must have a shared outlook that provides a common definition of situations that they are likely to encounter.

Discretion increases as one moves *down* the organizational hierarchy: patrol officers have the greatest amount of discretion in maintaining order and enforcing ambiguous laws such as disorderly conduct, public drunkenness, or breach of the peace. Officers exercise discretion in a number of ways including noninvolvement (i.e., doing nothing), arrest, or informal handling of incidents. Their decision typically involves a number of factors, including the nature of the crime, the relationship of the suspect to the complainant, the relationship of the police to the complainant or suspect, and demographic variables such as age, gender, class, and ethnicity.

C. **Domestic Violence**

Domestic violence perpetrated by men against women is consistent across racial and ethnic boundaries. African-American women, women aged 16-24, those living in urban areas, and those from lower income families are the most likely to be victims of violence by an intimate. It has been estimated that 30% of all female murder victims were killed by intimates.

Concerns were expressed that police intervention would make the situation worse for the victim by intervening into a "private family matter." Intervention in domestic disputes can also be dangerous to police officers. Domestic disturbances are volatile, emotional situations and citizens are typically hostile to the police.

Police in a democracy are organized mainly to be *reactive* (responding to citizen calls for service) rather than *proactive* (initiating activity on their own). Since police often arrive after the fact, reports by victims and observers have come to define the boundaries of policing. The public frequently expects that police will respond to every call, resulting in incident-driven policing. Police employ proactive strategies such as surveillance in some contexts. As more police personnel are allocated to proactive operations, the number of resulting arrests is likely to rise.

D. **Organizational Response**

A department's organization and administrative environment affect the way in which calls are processed as well as the nature of police response. The centralization of communications using technology such as 911 numbers and two-way radios changed the early police pattern of individual patrol officers observing and addressing crime problems in assigned neighborhoods. However, advocates of community policing believe that too much reliance on such technology further isolates the officers from the community and prevents them from building rapport. Police departments use *differential response strategies* for calls. Dispatchers make decisions about whether or not a patrol car needs to rush to the scene of each call. A delayed response may be just as effective depending on the nature of the call.

E. **Productivity**

Following the lead of New York City's Compstat program, several cities now emphasize accountability at the precinct level. Police have difficulty in measuring the quantity and quality of their work, and tend to focus on crime rates and clearance rates. Clearance rates vary according to the nature of the offense. Police often use "activity" (i.e., number of tickets issued, arrests made, suspects stopped for questioning) as a measure of productiveness, although this does not necessarily reflect the complete range of order maintenance functions. It may actually be more beneficial for society when police spend their time calming conflicts, becoming acquainted with citizens, and providing services and information for people.

II. DELIVERY OF POLICE SERVICES

Line functions, which directly involve field operations, account for the majority of police personnel. Within this group of officers, the patrol bureau is generally the largest.

A. <u>Patrol Functions</u>
Patrol officers make up two-thirds of all sworn officers. In small communities, the patrol force constitutes the entire department. The patrol function has three components: answering calls for assistance, maintaining a police presence, and probing suspicious circumstances. When not responding to calls, officers engage in preventive patrol, with the goal of deterring crime with their presence, which can also be a major factor in reducing citizen fear of crime. Patrol may also improve community relations and increase citizen cooperation with police.

B. <u>Investigation</u>
Most police departments have detective units, which are responsible for the investigation of criminal cases. Detectives are often organized by the type of crime they investigate (homicide, robbery, forgery, burglary, etc.). Detective work is largely reactive in that detectives typically wait until a crime is reported before their work can begin. Even though detectives are responsible for investigating most crimes in a jurisdiction, other officers (such as patrol, traffic, vice and juveniles) also have some investigative functions.

1. **Apprehension**: Apprehension of suspects has three stages. First, the crime is detected (either reported or discovered). Next, preliminary investigation is begun—usually by a patrol officer. Follow-up investigation, which on larger forces is usually performed by specialized detectives, is next. The final stages of apprehension are clearance and arrest, in which the crime is "solved" by arresting a suspect.

2. **Forensic Techniques**: This involves the application of scientific principles to the gathering and storage of physical evidence such as fingerprints, blood sample analysis, and DNA.

3. **Research on Investigation**: Police may have overrated the importance of investigation as a means of solving crimes; research reveals that most crimes are cleared because of arrests made by the patrol force at or near the scene. A key factor in crime clearance is identification of the offender by a victim or witness, which often has very little to do with investigation. However, good detective work can help improve police-community relations in that the police are seen as visibly working to solve a crime.

C. **Special Operations**

1. **Traffic** work is highly discretionary and essentially proactive, and the level of enforcement can be considered a direct result of departmental policies and norms. Traffic enforcement is one area in which departments enforce norms of productivity.

2. **Vice** officers work proactively to enforce laws against prostitution, gambling, and drug offenses. Because of the nature of the crimes, political influence is sometimes brought to bear to discourage enforcement. Police are increasingly using electronic surveillance and undercover work to clear vice crimes.

3. **Drug enforcement** is sometimes handled by a separate drug bureau within police departments. Such departments may periodically engage in aggressive patrol "round-ups," arresting drug dealers off the streets. However, some believe that a "war on drugs" is not necessarily the best way to combat drug-related crime.

III. **ISSUES IN PATROLLING**

Patrol officers utilize many different techniques to combat crime, which are typically defined by departmental policy. There is sometimes disagreement between researchers and police personnel about the most effective strategies for reducing crime.

A. **Assignment of Patrol Personnel**
It is important for departments to distribute officers geographically and by shift in the manner that is most effective in combating crime and keeping order. These decisions are usually made based on calls for service and crime problems.

1. **Preventive Patrol**: This method involves sending more police into neighborhoods to (1) actively look for criminal behavior, and (2) increase the visibility of the police. Unfortunately, research has indicated that preventive patrol does not seem to have a measurable effect on crime.

2. **Hot Spots**: Police can identify locations where crime is most likely to occur. These "hot spots" deserve more police attention, given their above-normal crime rates. This method of directed patrol can help to reduce crime, if that's where most crime is occurring. Knowledge of the seasonal and time-related variations in crime patterns can also be used to plan directed patrol.

106

3. **Rapid Response Time**: Most citizens believe rapid response time is important for controlling crime. Improvements in communication technology and the proliferation of cell phones have helped to decrease response time. However, there is little evidence that clearance rates increase if response time is decreased.

4. **Foot versus Motorized Patrol:** Most patrolling by police is done in cars, but sometimes it makes sense for police to patrol on foot or bicycle. Citizens feel better when officers are more "accessible", and patrol in police cars tends to distance police from citizens.

5. **One-Person versus Two-Person Patrol Units**: It is more cost-effective and efficient to place one officer in each police car, given that two officers in two police cars can cover twice as much area. However, it may be safer for two officers to ride together in one vehicle.

6. **Aggressive Patrol**: This proactive strategy involves the police aggressively attempting to reduce crime. There are many kinds of aggressive patrol, but most target specific types of crime. One strategy of aggressive patrol is based on the "broken windows" theory, which advocates control of small crime problems that might encourage larger crime problems to flourish. Unfortunately, these policies can lead to poor police-community relations.

7. **Community Policing:** Strategies for community policing involve problem-directed policing, in which officers are responsible for identifying community problems and working with community members to formulate solutions. The SARA strategy (Scanning, Analysis, Response, and Assessment) is often used for problem-solving in police work, and many departments train their officers to use these methods to reduce crime.

B. **The Future of Patrol**
   Improvements in technology, the shift to community policing, and the increasing importance of geographic crime analysis have changed the face of policing in the United States. The increased focus on fighting terrorism and the need for homeland security is also currently changing American policing in many ways.

IV. POLICE AND THE COMMUNITY

A. **Special Populations**
   Urban police have the complex task of working with social service agencies in dealing with special populations such as the homeless, runaways, mentally ill, drugs addicts, and alcoholics.

B. **Policing a Multicultural Society**

Policing can be a difficult task, especially in urban areas where there is distrust of police and a lack of cooperation among some citizens. The increasing ethnic diversity of the United States has resulted in poor police-citizen relations, which may be the result of stereotypes, cultural differences, and language barriers.

Some research has indicated that police officers may have biased attitudes toward the poor and members of racial minority groups. In addition, the military organization of police and the "war on crime" mentality many encourage violence by police toward inner city residents.

C. **Community Crime Prevention**

Police officers cannot control of crime and disorder without the assistance of citizens. There are currently many mechanisms for community involvement in crime control, including neighborhood watch, "crime stopper" programs on television and radio and "Weed and Seed" programs.

V. HOMELAND SECURITY

The terrorist attacks of September 11th have changed the face of American policing. Policing has become more focused on international cooperation and intelligence gathering.

A. **Preparing for Threats**

The Department of Homeland Security (DHS) was created to help protect the United States from terrorist attacks. One of their main concerns is law enforcement intelligence, which is the information needed to preempt crime, including terrorism. Local police have increased their training in law enforcement intelligence, and have begun cross-jurisdiction cooperation to adequately fight threats from terrorism. Fusion centers are used to coordinate inter-jurisdiction intelligence and encouraged communication between state and local agencies.

One consequence of the shift to homeland security-focused law enforcement is lack of funding for other programs, such as community policing. Experts warn that this shift needs to be planned carefully (such as using the Incident Command System) to avoid neglecting problems in other areas of law enforcement.

B. **New Laws and Controversies**

New laws and policies emerged following the terrorist attacks on September 11th. Some are concerned that our constitutional rights are at risk as the federal government attempts to prevent additional attacks.

1. **The USA Patriot Act** allows the government more liberty in searches and wiretaps, but some are concerned that the ability of the government to access library records (for example) is too intrusive. Despite criticisms from both liberals and conservatives, the Act was renewed with few changes in 2006. Since then, federal judges have struck down provisions of the Act as unconstitutional.

VI. SECURITY MANAGEMENT AND PRIVATE POLICING

Some private officers are merely watchmen who stand ready to call the police but others are deputized and granted arrest authority when a felony is committed in their presence. It is uncertain whether legal restrictions on police that protect individuals' constitutional rights also apply to actions by private police. There are indications that many private agencies are ready to assume increased responsibility for minor criminal incidents and that some governments are willing to consider letting private agencies handle some responsibilities (e.g. security at public buildings).

A. Functions of Security Management and Private Police
Top-level security managers have a range of responsibilities that call upon them to fulfill multiple roles that would be handled by a variety of separate individuals in the public sector. At lower levels, specific occupations in private security are more directly comparable to those of police officers. Many security personnel are the equivalent of private sector detectives. Other activities are more directly comparable to those of police patrol officers, especially for lower level security officers who must guard specific buildings, apartments, or stores.

B. Private Police and Homeland Security
Private police agencies are typically responsible for security around attractive terrorist targets, such as nuclear power plants, oil refineries and military manufacturing facilities. Some agencies, however, have not trained their personnel to be aware of terror threats. Private security officers are typically paid significantly less than police officers, and can even be without important technology (such as radios) that help them protect both buildings and individuals from harm.

C. Private Employment of Public Police
Many private agencies rely on public officers as employees. Off-duty police officers are frequently employed with private security firms, and there is a benefit of this to employers: off-duty police retain their full authority and powers to arrest, and stop and frisk while working for a private company.

1. **Conflict of Interest**: Police officers are banned from being process servers, bill collectors, repossessors, investigators for criminal defense attorneys and bail bondsmen, or employees at gambling establishments. Acting in these positions would create a conflict for them, as they may not be able to act in an unbiased way.

2. **Management Prerogatives**: departments require officers to gain permission to accept outside work, and department may deny permission if work degrading to department, physically exhausting, or dangerous.

Some departments control officer's work through a *department contract model* in which department pays the officer directly for off-duty work and the private business reimburses the department. This helps to maintain departmental control and protect departmental needs and interests. The *officer contract model* allows officers to contract independently with businesses if they have permission of the department. Finally, the *union brokerage model* lets union set pay scale and working conditions for outside employment. Generally, the more closely a department controls its officers' off-duty employment, the more liability it assumes for officers' actions when they work for private firms.

C. The Public-Private Interface

Private employers' interests may not always coincide with the goals and policies of the local police department. Lack of communication between public and private agencies can lead to botched investigations, loss of evidence, and overzealousness by private officers. Some cooperative efforts and investigations have occurred between security and police.

Private agencies tend to report UCR index crimes, but do not report fraud, commercial bribery, employee theft, and other "white collar" type offenses in the companies for which they work. This tends to provide more lenient private justice for corporate employees caught in wrongdoing and is never reported to law enforcement authorities. Internal punishment through payroll deduction restitution or firing is usually much quicker than providing evidence for police and prosecutors.

D. Recruitment and Training

There are serious concerns on the part of law enforcement officials and civil libertarians about the recruitment and training of private officers, given that there is relatively little training provided in most places. Fewer than half of the states have licensing requirements. Because pay is low and many private officers work only temporarily, work is often done by the young or the retired, with few formal qualifications. Regulations that exist tend to be aimed at contractual private police (agencies that work for fees) rather than proprietary (officers hired by a company to provide security for that company).

REVIEW OF KEY TERMS

Define each of the following:

discretion

domestic violence

reactive

proactive

incident-driven policing

differential response

clearance rate

line functions

sworn officers

preventive patrol

directed patrol

aggressive patrol

problem-oriented policing

law enforcement intelligence

USA Patriot Act

111

SELF-TEST SECTION

KEY TERMS

Fill in the appropriate term for each statement:

1. _____ is an approach in which officers seek to identify, analyze, and respond to the underlying circumstances that create the incidents that generate citizens' calls for police assistance.

2. The _____ is used as a measure of officer success at solving crimes.

3. _____ policing strategies involve officers actively seeking out crime.

4. Officers who have taken an oath to uphold the law and protect society are called _____.

5. _____ are basic police operations performed by units such as patrol and traffic.

6. _____ policing is the typical American patrol strategy that involves officers responding to citizens' calls.

7. _____ policing occurs in response to crime.

8. _____ is a strategy designed to focus patrol resources in a proactive manner against known high crime areas

9. _____ sets priorities for officer response to calls for service.

10. The goal of _____ is to make officer presence known in neighborhoods in order to deter crime.

11. _____ is a proactive patrol strategy which may involve greater numbers of on-street interrogations and traffic stops.

12. The _____ was enacted after September 11th in order to more easily conduct searches and wiretaps.

13. _____ is collected and analyzed to learn about illegal activities such as terrorism.

FILL-IN-THE-BLANK EXERCISE

When police decide to allocate resources to crime "hot spots," they use **1.** ____________________, which is a form of **2.** ____________________ patrol because it involves police initiative rather than reaction.

Police may directly address problems in a community through **3.** ____________________, which involves in-depth examination recurring problems as well as through **4.** ____________________, which will bring officers in closer contact with citizens in their neighborhoods.

5. ____________________ is not a particularly good measure of **6.** ____________________ because it is so heavily dependent on prompt reports from victims and witnesses and because impressive performance will not necessarily increase the rate of arrests.

Because of the power gained through the police union movement that has affected police departments in the past twenty years, police officers have greater input into policy decisions affecting law enforcement. In some cities, this power carries over into the organization of opportunities to gain extra income through **7.** ____________________, although some departments do not allow officers to work for private firms.

MULTIPLE CHOICE

5.1. Which of the following is a line function?
a) patrol
b) investigation
c) traffic control
d) vice
e) all of the above

5.2. Why do proactive responses to crime usually have a clearance rate of 100%?
a) these crimes are always reported to police
b) evidentiary problems usually reduce arrest rates
c) there are always witnesses to these kinds of events
d) these crimes are impossible to solve
e) because they are initiated in police, they usually result in arrest

5.3. Which of the following statements is true about detective work?
a) They engage in law enforcement as well as service and order maintenance
b) They are usually receive lower pay than patrol officers
c) They must wear uniforms to work
d) Their work is similar to federal investigative positions
e) They are likely reactive in their duties

5.4. What is the origin of the word "patrol"?
a) from a Scottish word meaning "rolling police"
b) from a German word meaning "police action"
c) from a French word meaning "to tramp around in the mud"
d) from a Spanish word meaning "to dance in the streets"
e) from a Latin word meaning "walking with authority"

5.5. How many instances does rapid police response really make a difference?
a) none
b) a small fraction
c) about one-half
d) a great many
e) all

5.6. Which of the following delays slow the process of calling the police?
a) ambiguity delays
b) coping delays
c) conflict delays
d) all of the above
e) none of the above

5.7. In the past, patrols were organized by "beats" because it was assumed that...
a) crime could happen anywhere
b) police could "beat" criminals at their game
c) police could use timing techniques to solve crimes
d) criminals were all "deadbeats"
e) all of the above

5.8. Which of the following is an example of a proactive strategy?
a) responding to a citizens' call
b) undercover work
c) citizen approaching police on the street with information
d) all of the above
e) none of the above

5.9. Which of the following is an example of a reactive strategy?
a) surveillance
b) undercover work
c) waiting for a citizen to approach police on the street with information
d) all of the above
e) none of the above

5.10. According to research, what is a crucial factor in solving crimes?
a) DNA evidence
b) Tips from informants
c) Offender line-ups
d) Identification of the perpetrator by the victim
e) Fingerprint analysis

5.11. A police officer driving through a neighborhood spots a citizen waiving at her to stop. If the officer stops to talk with the citizen, this type of policing is considered to be:
a) Proactive policing
b) Reactive policing
c) Informal policing
d) Formal policing
e) Occupational policing

5.12. What is the primary action by police in incident-driven policing?
a) Responding quickly to calls from citizens
b) Driving around, looking for crime
c) Gathering intelligence about criminal activity
d) Cracking down on problem areas
e) Identifying problems and generating solutions

5.13. Which of the following are measures of police productivity?
a) Clearance rate
b) Number of arrests
c) Tickets issued
d) Cars ticketed
e) All of the above are measures of productivity

5.14. Which statement regarding homeland security is FALSE?
a) Since September 11th 2001, American policing has focused less on international cooperation and intelligence gathering.
b) Funding has been shifted away from community policing to strengthen homeland security
c) The Department of Homeland Security focuses on gang-related crime in addition to threats from terrorism
d) The Department of Homeland Security was created, in part, to increase inter-agency communication
e) After September 11th 2001, New York City and Washington, DC received cuts to their federal funding.

5.15. Why are some Americans critical of the USA Patriot Act?
a) It limits funding to the Department of Homeland Security
b) It weakens the federal government by increasing offender's rights
c) It increases the ability of the government to conduct warrantless searches and wiretaps
d) It was passed too long after September 11th to have any effect on terrorism
e) It was passed by a very small number of members in the Congress

5.16. The focus of domestic terrorism is the use of:
a) Violence
b) Intimidation
c) Peaceful protest
d) Suicide bombings
e) Litigation

5.17. Which of the following private employment opportunities would NOT be a conflict of interest for public police officers looking for extra work?
a) Working security in the mall at during the holiday season
b) Doing background checks for criminal defense attorneys
c) Acting as a bail bondsman
d) Acting as a process server
e) Working security in a casino

TRUE/FALSE

5.1.   _____   Most police work generally is reactive.

5.2.   _____   Patrol officers account for two-thirds of all sworn officers.

5.3.   _____   Line functions are those that directly involve field operations.

5.4.   _____   A small number of hot spots can be responsible for a great deal of crime in a jurisdiction.

5.5.   _____   Even though many people today have cellular phones, very few 911 calls come from cell phones.

5.6.   _____   Police do not use proactive strategies.

5.7.   _____   Most police action is initiated by an officer in the field.

5.8.   _____   All police departments have vice squads.

5.9.   _____   Rewarding officers through the use of traffic ticket quotas is one way to encourage them to use incident-directed patrol more often.

5.10.   _____   The clearance rate is the percentage of crimes solved through an arrest.

5.11.   _____   Arrests for drug selling has a 100 percent clearance rate.

5.12.   _____   Rapid response time is valuable for only a small fraction of police calls.

ANSWER KEY

Key Terms

1. problem-oriented policing [p. 148, LO4]
2. clearance rate [p. 135, LO4]
3. proactive [p. 133, LO1]
4. sworn officers [p. 137, LO3]
5. line functions [p. 136, LO3]
6. incident-driven policing [p. 133, LO4]
7. reactive [p. 133, LO1]
8. directed patrol [p. 143, LO4]
9. differential response [p. 134, LO4]
10. preventive patrol [p. 137, LO4]
11. aggressive patrol [p. 145, LO4]
12. USA Patriot Act [p. 157, LO6]
13. law enforcement intelligence [p. 154, LO6]

Fill-in-the-Blank

1. directed patrol [p. 143, LO4]
2. proactive patrol [p. 133, LO4]
3. problem-oriented policing [p. 148, LO4]
4. community-oriented policing [p. 146, LO4]
5. response time [p. 143, LO2]
6. productivity [p. 143, LO4]
7. private policing [p. 160, LO7]

Multiple Choice

5.1. A [p. 136, LO3]
5.2. E [p. 133, LO1]
5.3. E [p. 138, LO3]
5.4. C [p. 136, LO3]
5.5. B [p. 143, LO2]
5.6. D [p. 144, LO2]
5.7. A [p. 143, LO4]
5.8. B [p. 133, LO4]
5.9. C [p. 133, LO4]
5.10. D [p. 138, LO3]
5.11. B [p. 133, LO4]
5.12. A [p. 133, LO4]
5.13. E [p. 143, LO2]
5.14. A [p. 161, LO6]
5.15. C [p. 157, LO6]
5.16. B [p. 157, LO6]
5.17. A [p. 162, LO7]

True/False

5.1. T [p. 133, LO1]
5.2. T [p. 137, LO3]
5.3. T [p. 136, LO3]
5.4. T [p. 143, LO4]
5.5. F [p. 144, LO5]
5.6. F [p. 145, LO4]
5.7. F [p. 133, LO4]
5.8. F [p. 141, LO3]
5.9. F [p. 146, LO3]
5.10. T [p. 135, LO1]
5.11. T [p. 135, LO1]
5.12. T [p. 143, LO2]

WORKSHEET 5.1: DETECTIVES

A study has raised questions about whether or not your police department should keep a separate investigation division containing detectives. There are questions about how much detectives contribute to overall crime clearance, because most arrests result from the work of patrol officers or the assistance of citizens. Pretend that you have to draft a report making recommendations about the future of the detective bureau. How would you address the following questions?

1. What is the job of the detectives? (Write a job description.)

_____

_____

_____

_____

_____

2. How are investigations conducted and what is the role of the detectives in investigations?

_____

_____

_____

3. What would be the consequences to the police department if there were no detectives?

_____

_____

_____

4. What would be the advantages of eliminating the detective function? Would you recommend doing so? Why or why not?

_____

_____

_____

_____

WORKSHEET 5.2: SPECIAL LAW ENFORCEMENT CHALLENGES

Consider the special challenges and problems police officers face in dealing with the following issues. What suggestions would you make for handling these issues?

Domestic violence: _____

_____

_____

People who are homeless and mentally ill: _____

_____

_____

Ethnic communities in which many people do not speak English: _____

_____

_____

Lack of financial resources allowing small-town forces to invest in the latest technology:

_____

_____

_____

WORKSHEET 5.3: MEASURING POLICE PRODUCTIVITY

Police departments have struggled to identify good ways to measure productivity. What are the pros and cons of using the following methods to measure police productivity?

Number of Arrests: _____

_____

_____

_____

_____

_____

Number of Traffic Tickets: _____

_____

_____

_____

_____

_____

Number of convictions resulting from a particular officer's arrests: _____

_____

_____

_____

_____

_____

POLICE AND LAW

OUTLINE

- Legal Limitations on Police Investigations
- Plain View Doctrine
- Warrantless Searches
- Questioning Suspects
- The Exclusionary Rule
- Police Abuse of Power
- Civic Accountability

CHAPTER 6
POLICE AND LAW

LEARNING OBJECTIVES

After reading the material in this chapter, students should be able to:

1. Know the extent of police officers' authority to stop people and to conduct searches of people, their vehicles, and other property

2. Recognize how police officers seek warrants in order to conduct searches and make arrests

3. Identify situations in which police officers can examine property and conduct searches without obtaining a warrant

4. Analyze the purpose of the privilege against compelled self-incrimination

5. Understand the exclusionary rule and situations in which it applies

6. Analyze the problems of police abuse and corruption

7. Recognize the mechanisms used to hold police accountable when they violate laws and policies

CHAPTER SUMMARY

The Supreme Court has defined rules for the circumstances and justifications for stops, searches, and arrests primarily with reference to the Fourth Amendment's prohibition on "unreasonable searches and seizures." Most stops must be supported by reasonable suspicion, while arrests, like search warrants, must be supported by enough information to constitute probable cause. The plain view doctrine permits officers to visually examine and seize any contraband or criminal evidence that is in open sight when they are in a place that they are legally permitted to be. Searches are considered "reasonable" and may be conducted without warrants in a number of specific circumstances such as borders, airports, and other situations where they are required by special needs beyond the normal purposes of law enforcement. Limited searches may be conducted without warrants when officers have reasonable suspicions to justify a stop-and-frisk for weapons on the streets, when officers make a lawful arrest, when exigent circumstances exist, when people voluntarily consent to searches of their persons or property, and in certain situations involving automobiles. The Fifth Amendment privilege against compelled self-incrimination helps protect citizens against violence and coercion by police as well as maintain the legitimacy and integrity of the legal system. The Supreme Court's decision in *Miranda v. Arizona* (1966) required officers to inform suspects of specific rights before custodial questioning, although officers have adapted their practices to accommodate this rule, and several exceptions have been created. The exclusionary rule is a remedy designed to deter police from violating citizens' rights during criminal investigations by barring the use of illegally obtained evidence in court. The Supreme Court has created several exceptions to the exclusionary rule, including the inevitable discovery rule and the "good faith" exception in defective warrant situations.

Police corruption and misuse of force and corruption may cause erosion of support among the community a police department serves. The four major approaches employed to increase police accountability to citizens are internal affairs units, civilian review boards, standards and accreditation, and civil liability suits. The development of new technologies has assisted police investigations through the use of computers, databases, surveillance devices, and methods to detect deception. Police departments are seeking to identify non-lethal weapons that can incapacitate suspects and control unruly crowds without causing serious injuries and deaths. After September 11th, federal and local law enforcement have refocused their efforts on intelligence and protecting the public from terrorist attacks. The expansion of security management and private policing reflects greater recognition of the need to protect private assets and plan for emergencies, but it also produces new issues and problems concerning the recruitment, training, and activities of lower-level private security personnel.

CHAPTER OUTLINE

I. LEGAL LIMITS OF POLICE INVESTIGATIONS

In a democratic society, police are expected to control crime while complying with the rule of law as it protects the rights of citizens, including criminal suspects. To be admissible against a suspect in court, evidence must have been obtained in accordance with certain rules which have been implemented to ensure the police do not step beyond the bounds of their authority.

A. Search and Seizure Concepts

The Fourth Amendment prohibits unreasonable searches and seizures. The Supreme Court defines searches as actions by law enforcement officials that intrude upon people's reasonable expectations of privacy. The plain view doctrine permits officers to notice and use as evidence items that are visible to them when they are in a location where they are permitted to be, such as a public sidewalk. Similarly, police can see what is in open area, including private property, either by walking through open fields or by flying a helicopter over people's houses and yards. Officers may not break into a home and then claim that the drugs found inside were in plain view on a table. However, if a homeowner invited officers into his home in order to file a report about a burglary, the officers do not need to obtain a warrant in order to seize drugs that they see lying on the kitchen table.

In defining seizures, the Supreme Court focuses on the nature and extent of officers' interference with people's liberty and freedom of movement. A stop is a brief interference with a person's freedom of movement for a duration that can be measured in minutes. In order to be permissible under the Fourth Amendment, stops must be justified by reasonable suspicion—a situation in which specific articulable facts lead officers to conclude that the person may be engaging in criminal activity.

B. **The Concept of Arrest**

An arrest is the seizure of an individual by a government official who takes the suspect into custody. Courts prefer arrest warrants for felonies, but have not required them. According to the Fourth Amendment, arrests must be based on probable cause.

C. **Warrants and Probable Cause**

An officer must show reliable information establishing that there is probable cause to believe that a crime has been or is being committed. The particular premises and pieces of property to be seized must be specifically identified, and the officer must swear under oath that they are correct to the best of their knowledge.

Search warrants can be obtained when officers present an affidavit that the information they present to obtain the warrant is believed to be correct.

II. WARRANTLESS SEARCHES

During a search, incident to arrest or with a warrant, officers can seize and examine items that are in plain view, even if they are not listed on the warrant, if those items may be evidence of illegal activity.

A. **Open Fields Doctrine**

Property owners have no reasonable expectation of privacy in open areas on and around their property.

B. **Plain Feel and Other Senses**

Police officers can justify a warrantless search based upon smell or odor and also based upon feel.

III. WARRANTLESS SEARCHES

A. **Special Needs beyond the Normal Purpose of Law Enforcement**

Officers do not need any suspicion to justify a search in specific contexts, such as airline passengers or border searches. U.S. Customs and Border Patrol agents (CBP) can use random searches at the Canadian and Mexican borders, and these agents can use the standard of "reasonable suspicion" to identify individuals to search.

Some states can use vehicle checkpoints to apprehend drunk drivers, but not every state allows this type of warrantless search due to differences in state statutes and court decisions.

B. **Stop and Frisk on the Streets**

Brief questioning and pat-down searches (stop-and-frisk) are permitted based on reasonable judgment of police officers that a crime has occurred or is about to occur, and that the stopped person may have a weapon (*Terry v. Ohio*, 1968). However, an anonymous tip is insufficient justification for a stop-and-frisk search [*Florida v. J.L.* (2000)].

C. **Search Incident to Lawful Arrest**

Police can search people and areas in the immediate vicinity for weapons when a lawful arrest is made [(*Chimel v. California*, (1969)].

D. **Exigent Circumstances**

Officers might find themselves in the middle of an urgent situation where they must act swiftly and do not have time to request a warrant from the court.

E. **Consent**

A citizen may waive his or her Fourth Amendment and other rights and allow police to conduct a search. Police officers do not have to inform citizens of their right to decline a request to search [(*United States v. Drayton* (2002)].

F. **Automobile Searches**

Automobiles differ from homes in terms of people's expectations of privacy and the risk that evidence may be contained in a mobile vehicle. Officers may search automobiles and containers in such vehicles if they have probable cause to do so.

IV. QUESTIONING SUSPECTS

Upon arrest, suspects must be informed of their rights. This is vitally important, given the constitutional protection against self-incrimination guaranteed by the Fifth Amendment.

A. ***Miranda* Rules**

In *Miranda v. Arizona* (1966), the Supreme Court stated that subjects in police custody must be notified of the following: (1) they have the right to remain silent; (2) if they choose to make a statement, it can and will be used against them in court; (3) they have the right to have an attorney present during interrogation, or have an opportunity to consult with an attorney; and (4) if they cannot afford an attorney, the state will provide one.

In *Escobedo v. Illinois* (1964), the Court linked the Fifth and Sixth Amendments, stating that the right to counsel and the right against self-incrimination are interrelated.

B. **The Consequences of *Miranda***

Police officers have adapted their techniques in various ways to question suspects and get information despite *Miranda* limitations. *Miranda* rights must be provided *before questions are asked* during custodial interrogations.

Departments train officers to read the *Miranda* warnings to suspects as soon as an arrest is made. This is done in order to make sure the warnings are not omitted as the suspect in processed in the system. The warnings may be read off a standard "Miranda card" to make sure that the rights are provided consistently and correctly. However, the courts do not require that police inform suspects of their rights immediately after arrest.

Officers are also trained in interrogation techniques that are intended to encourage suspects to talk despite *Miranda* warnings immediately after arrest. The Supreme Court has ruled that officers may use such tactics to encourage suspects to confess, even if those tactics are dishonest.

V. THE EXCLUSIONARY RULE

If evidence used in criminal trials is obtained illegally, that evidence cannot be used against an offender in court. The Supreme Court created the exclusionary rule as a judicial remedy to guard against police corruption.

A. Application of the Exclusionary Rule to the States
One of the most important cases in the Warren Court, the case of *Mapp v. Ohio* (1961), applied the exclusionary rule to the states.

B. Exceptions to the Exclusionary Rule
As composition of the Supreme Court became more conservative in the 1970s and 1980s, a number of decisions limited or created exceptions to the exclusionary rule. Among the modifications created were exceptions for public safety, inevitable discovery [*Nix v. Williams* (1984)], and "good faith" exceptions.

VI. POLICE ABUSE OF POWER

A. Use of Force
Citizens use the term "police brutality" to describe a wide range of practices, from the use of profane or abusive language to physical force and violence. However, police use of deadly force often causes great emotional upheaval within a community. The typical victim of police force is an African American male.

In *Tennessee v. Garner* (1985), the Supreme Court ruled for the first time that police use of deadly force to apprehend an unarmed, nonviolent, fleeing felony suspect violated the Fourth Amendment guarantee against unreasonable seizure. Previously, police in many states followed common law principle that allowed the use of any force necessary to arrest a fleeing felon. The risk of significant lawsuits by victims of improper police shootings looms over contemporary police departments and creates incentives for administrators to set and enforce standards for the use of force.

B. Corruption
Corruption is not easily defined—it can range from accepting free items from local businesses to murder.

"Grass eaters" are officers who accept payoffs that circumstances of police work bring their way. This is the most common form of corruption. "Meat eaters" aggressively misuse their power for personal gain. Recent examples of officers getting actively involved in crimes related to illegal drug trafficking, either working with drug dealers or else robbing drug dealers.

Such corruption has multiple effects: criminals are left free to pursue their illegal activities, departmental morale and supervision drop, and the public image of the police suffers.

VII. CIVIC ACCOUNTABILITY

A. Internal Affairs Units

These units investigate complaints against officers. Investigations by internal affairs units do not often fit the Hollywood model, frequently investigating allegations of sexual harassment, substance abuse problems, or misuse of physical force rather than grand corruption. Working in internal affairs offices can be stressful, as it places a strain on the relationship of these officers with their counterparts outside the unit. Moreover, those conducting an investigation often find it difficult to obtain information from other officers.

B. Civilian Review Boards

Such boards are a politically sensitive issue, because police oppose civilian evaluation or control of their actions. Nonetheless, such boards exist in 36 of the 50 largest cities and in 13 of the next 50 largest cities. Although officers believe such boards cannot understand and judge them fairly, the boards have not been harsh on police. Because of the low visibility of actions that result in complaints, most complaints cannot be substantiated.

C. Standards and Accreditation

Communities can gain greater accountability if they require that operations be conducted by nationally recognized standards. For example, the Commission on Accreditation for Law Enforcement Agencies (CALEA) includes the creation of standards for the use of discretion. Accreditation is voluntary. Certification may increase public confidence in the department while providing its management with tools that serve as a basis for educating officers about being accountable for their actions.

D. Civil Liability Suits

Civil lawsuits against departments for misconduct are another avenue for civic accountability. Lawsuits for brutality, false arrest, and negligence are increasingly common. Such suits were first approved by the Supreme Court in 1961. Successful lawsuits, or even the threat of lawsuits, affect the development of departmental policies. Insurance companies that provide civil liability coverage for police departments now give discounts to departments that obtain accreditation.

REVIEW OF KEY TERMS

<u>Define each of the following:</u>

affidavit

exclusionary rule

exigent circumstances

"good faith" exception

inevitable discovery rule

open fields doctrine

plain view doctrine

probable cause

"public safety" exception

reasonable expectation of privacy

reasonable suspicion

search

seizure

stop

stop-and-frisk search

totality of circumstances test

Chimel v. California (1969)

Miranda v. Arizona (1966)

Nix v. Williams (1984)

Terry v. Ohio (1968)

United States v. Drayton (2002)

internal affairs units

SELF-TEST SECTION

KEY TERMS

Fill in the appropriate term for each statement:

1. _____ established the "stop and frisk" doctrine permitting pat-down searches during field interrogations.

2. In the case of _____ the Supreme Court determined that officers are not required to inform suspects that they may decline a search by the police.

3. A _____ occurs when an official examines and hunts for evidence in or on a person or place in a manner that intrudes on reasonable expectation of privacy.

4. A court must use the _____ test before granting a search warrant.

5. _____ established that a gun protruding from under seat is within the scope of the plain view doctrine.

6. The landmark case mandating that suspects must be informed of their rights prior to questioning is _____.

7. When a government official interferes with an individual's freedom of movement, it is considered a _____.

8. _____ established the inevitable discovery exception to the exclusionary rule.

9. When officers have _____ to believe a crime has been committed, they are allowed to conduct a search.

10. The _____ prevents police and prosecutors from using evidence that has been obtained through improper procedures.

11. In *Terry v. Ohio*, the Supreme Court allowed police officers to conduct _____ if they have reasonable suspicion to believe a crime has occurred.

12. The standard used to determine whether an action actually constitutes a search is called _____.

13. In the case of _____ , the Supreme Court decided that officers could not stop-and-frisk a suspect based on an anonymous tip.

14. A _____ is based on the idea that evidence should not be excluded when police officers did everything that they thought they were supposed to do even though a mistake occurred.

15. If officers can see evidence of a crime on private property, they can seize it under the _____.

16. _____ occurs when officers obtain reliable information indicating that evidence will be found somewhere or someone has committed a crime.

17. Officers may search, arrest, or question suspects when there is a threat to public safety or risk evidence will be destroyed when there are _____.

18. _____ allows courts to use evidence collected if officers took necessary actions to protect citizens, even if no warrant was issued.

19. _____ permits the use of improperly obtained evidence that would have been found by the police eventually through proper means.

20. In _____, the Supreme Court decided that evidence obtained illegally must be excluded at trial.

21. _____ are sometimes used by police to obtain search warrants.

22. _____ occurs when the police deprive people of their liberty or property in a reasonable manner.

23. Under the _____, an exception to the warrant requirement exists because officers need not ignore illegal objects that are clearly visible.

24. _____ are the divisions within a police department responsible for investigating officers' misconduct.

FILL-IN-THE-BLANK EXERCISE

Legal limitations are placed on the ability of the police to conduct searches of citizens and seizures of property. Warrants are usually necessary in order to search property, unless officers can see the evidence in **1.**_____. In what is sometimes known as a "Terry stop", officers can stop citizens and frisk them under the Court's decision in the case of **2**_____. Officers are also allowed to search when **3.**_____ exist that indicates the public is at risk or evidence is about to be destroyed. Offenders must be read their Constitutional rights prior to any questioning, in accorance with the verdict in the case of **4.**_____.

One of the most important Supreme Court decisions in the twentieth century was the finding that evidence obtained illegally cannot be used in court. This rule, called the **5.**_____, was later applied to the states in the court case **6.**_____. There are several exceptions to this rule, for instance, the one allowing a **7.**_____ exception when officers act honestly even if the warrant is later found to be in error.

Police officers occasionally become involved in **8.**_____, in which they abuse their power to gain money and other rewards. They can be investigated by **9.**_____, which have the power to investigate police officers engaged in wrongdoing. Some officers occasionally use excessive force, also known as **10.**_____. Some communities have increase officer accountability by creating **11.**_____, in which community members review complaints against officers.

MULTIPLE CHOICE

6.1.   How does the U. S. Supreme Court define a "search"?
   a) an action by a law enforcement official that creates tension between the official and a citizen
   b) an action by a law enforcement official that intrudes upon people's "reasonable expectations of privacy"
   c) when a law enforcement official speaks to a person
   d) when a law enforcement official informs a person that a search is taking place
   e) when a law enforcement official looks at a person

6.2.   What practice of questioning suspects was declared unconstitutional by the Supreme Court in 2004?
   a) Asking suspects to repeat earlier incriminating statements after being read their Miranda rights
   b) Using physical force to coerce confessions from suspects
   c) Lying to suspects about having the right to an attorney
   d) Telling suspects they held incriminating evidence against them when no such evidence ever existed
   e) Holding suspects for more than 24 hours without counsel

6.3.   All arrests must be supported by ...
   a) reasonable suspicion
   b) reasonable doubt
   c) preponderance of the evidence
   d) probable cause
   e) real evidence

6.4.   What is a written statement confirmed by oath or affirmation?
   a) warrant
   b) perjury
   c) interrogatory
   d) booking
   e) affidavit

6.5.   If a judicial officer makes a generalized determination about whether the evidence is both sufficient and reliable enough to justify a warrant, this is called the standard of..
   a) reasonable suspicion
   b) reasonable doubt
   c) preponderance of the evidence
   d) the totality of the circumstances
   e) real evidence

6.6. Which of the following is not something police have to do before conducting a stop and frisk search?
   a) Identify themselves as a police officer
   b) Observe unusual conduct
   c) Read the suspect *Miranda* warnings
   d) Draw reasonable conclusions that crime may be afoot
   e) Make inquiries of the suspect before searching

6.7. In what case did the U. S. Supreme Court rule that an unverified anonymous tip is not adequate as basis for a stop and frisk search?
   a) *Maryland v. Wilson* (1997)
   b) *Michigan v. Sitz* (1991)
   c) *Minnesota v. Dickerson* (1993)
   d) *New York v. Quarles* (1984)
   e) *Florida v. J.L.* (2000)

6.8. If a citizen gives a police officer consent to search his or her property, then…
   a) The officer no longer needs a search warrant
   b) The officer still must obtain a search warrant
   c) The officer must ask three times in order to search the property
   d) The officers is violating the citizen's Fourth Amendment rights
   e) The officer is in the wrong

6.9. Why does the Fifth Amendment contain the privilege against self-incrimination?
   a) because suspects do not tell the truth and this infringes upon an investigation
   b) because police officers often ask the wrong questions
   c) because suspects can talk too much and this interferes with the investigation
   d) to discourage police officers from using violent or coercive means to get suspects to confess
   e) because police officers often fail to remember what suspects have to say

6.10. In the landmark case of *Terry v. Ohio*, what was Terry doing that made officers suspicious?
   a) Keeping pornography in his home
   b) Driving in an unsafe manner
   c) Preparing to rob a store
   d) Using the Internet to lure minors into sexual relationships
   e) Having loud parties in his home

6.11. In what case did the U. S. Supreme Court rule that officers could forego Miranda warnings if there would be a threat to "public safety"?
   a) *Minnesota v. Dickerson* (1993)
   b) *Flippo v. West Virginia* (1999)
   c) *Florida v. J.L.* (2000)
   d) *Warden v. Hayden* (1967)
   e) *New York v. Quarles* (1984)

6.12. Which of the following statements regarding automobile searches is true?
   a) The trunk of a car can be treated the same as the rest of a car in a search
   b) The trunk of a car must be treated differently as the rest of a car in a search
   c) Police officers cannot open the hood of a car, even if they have a warrant to search the vehicle
   d) Police officers must always have a warrant to search a car
   e) Police officers cannot search a car, even if they arrest the driver for illegal behavior

6.13. Which of the following is FALSE regarding the Miranda warnings?
   a) police must inform suspects of their rights immediately after arrest
   b) the warnings do not have to be provided until the police begin to ask questions
   c) the warnings involve the Fifth and Sixth Amendments to the Constitution
   d) the warnings are designed to deter police misconduct
   e) all of the above are TRUE

6.14. Why must officers read suspects their *Miranda* rights prior to questioning?
   a) So the offender does not confess to the crime
   b) To make sure the offender gives an honest confession
   c) To force the offender to implicate a co-conspirator
   d) To make sure any information is provided voluntarily
   e) To force the offender to testify against himself in court

6.15. Under which exception can officers forgo using the Miranda warning and still question suspects?
   a) Inevitable discovery
   b) "public safety" exception
   c) "exigent circumstances" exception
   d) The Exclusionary rule
   e) "early warning" exception

6.16. Which of the following is TRUE about the exclusionary rule?
   a) it is specifically mentioned in the Fourth Amendment
   b) it currently applies only to the federal courts
   c) the Rehnquist Court has expanded criminal defendants' rights by supporting the exclusionary rule
   d) it was created by the judiciary to prevent police misconduct
   e) all of the above are TRUE

6.17. The term "police brutality" refers to which actions by police officers?
   a) offensive language
   b) physical force
   c) violence
   d) racial discrimination
   e) all of the above

6.18. Which of the following statements about police use of force is FALSE?
a) it is used infrequently
b) when used, it is less serious force
c) it is usually done in response to force
d) force usually involves an officer's weapon
e) excessive use of force is against policy

6.19. Police officers who act improperly must be responsible for their actions. This is known as:
a) Civil reliability
b) Criminal instability
c) Civil accountability
d) Occupational validity
e) In-service acceptability

6.20. Which of the following techniques are used to control the police?
a) internal affairs units
b) civilian review boards
c) standards and accreditation
d) civil liability lawsuits
e) all of the above

6.21. Which of the following offenses is the internal affairs unit most likely to investigate?
a) Murder
b) Sexual harassment
c) Drug use
d) Drug distribution
e) Sexual assault

6.22. "Grass Eaters" are police officers who:
a) actively use their power for personal gain
b) frequently use physical force against citizens
c) are vegetarians
d) regularly accept payoffs that the routines of police work bring their way
e) are not corrupt

6.23. Which of the following is NOT an effect of police corruption on law enforcement?
a) Morale among officers is damaged and supervision becomes lax
b) Suspects are free to engage in future crime
c) Police salaries could be increased to dissuade officers from engaging in corrupt behavior
d) The image of police suffers
e) Police-community relations are damaged

6.24. Which of the following is not a valid criticism of civilian review boards?
   a) Civilians might not understand the issues faced by police officers
   b) Civilian review boards can lower officer morale
   c) Civilian review boards can hinder officer performance
   d) Officers cannot do their jobs if they are worried about disciplinary actions
   e) Civilian review boards have been overly harsh in punishing officers

TRUE/FALSE

6.1. _____ A warrant must be signed by a judicial officer.

6.2. _____ Border searches without a warrant are an automatic violation of the Fourth Amendment.

6.3. _____ The exclusionary rule applies to federal and state courts.

6.4. _____ Police can stop and frisk a person without a warrant if reasonable suspicion exists.

6.5. _____ The Fourth Amendment does not contain the word "warrant."

6.6. _____ The Fifth Amendment contains the right against unreasonable search and seizure.

6.7. _____ The Sixth Amendment contains the right to counsel.

6.8. _____ A seizure and a stop are essentially the same thing.

6.9. _____ Evidence that was obtained illegally will not be thrown out if a police officer acted in good faith.

6.10. _____ Warrantless searches are justified if exigent circumstances exist.

6.11. _____ Sobriety checkpoints violate the Fourth Amendment rights of citizens.

6.12. _____ Most suspects talk to the police even after they have been informed of their right to remain silent.

6.13. _____ Abuse of police power is a major issue on the public's agenda.

6.14. _____ Police may use "legitimate" force to do their job.

6.15. _____ Police scandals rarely have occurred in the last quarter-century.

6.16. _____ Grass eaters" are more of a problem than "meat eaters" because they are greater in number.

6.17. _____ Internal Affairs officers usually have good relationships with officers outside of their department.

ANSWER KEY

Key Terms

1. *Terry v. Ohio* [p. 173, LO1]
2. *United States v. Drayton* [p. 176, LO1]
3. search [p.169, LO1]
4. totality of circumstances [p. 171, LO1]
5. *Chimel v. California* [p. 175, LO2]
6. *Miranda v. Arizona* [p. 175, LO4]
7. stop [p. 170, LO1]
8. *Nix v. Williams* [p. 185, LO2]
9. reasonable suspicion [p. 170, LO1]
10. exclusionary rule [p. 183, LO5]
11. stop-and-frisk searches [p. 174, LO2]
12. reasonable expectation of privacy [p. 169, LO1]
13. *Florida v. J.L.* [p. 175, LO2]
14. "good faith" exception [p. 184, LO3]
15. Plainview Doctrine [p. 169, LO2]
16. probable cause [p. 170, LO2]
17. exigent circumstances.[p. 176, LO3]
18. "public safety" Exception [p. 180, LO3]
19. "inevitable discovery" Exception [p. 185, LO5]
20. *Mapp v. Ohio* [p. 184, LO2]
21. affidavits [p. 171, LO2]
22. seizure [p. 169, LO1]
23. plain view doctrine [p. 169, LO3]
24. internal affairs [p. 192, LO7]

Fill-in-the-Blank

1. plain view [p. 169, LO3]
2. *Terry v. Ohio* [p. 173, LO1]
3. exigent circumstances [p. 176, LO2]
4. *Miranda v. Arizona* [p. 180, LO4]
5. exclusionary rule [p. 183, LO5]
6. *Mapp v. Ohio* [p. 184, LO2]
7. "good faith" [p. 184, LO3]
8. corruption [p. 190, LO7]
9. internal affairs units [p. 192, LO7]
10. police brutality [p. 187, LO6]
11. civilian review boards [p. 192, LO7]

Multiple Choice

6.1. B [p. 169, LO1]
6.2. A [p. 182, LO4]
6.3. D [p. 170, LO1]
6.4. E [p. 171, LO2]
6.5. D [p. 171, LO2]
6.6. C [p. 174, LO2]
6.7. E [p. 175, LO2]
6.8. A [p. 176, LO3]
6.9. D [p. 179, LO3]
6.10. C [p. 173,174, LO3]
6.11. E [p. 180,181, LO4]
6.12. A [p. 177, LO3]
6.13. A [p. 180, LO4]
6.14. D [p. 180, LO4]
6.15. B [p. 180,181, LO4]
6.16. D [p. 183, 184, LO5]
6.17. E [p. 187, LO6]
6.18. D [p. 187,188, LO6]
6.19. C [p. 192, LO7]
6.20. E [p. 194, LO7]
6.21. B [p. 192, LO7]
6.22. D [p. 190, LO6]
6.23. C [p. 190,191, LO6]
6.24. E [p. 192,193, LO7]

True/False

6.1.T [p. 171, LO2]
6.2. F [p. 172, LO2]
6.3.T [p. 184, LO5]
6.4. T [p. 172, LO3]
6.5. F [p. 171, LO2]
6.6. F [p. 169, LO2]
6.7. F [p. 180, LO3]
6.8. F [p. 170, LO2]
6.9. T [p. 184, LO5]
6.10 T [p. 176, LO3]
6.11.F [p. 172, LO2]
6.12. T [p. 182, LO3]
6.13. T [p. 186, LO6]
6.14. T [p. 187, LO6]
6.15. F [p. 186, LO6]
6.16. T [p. 190, LO7]
6.17. F [p. 192, LO7]

WORKSHEET 6.1: POLICE ACCOUNTABILITY

What are the pros and cons of each of the following mechanisms for police accountability?
Which one is best? Why?

Internal affairs units: _____

_____

_____

_____

_____

_____

Civilian review boards: _____

_____

_____

_____

_____

_____

Standards and accreditation: _____

_____

_____

_____

_____

_____

Civil liability lawsuits: _____

_____

_____

_____

_____

WORKSHEET 6.2: PRIVATE POLICING

What suggestions would you make to deal with each of the following issues concerning private policing and security management?

Coordination and cooperation between public and private police: _____

_____

_____

_____

_____

Public police "moonlighting" off-hours as private security guards: _____

_____

_____

_____

_____

Hiring standards and training for security guards: _____

_____

_____

_____

_____

International criminal efforts to steal trade secrets, commit online fraud, and engage in other types of criminal activity primarily targeting public corporations:

_____

_____

_____

_____

COURTS AND ADJUDICATION

OUTLINE

CHAPTER 7
COURTS AND ADJUDICATION

LEARNING OBJECTIVES

After covering the material in this chapter, students should be able to:

1. Recognize the structure of the American court system

2. Analyze the qualities that we desire in a judge

3. Identify the ways that American judges are selected

4. Understand the roles of the prosecuting attorney

5. Analyze the process by which criminal charges are filed and what role the prosecutor's discretion plays in that process

6. Identify those with whom the prosecutor interacts in decision making

7. Understand the day-to-day reality of criminal defense work in the United States

8. Know how counsel is provided for defendants who cannot afford a private attorney

9. Understand the courtroom workgroup and how it functions

CHAPTER SUMMARY

The United States has a dual court system consisting of state and federal courts that are organized into separate hierarchies. Trial courts and appellate courts have different jurisdictions and functions. The judge is a key figure in the criminal justice process who at various times assumes the roles of adjudicator, negotiator, and administrator. State judges are selected through varying methods including partisan elections, nonpartisan elections, gubernatorial appointment, and merit selection. Merit selection methods for choosing judges have gradually spread to many states. Such methods normally rely on a screening committee to make recommendations of potential appointees who will, if placed on the bench by the governor, go before the voters for approval or disapproval of their performance in office.

American prosecutors at all levels have considerable discretion to determine how to handle criminal cases. In most cases, there is no higher authority that can overrule a prosecutor's decision to decline to prosecute (*nolle prosequi*), or to pursue multiple counts against a defendant. The prosecutor occupies a variety of roles, including trial counsel for the police, house counsel for the police, representative of the court, and elected official. Prosecutors' decisions and actions are affected by their exchange relationships with many other important actors and groups, including police, judges, victims and witnesses, and the public.

The image of defense attorneys portrayed in the media as courtroom advocates is often vastly different from the reality of pressured, busy negotiators constantly involved in bargaining with the prosecutor over guilty plea agreements. Relatively few private defense attorneys make significant incomes from criminal work, but larger numbers of private attorneys accept court appointments to handle indigent defendants' cases quickly for relatively low fees. The quality of representation provided to criminal defendants is a matter of significant concern, but U.S. Supreme Court rulings have made it difficult for convicted offenders to prove that their attorneys did not provide a competent defense.

The outcomes in criminal cases are largely influenced by a court's local legal culture, which defines the "going rates" of punishment for various offenses. Courtrooms are work groups composed of judges, prosecutors, and defense attorneys who work together to handle cases through cooperation.

CHAPTER OUTLINE

I. THE FUNCTIONS AND STRUCTURE OF AMERICAN COURTS

Both the federal and state court systems in the U.S. have trial and appellate courts. Native Americans have tribal courts, with jurisdiction over crimes committed on tribal land.

Trial courts of limited jurisdiction handle less serious cases, while courts of general jurisdiction handle the more serious criminal cases and civil cases. Appellate courts hear appeals from the lower courts, when defendants claim that errors were made in their original trial. While all jurisdictions employ this court system, they do not always refer to them using the same terms.

II. TO BE A JUDGE

A. Who Becomes a Judge?
Judges enjoy high status and salaries that are significantly higher than those paid to most American workers, yet still lower than pay for partners at large law firms. Judges in the U.S. tend to be overwhelmingly white and male, although the demographics of the group have begun to shift in the past few years. In many cities, political factors dictate that judges be drawn from specific racial, religious, and ethnic groups.

B. Functions of the Judge
1. **Adjudicator**: In the role of the adjudicator, judges are neutral actors between prosecution and defense in making decisions on bail, pleas, sentencing, and motions. They must avoid any appearance of bias.
2. **Negotiator**: In the negotiator role, judges spend much of their time talking to prosecutors, defense attorneys, and other court personnel.
3. **Administrator**: As administrators, judges are responsible for managing the courthouse. In urban areas, there may be a professional court administrator to assist

145

the judge. In rural areas, the administrative burdens on judges may be more substantial.

C. How to Become a Judge

The quality of courts and justice depends on having judges with proper skills and qualities. Public confidence in courts is diminished by poor performance or apparent lack of competence. There are five methods of selection for state trial judges: gubernatorial selection, legislative selection, merit selection, nonpartisan election and partisan election. Selection by public voting is most common.

Merit selection is used in several states. Under this process, a nominating commission of lawyers and citizens sends the governor a list of three recommended names and the governor chooses one of them to fill a vacant seat. After one year, the citizens vote in a retention election on whether to approve the judge's continued service.

III. THE PROSECUTORIAL SYSTEM

United States attorneys are federal prosecutors, appointed by the President in each of 94 districts around the country. They are responsible for prosecuting federal crimes. Attorneys General are elected in most states. The number of assistant prosecutors will vary by size of office (as many as 500 in Los Angeles).

A. Politics and Prosecution

The process and organization of prosecution is inescapably political. For example, the appointment of deputies may serve a political party's purposes. In addition, the decision about whether to prosecute may include consideration of prosecutor's or political party's electoral interests. Historically, some groups (e.g., racial minorities) received harsher treatment when prosecutors used their discretion to pursue their cases while not pursuing others' cases.

B. The Prosecutor's Influence

The low visibility of prosecutors' decisions increases their power in making discretionary decisions. Voters cannot easily hold elected prosecutors accountable because they do not generally know the true range and nature of prosecutors' decisions. State statutes generally state that all crimes shall be prosecuted, but it is really up to the prosecutor to decide if and how that will really happen. Prosecutors may decline to prosecute crimes if they believe that the local community no longer considers such behavior worthy of punishment, even if the law is still on the books. Because most prosecutors are in smaller counties, they can be highly influenced by local public opinion—especially with regards to the discretionary enforcement of laws against victimless crimes (such as gambling and drug use).

C. The Prosecutor's Roles

The "prosecutor's dilemma" is that prosecutors, as lawyers for the state, are expected to do everything in their power to win the public's case, but as officers of the court and members of the local legal profession, they are also obligated to see that justice is done. This environment can create a "prosecution complex," in which prosecutors come to consider themselves primarily as instruments of law enforcement although they are supposed to represent all people, including the accused. Prosecutors sometimes make mistakes, but they are immune from lawsuits if they prosecute innocent people.

The prosecutor's role is defined by a variety of factors in addition to formal professional responsibilities, such as the individual prosecutor's personality, the political and social environment in which the prosecutor operates, and the individual prosecutor's expectations concerning the attitudes of other actors. Four basic role conceptions exist among prosecutors: trial counsel for the police, house counsel for the police, representative of the court, and elected official.

D. Discretion of the Prosecutor

Autonomy, lack of supervision, and low visibility of decisions give prosecutors broad discretionary authority to make decisions at each step of the criminal justice process. Prosecutors have the discretion to: file or not file charges, determine the type of charge, and determine the number of charges for an offender.

Discovery is the legal requirement that information be made available to the defense attorney. It is part of the prosecutor's obligation to act impartially in seeking justice rather than in seeking only convictions on behalf of the state. Prosecutors may also drop charges (*nolle prosequi* or nol. pros.), which essentially dismisses the criminal case against an offender.

E. Key Relationships of the Prosecutor

The decisions made by the prosecuting attorney's office reflect the personal and organization clients with whom it interacts. Precise decisions and procedures will vary with each environment.

1. **Police**: Prosecutors are dependent on the police to bring them cases that are strong enough to prosecute. They depend on the investigative function of the police, and they can affect police workload by returning cases for further investigation or by refusing to approve arrest warrants.

2. **Victims and Witnesses**: Victims and witnesses are vital components of evidence in prosecuting criminal cases. Prosecutors must make important decisions about the credibility of victims and witnesses, as that affects the likelihood that cases will be prosecuted.

3. **Judges and Courts**: The sentencing history of each judge may influence prosecutors' decisions about which charges to file and whether to prosecute.

4. **The Community**: Like other elected officials, prosecutors cannot remain unresponsive to public opinion—otherwise, they risk losing their jobs. Prosecutors' decisions are also affected by their relationships with the news media, state and federal officials, legislators, and political party officials.

F. Decision-Making Policies

Prosecutors approach their tasks in different ways, even within the same state. Some prefer to use plea bargaining frequently to process cases, others take more cases to trial. It is through the accusatory process that cases progress through the criminal justice system.

IV. THE DEFENSE ATTORNEY: IMAGE AND REALITY

The defense attorney represents individuals accused of committing a crime. Defense attorneys typically handle a large load of cases and process them quickly, for low pay. They are sometimes considered 'partners' with the prosecutor, due to the bargaining they engage in with the prosecutor to arrive at plea bargains.

A. The Role of the Defense Attorney

Criminal defense lawyers are the essential advocates for defendants, on whose behalf they employ pretrial investigative skills as well as verbal skills in plea negotiations and courtroom proceedings. In addition to advocacy functions, defense counsel provides psychological support to the defendant and the defendant's family.

B. Realities of the Defense Attorney's Job

The provision of defense counsel does not automatically create the adversarial nature assumed by the due process model. Defense attorneys' actual behavior will depend on exchange relations and organizational setting of the court. Defense attorneys may, in fact, act as mediators between the defendant, judge, and prosecutor. By facilitating the smooth processing of cases, the defense counsel may be able to bargain for a better deal for his client.

C. The Environment of Criminal Practice

Much of the service provided by defense counsel involves preparing clients and relatives for possible negative outcomes of cases. The low pay for such work is a key factor in the environment, along with spending large amounts of time in jails at all hours.

D. Counsel for Indigents

The Supreme Court requirement that counsel be appointed early in criminal process for all defendants facing incarceration has drastically raised the percentage of defendants relying on publicly supported criminal defense lawyers. In some jurisdictions, 90 percent of the accused must be provided with counsel. Unfortunately, the quality of representation for the poor often remains in question.

1. Ways of Providing Indigents with Counsel

Counsel for indigents can be assigned, contracted, or a public defender. Counties are most likely to use assigned counsel, public defenders, or a combination of both. Contract counsel is used the least often.

2. **Assigned Counsel**: method in which the court appoints a private practice attorney to represent indigent defendants. Courts may use an ad hoc system to assign counsel, in which a judge selects lawyers at random from a prepared list or appoints lawyers who are present in the courtroom; or a coordinated system, in which a court administrator oversees the appointment of counsel.

3. **Contract System**: a method currently in use in about 200 counties, in which the government enters into a contract with a law firm, individual attorney, or non-profit organization that will provide representation for all indigent defendants.

4. **Public Defender**: Public defenders are salaried government employees who handle indigents' criminal cases. Public defender systems predominate in large cities, and are typically overburdened with cases.

5. **Attorney Effectiveness and Competence**: The right to counsel may be meaningless if the attorney is incompetent or ineffective. It is difficult to define inadequate representation, especially when many defense attorneys struggle with high caseloads or make tactical decisions which turn out to be unsuccessful.

   The Supreme Court has decided that attorneys must demonstrate "reasonable competence" if issues of inadequate representation arise. Poor performance can only be considered legally defective if a reasonably competent attorney would not have acted as the trial counsel did, and if specific errors resulted in an unfair proceeding and an unreliable result.

V. THE COURTROOM: HOW IT FUNCTIONS

Guilt or innocence is determined in much the same fashion in every state, although the definitions of crimes and practices in setting punishments may vary significantly. The local legal culture, which refers to the totality of beliefs, attitudes, and norms shared by a court community, greatly influences events. This is why courts operate differently from one another even though they have the same formal rules and procedures. The norms of a court community define the going rate, or the typical expected sentence for a crime.

Although our court system is adversarial, the actors in the courtroom (judge, prosecutor, defense attorney) tend to act more as a group. They work together to process cases quickly while also trying to use fairness in sentencing. Judges tend to lead the workgroup, ensuring that everyone follows procedure. Different judges tend to define their roles in the workgroup according to different terms.

REVIEW OF KEY TERMS

__Define each of the following:__

accusatory process

adversary process

appellate courts

assigned counsel

continuance

contract counsel

count

defense attorney

discovery

going rate

inquisitorial system

jurisdiction

local legal culture

merit selection

nolle prosequi

nonpartisan election

partisan election

prosecuting attorney

public defender

state attorney general

trial court of limited jurisdiction

trial court of general jurisdiction

United States attorneys

workgroup

SELF-TEST SECTION

KEY TERMS

Fill in the appropriate term for each statement:

1. _____ is a judicial selection method in which the selection of candidates is controlled by the political parties.

2. _____ is the trial court that handles specific categories of less serious cases.

3. A court's _____ defines the boundaries of its authority over people, places, and types of legal actions.

4. _____ is a method of selecting judges that attempts to remove partisan politics, but merely replaces those politics with the political conflicts within the legal profession.

5. _____ is the level of the judicial hierarchy that looks for errors by trial judges.

6. The United States court system uses the _____ to try cases.

7. _____ is the trial court that handles felony cases.

8. _____ is a method of selecting judges that attempts but fails to remove politics because, for example, so many judges initially gain their judgeships through gubernatorial mid-term appointments to fill vacancies created by deaths and retirements.

9. In the _____ , judges participate in investigation of cases.

10. A _____ is a salaried government employee who represents indigent criminal defendants in most large cities.

11. The _____ is the lawyer who represents the accused in the criminal justice process.

12. The _____ is a private attorney among a list of attorneys appointed to represent an indigent defendant for a relatively small fee.

13. The _____ is a private attorney who successfully submits a bid to represent all indigent defendants in a county for one year.

14. The _____ is the prosecutor responsible for federal crimes in each federal district court.

15. The _____ is the series of activities from arrest through the filing formal charges.

16. A _____ is an individual charge filed against a defendant.

17. _____ is the discretionary decision to decline to initiate a prosecution.

18. _____ is the process that permits defense attorneys to gain access to information possessed by the prosecutor.

19. The _____ is regarded as the most powerful figure in the criminal justice system.

20. The _____ is the chief legal officer of a state.

21. Attorneys who need more time to prepare their case might request a _____.

22. The typical sentence in a jurisdiction (which varies by type of crime) is known as the _____ _____.

23. The individual actors in a courtroom who share goals and norms are known as a _____.

24. The _____ _____ _____ defines how actors work together when "doing justice".

FILL-IN-THE-BLANK EXERCISES

Although reformers have hoped that **1.** _____ would minimize the influence of politics on the selection of judges, they still face problems with special interest groups who try to unseat judges.   A large number of states also use **2.** _____ in an attempt to avoid such problems.

In many counties and cities that use the **3.** _____ system to represent **4.** _____ defendants, virtually any attorney can have the opportunity to participate. By contrast, in some other countries, attorneys are carefully selected because of the emphasis on quality.

Larger cities tend to use the **5.** _____ system, and some places have a state-wide system in place to use this mechanism. Although many observers believe this approach provides the highest quality representation because of the attorneys' interest and expertise, large caseloads can prevent careful attention to individual cases.

Because exchange relations influence a prosecutor's decisions about charging and plea bargaining, victims who refuse to cooperate in providing testimony against defendants can lead prosecutors to end the case by entering a notation of **6.** _____ .

While the United States uses a two-sided, **7.** _____ for trying cases, the courtroom actually functions more like a **8.** _____, with common goals and interests. Actors agree on the **9.** _____ for an offense, defined as such by the courtroom workgroup.

MULTIPLE CHOICE

7.1. Federal criminal laws are prosecuted by:
a) the state attorney general
b) the United States Attorney
c) the local police
d) the prosecuting attorney
e) the Federal Bureau of Investigation

7.2. In all states except Connecticut and New Jersey, prosecutors are:
a) elected
b) appointed
c) represented
d) prosecuted
e) regurgitated

7.3. The vast majority of criminal cases are handled in...
a) city level offices of the prosecuting attorney
b) state level offices of the prosecuting attorney
c) township level offices of the prosecuting attorney
d) county level offices of the prosecuting attorney
e) federal offices of the prosecuting attorney

7.4. Which of the following is NOT a reason to become a judge?
a) perform public service
b) gain political power
c) gain prestige
d) gain wealth
e) all of the above are reasons to become a judge

7.5. Which of the following best describes the role of prosecutors within the criminal justice system?
a) prosecutors are involved in every aspect of the criminal justice system
b) prosecutors are only involved with adjudication
c) prosecutors are concerned with pre-trial processes and adjudication
d) prosecutors define their own roles for themselves
e) state law defines the role of a prosecutor

7.6. Which of the following is a seldom-recognized function of most judges?
  a) negotiating
  b) managing the courthouse
  c) adjudicating
  d) all of the above
  e) none of the above

7.7. When are prosecutors less inclined to drop charges?
  a) if the damage (monetary value or physical injuries) was considerable
  b) if the suspect had previously been convicted
  c) if the evidence is strong
  d) all of the above
  e) none of the above

7.8. What type of relationship exists between the prosecutor and police?
  a) conflictual relationship
  b) informal relationship
  c) exchange relationship
  d) no relationship at all
  e) unethical relationship

7.9. Which of the following traits of a victim will affect whether a prosecutor pursues charges?
  a) criminal record of the victim
  b) victim's role in his or her own victimization
  c) credibility of the victim
  d) all of the above
  e) none of the above

7.10. If a prosecutor decides not to prosecute a case, this is known as a:
  a) *means rea*
  b) *actus rea*
  c) *nolo contendere*
  d) *e pluribus unum*
  e) *nolle prosequi*

7.11. In which of the following roles does the prosecutor give legal advice to police officers?
  a) Trial counsel for the police
  b) House counsel for the police
  c) Defense attorney
  d) Representative of the court
  e) Elected official

7.12. How many assistant prosecutors serve in a prosecutor's office?
   a) two
   b) five
   c) ten
   d) twenty
   e) it varies based upon the size of the office

7.13. At what stage is evidence presented to a grand jury made up of citizens who determine whether to issue a formal charge?
   a) arrest
   b) booking
   c) sentencing
   d) appeal
   e) indictment

7.14. What is the main reason for declining to prosecute a case?
   a) lack of resources
   b) insufficient evidence
   c) politics
   d) lack of prison space
   c) defendant's lack of a criminal record

7.15. Prosecuting attorneys represent the _____ in criminal trials.
   a) Accused
   b) Victim
   c) Defense
   d) Government
   e) Judge

7.16. Which of the followings is NOT a basic duty of the defense attorney?
   a) to save criminals from punishment
   b) to protect constitutional rights
   c) keep the prosecution honest in preparing and presenting cases
   d) prevent innocent people from being convicted
   e) all of the above are basic duties

7.17. Most criminal defense attorneys interact with...
   a) upper class clients
   b) middle class clients
   c) lower class clients
   d) upper and middle class clients
   e) upper and lower class clients

7.18. The right to an attorney is found in the _____ Amendment.
a) First
b) Second
c) Fourth
d) Fifth
e) Sixth

7.19. When does the U. S. Supreme Court require that attorneys be appointed to defend suspects?
a) early in the criminal justice process
b) immediately prior to jury selection
c) immediately prior to a trial
d) immediately prior to sentencing
e) the Court has no such requirement

TRUE/FALSE

7.1. _____ Prosecutors in America have very little discretion.

7.2. _____ Prosecutors in America are active only at the adjudication stage of the criminal justice process.

7.3. _____ Most prosecutors in America are elected officials.

7.4. _____ Prosecutors might not file charges if a victim is dressed shabbily.

7.5. _____ The American Bar Association has prohibited the control of court jobs by political parties and judges.

7.6. _____ Most charges are filed by county prosecutors in the United States.

7.7. _____ Under the adversary process of justice in the U. S., each side (prosecution and defense) is represented by an attorney.

7.8. _____ Most criminal defense attorneys have wealthy clients.

7.9. _____ The work of a judge is limited to presiding at trials.

7.10. _____ The main reason that charges are dropped by prosecutors is insufficient evidence.

7.11. _____ It is easy for convicted offenders to prove that their attorneys did not provide a competent defense.

7.12. _____ One disadvantage of the courtroom workgroup is the long amount of time usually taken to dispose of cases.

7.13. _____ Defense attorneys rarely have to visit jails.

7.14. _____ The sentencing history of a judge may influence prosecutors' decisions about which charges to file.

7.15. _____ There are 75 state attorneys general in the United States.

7.16. _____ The service provided by defense counsel usually involves preparing clients for positive outcomes of cases.

7.17. _____ Some judges are responsible for managing the administrative affairs at their courthouses.

7.18. _____ Prosecutors may reduce charges in exchange for a plea bargain.

7.19. _____ If a person is too poor to pay for legal counsel, the state will not provide an attorney.

ANSWER KEY

Key Terms

1. partisan election [p. 207, LO3]
2. trial court of limited jurisdiction [p. 202, LO1]
3. jurisdiction [p. 202, LO1]
4. merit selection [p. 210, LO3]
5. Appellate court [p. 202, LO1]
6. adversarial process [p. 202, LO1]
7. trial court of general jurisdiction [p. 202, LO1]
8. nonpartisan election [p. 207, LO3]
9. inquisitorial process [p. 201, LO1]
10. public defender [p. 222, LO7]
11. defense attorney [p. 218, LO7]
12. assigned counsel [p. 222, LO7]
13. contract counsel [p. 222, LO7]
14. United States Attorney [p. 210, LO4]
15. accusatory process [p. 217, LO5]
16. count [p. 215, LO5]
17. *nolle prosequi* [p. 215, LO5]
18. discovery [p. 215, LO5]
19. prosecuting attorney [p. 210, LO4]
20. state attorney general [p. 210, LO4]
21. continuance [p.226, LO5]
22. going rate [p. 226, LO5]
23. workgroup [p. 226, LO9]
24. local legal culture [p. 226, LO9]

Fill-in-the-Blank

1. merit selection [p. 210,LO3]
2. nonpartisan election [p. 207, LO3]
3. assigned counsel [p. 222, LO8]
4. indigent [p. 220, LO8]
5. public defender [p. 222, LO8]
6. *nolle prosequi* [p. 215, LO5]
7. adversarial process [p. 201, LO1]
8. workgroup [p. 226, LO9]
9. going rate [p. 226, LO5]

Multiple Choice

7.1. B [p. 211, LO4]
7.2. A [p. 212, LO4]
7.3. D [p. 211, LO4]
7.4. E [p. 205, LO2]
7.5. A [p. 213,214, LO4]
7.6. B [p. 207, LO2]
7.7 D [p. 214, LO5]
7.8. C [p. 214,215, LO5]
7.9. D [p. 215,LO4]
7.10. E [p. 215, LO4]
7.11. B [p. 220, LO4]
7.12. E [p. 214, LO6]
7.13. E [p. 216, LO5]
7.14. B [p. 217, LO5]
7.15. D [p. 217, LO5]
7.16. A [p.218,219, LO7]
7.17. C [p. 215,216 LO7]
7.18. E [p. 221, LO7]
7.19. A [p. 221, LO7]

True/False

7.1. F [p. 210, LO4]
7.2. F [p. 211, LO4]
7.3. T [p. 212, LO4]
7.4. T [p.214,215, LO5]
7.5. F [p. 224, LO5]
7.6. T [p. 217, LO5]
7.7. T [p. 218, LO6]
7.8. F [p. 220, LO7]
7.9. F [p. 207,208, LO2]
7.10. T [p. 217, LO5]
7.11. F [p. 228, LO8]
7.12. F [p. 226, LO9]
7.13. F [p. 221, LO7]
7.14. T [p. 216, LO5]
7.15. F [p. 210, LO4]
7.16. F [p. 221,222, LO7]
7.17. T [p. 207, LO2]
7.18. T [p. 213,214, LO5]
7.19. F [p. 221, LO8]

WORKSHEET 7.1: JUDICIAL SELECTION

Respond to the following questions in light of the text's discussion of the importance of judicial selection methods. Think about the implications and consequences of each selection method (Gubernatorial Appointment, Legislative Appointment, Partisan Election, Nonpartisan Election, Merit Selection)

1. What are the four most important qualities that we should look for in the people we select to be judges?

_____

_____

_____

_____

2. How do we know which people possess these qualities?

_____

_____

_____

3. Which judicial selection method would provide the best means to identify and select the people who possess these qualities?

_____

_____

_____

_____

4. What are the drawbacks to this judicial selection method?

_____

_____

_____

_____

5. Which judicial selection method is used in the state where you live or go to school? Why do you think that your state uses this selection method instead of one of the other methods?

_____

_____

_____

_____

_____

WORKSHEET 7.2: PROSECUTORIAL DECISION-MAKING

Imagine that you are a prosecutor. Consider the following scenarios. For each, decide whether you would dismiss charges, offer a plea agreement, or insist that the case go to trial. If you offered a plea agreement, what punishment would be appropriate?

An affluent suburban woman—the wife of a bank president—with no prior record, strikes and kills an unemployed laborer with her car as he is walking along the side of an unlit road at night. The woman claimed that she thought she sideswiped a deer or a construction barrel; she says she did not know that she had hit a person and that's why she kept driving after the collision. Evidence indicates that she was returning home from a bar where she had several drinks, but when she was contacted by the police two days later, the alcohol had already passed through her system; there is no way to know her precise blood alcohol level at the time of the collision.

_____

_____

_____

_____

_____

_____

A man released on parole after serving five years in prison for a series of burglaries becomes enraged when he discovers that his long-time girlfriend has become involved with another man while he was in prison. In an angry state, he punches her several times–causing facial bruises and a bloody nose–but then feels remorseful, apologizes, and begs for her forgiveness. He calls his parole officer immediately to admit what he has done. The girlfriend pleads with the police and prosecutor to dismiss any charges and vows not to testify against him.

_____

_____

_____

_____

_____

_____

A seventeen-year-old suburban boy out joyriding with friends steals several mailboxes and throws them into a lake. Some of the mailboxes contained mail, which raises the possibility of a federal crime in addition to the state destruction of property charge. Investigation reveals that the boy defies his parents' rules and stays out all night when he gets angry at them. The defense attorney reports that the parents believe the boy has psychological problems that may be helped with medication and, moreover, they believe the arrest and threat of prosecution will now motivate the boy to agree to meet with the psychiatrist that the parents have hired. The people who lost the mailboxes and mail are angry, but they do not wish to see the boy end up with a criminal record for youthful misbehavior. The boy's parents have already paid to replace the mailboxes.

_____

_____

_____

_____

_____

_____

_____

_____

A seventeen-year-old youth from an inner-city neighborhood steals a football jersey from a sporting goods store. He has a prior record for shoplifting candy from a grocery store. The owner of the sporting goods store wants him to be prosecuted and given the most serious possible punishment in order to warn other potential thieves to leave his store alone.

_____

_____

_____

_____

_____

_____

_____

_____

WORKSHEET 7.3: COUNSEL FOR INDIGENTS

If you were given the responsibility for selecting the method of providing counsel for indigent defendants within your local courthouse, which method would you choose? For each method listed below, state whether you would select that method and explain why or why not.

Assigned counsel: _____

_____

_____

_____

_____

Contract counsel: _____

_____

_____

_____

_____

_____

Public defender: _____

_____

_____

_____

_____

Is there some other feasible alternative?: _____

_____

_____

_____

_____

WORKSHEET 7.4. COURTROOM WORKGROUP

A newly elected prosecutor has hired you as a consultant. She wants to know whether she should assign assistant prosecutors to single courtrooms to handle all cases before a specific judge or, alternatively, rotate assistant prosecutors to different courtrooms and other assignments every week. She says, "I've heard that these 'courtroom workgroups,' whatever they are, form if you keep assistant prosecutors in one courtroom. What should I do?"

1. Explain the concept of the courtroom workgroup.

_____

_____

_____

_____

2. Describe how courtrooms will work if an assistant prosecutor is permanently assigned to one courtroom. What are the consequences?

_____

_____

_____

_____

3. How will courtrooms work if assistant prosecutors are rotated? What are the consequences?

_____

_____

_____

_____

4. Which approach do you recommend? Why?

_____

_____

_____

_____

_____

167

PRETRIAL PROCEDURES, PLEA BARGAINING, AND THE CRIMINAL TRIAL

OUTLINE

CHAPTER 8
PRETRIAL PROCEDURES,
PLEA BARGAINING AND THE CRIMINAL TRIAL

LEARNING OBJECTIVES

After reading the material in this chapter, students should be able to:

1. Understand the pretrial process in criminal cases

2. Recognize how the bail system operates

3. Understand the context of pretrial detention

4. Analyze how and why plea bargaining occurs

5. Know why cases go to trial and how juries are chosen

6. Identify the stages of a criminal trial

7. Understand the basis for an appeal of a conviction

CHAPTER SUMMARY

The accused first appears in court at the arraignment, at which point a plea of guilty or not guilty is entered. The bail process provides opportunities for many defendants to gain pretrial release, but poor defendants may be disadvantaged by their inability to come up with the money or property needed to secure release. Preventive detention statutes may permit judges to hold defendants considered dangerous or likely to flee. Bail bondsmen are private businesspeople who provide money for defendants' pretrial release, in exchange for a fee. Although judges bear the primary responsibility for setting bail, prosecutors are especially influential in recommending amounts and conditions for pretrial release. Initiatives to reform the bail process include release on own recognizance (ROR), police-issued citations, and bail guidelines. Pretrial detainees, despite the presumption of innocence, are held in difficult conditions in jails containing mixed populations of convicted offenders, detainees, and troubled people.

Most convictions in criminal cases are obtained through plea bargains, a process that continues to exist in part because it serves the self-interest of prosecutors, judges, defense attorneys, and defendants. Plea bargaining is facilitated by exchange relations between prosecutors and defense attorneys. In many courthouses, there is little actual bargaining, as outcomes are determined through the implicit bargaining process of settling the facts and assessing the "going rate" of punishment according to the standards of the local legal culture.

The U.S. Supreme Court has endorsed plea bargaining and addressed legal issues concerning the voluntariness of pleas and the obligation of prosecutors and defendants to uphold agreements. Plea bargaining has been criticized both for pressuring defendants to surrender their rights and for reducing the sentences imposed on offenders. Although the general public presumes that dramatic courtroom battles between the prosecution and defense are both common practice and the best means of arriving at the truth, less than 10 percent of cases actually go to trial, and half of these are typically bench trials in front of a judge, which do not involve juries. Juries serve a vital function in the criminal justice system as well as the larger society by preventing arbitrary action by prosecutors and judges, educating citizens about the justice system, symbolizing the rule of law, and involving citizens from diverse segments of the community in judicial decision making.

The jury selection process, especially in the formation of the jury pool and the exercise of peremptory challenges, often creates juries that do not fully represent all segments of a community. The trial process consists of a series of steps: jury selection, opening statements, presentation of prosecution's evidence, presentation of defense evidence, presentation of rebuttal witnesses, closing arguments, judge's jury instructions, and the jury's decision. The federal rules of evidence dictate what kinds of information may be presented in court for consideration by the jury.

Convicted offenders have the opportunity to appeal, although defendants who plead guilty—unlike those convicted through a trial—often have few grounds for an appeal. Appeals focus on claimed errors of law or procedure in the investigation by police and prosecutors or the decisions by trial judges. Relatively few offenders win their appeals, and most of those simply gain an opportunity for a new trial, not release from jail or prison. After convicted offenders have used all of their appeals, they may file a habeas corpus petition to seek federal judicial review of claimed constitutional rights violations in their cases. Very few petitions are successful.

CHAPTER OUTLINE

I. FROM ARREST TO TRIAL OR PLEA

After arrest, the suspect is taken to the station for booking, including photographs and fingerprints. For warrantless arrests, a probable cause hearing must be held within forty-eight hours. At the subsequent arraignment, the formal charges are read and the defendant enters a plea. Prosecutors evaluate the evidence and make discretionary determinations about what charges to pursue or whether the charges should be dropped. Decisions to drop charges may be influenced by the defendant's age, prior record, seriousness of offense, or jail overcrowding. Such decisions may also be influenced by bias based on race or some other factor.

A motion is an application to a court requesting an order to be issued to bring about a specified action. Motions are filed in only about 10% of felony cases and 1% of misdemeanor cases. They may be filed when a defense attorney believes that evidence was obtained illegally, or for a number of other reasons. The defense may attempt to use motions to its tactical advantage, by seeking, for example, to suppress evidence or to learn about the prosecutor's case.

II. BAIL: PRETRIAL RELEASE

Bail is a sum of money or property specified by the judge that will be posted by the defendant as a condition of pretrial release, and that will be forfeited if the defendant does not appear in court for scheduled hearings. Bail is a mechanism that permits presumptively innocent defendants to avoid loss of liberty pending the outcome of the case. The Eighth Amendment to the U.S. Constitution forbids excessive bail, but does not establish a right to bail. Congress and some states have reformed bail's underlying purpose (i.e., return of the defendant) to allow preventive detention in order to permit holding some defendants in jail without bail, especially if they might pose a danger to the community upon release

A. The Reality of the Bail System
The amount of bail is normally based on the judge's perception of the seriousness of the crime and the defendant's record. Because bail is set within 24 to 48 hours after arrest, there is little time to seek background information about the defendant. Within particular localities, judges in effect develop standard rates for particular offenses. To post bail, a prisoner must give the court some form of monetary surety, usually cash, property, or bond from a bonding company.

Bondsmen provide bail for defendants for a fee, normally ranging from 5% to 10% of the bail amount. They may track down and return bail jumpers without extradition and by force if necessary. Bondsmen exert influence on the court through their ability to cooperate with police officers, who recommend their services rather than those of other bondsmen. In return, bondsmen may refuse to provide bail for defendants whom the police would like to keep in jail.

Bondsmen have a positive impact on the system, by maintaining social control over defendants during the pretrial period; reminding clients about court dates; or putting pressure on defendant's friends and family to make sure the defendant appears for court. However, they also cause problems by using bounty hunters to retrieve clients who have jumped bail.

C. Setting Bail
Bail for misdemeanors is sometimes determined according to a set schedule, but other factors, such as severity of offense. are usually taken into account for felonies. Judges also consider the characteristics of the defendant in setting bail. The police may be particularly active in attempting to influence the bail decision if they do not want to see a particular defendant released. Bail amounts also vary by race and class.

D. **Reforming the Bail System**

Reformers are concerned that judges have too much discretion in setting bail, and that the poor are discriminated against in setting bail. The following alternatives to bail have been suggested:

1. **Citation**: a citation or summons issued by a police officer. This method avoids booking, arrest, bail, and jailing. In some jurisdictions, only a small percentage of offenders fail to appear. Bail bondsmen have opposed this method as a threat to their livelihood.

2. **Release on Own Recognizance (ROR)**: Court personnel talk to defendants about their family ties and roots in the community (i.e., job, family, prior record, length of time in local area), then recommend ROR if sufficient contacts exist.

3. **Ten Percent Cash Bail**: Many judges are unwilling to use ROR, so some states have instituted policy in which defendants deposit a percentage of bail as collateral. When they return to court, they receive 90% of this back.

4. **Bail Guidelines**: Guidelines developed to establish criteria that will produce more consistency in bail decisions

5. **Preventive Detention**: Although considered a basic threat to liberty by civil libertarians, it was approved by Congress for federal court in Bail Reform Act of 1984. Judges can consider whether a defendant poses a danger to community and decide not to set bail. The decision is made at a hearing, at which the prosecution contends that there is risk of flight, or a risk that defendant will obstruct justice by threatening a witness or juror. The defendant must be accused of a crime of violence or one punishable by life imprisonment or death. The Supreme Court has upheld the use of preventive detention as constitutional (*United States v. Salerno and Cafero*).

III. PRETRIAL DETENTION

Defendants awaiting trial are typically held in jail. About half of the 600,000 people in jail at any given moment in the U.S. are in pretrial detention, while the other half are serving short sentences; nearly all are poor. Conditions in jails may be much worse than those in prisons, given the transient population and constant overcrowding.

The ultimate outcome of a case can be affected by whether the defendant was held in jail. Jailed defendants may look guiltier in the eyes of the judge and jury when escorted into court by guards rather than by friends and family. Some research shows a greater likelihood of conviction and incarceration for those jailed prior to trial, but it is difficult to know if the pretrial detention itself increases the severity of the outcome.

IV. PLEA BARGAINING

Plea bargaining is the most important step in the criminal justice process. 90% of felony defendants generally plead guilty. Plea bargaining helps to reduce heavy caseloads, moves cases along quickly, and reduces the time that pretrial detainees spend in jail. In addition, offenders who are processed quickly can move to treatment very quickly. Supporters of plea bargaining also note that plea bargaining helps to individualize punishment, and allows the punishment to "fit the crime".

A. Exchange Relationships in Plea Bargaining
Plea bargaining is a process that can sometimes take surprising amounts of time. One benefit of this process is that the prosecutor or defense attorney may find evidence that helps their respective cases.

B. Tactics of Prosecutor and Defense
One common tactic used by prosecutors is the multi-count indictment. Even when they cannot prove all of the charges in the indictment, it puts greater pressure on defendant to plead guilty and gives prosecutor more items to negotiate away. On the other hand, defense attorneys may threaten to move ahead with a jury trial or threaten delays, during which witnesses' memories may fade. However, other defense attorneys feel more effective bargaining on a friendly basis rather than trying to pin down or threaten the prosecutor.

C. Pleas without Bargaining
Both prosecutor and defense attorney may be members of the same local legal culture, with shared values and understandings about the punishments for particular offenses. Implicit plea bargaining may be less likely to occur when there is personnel turnover in a court community that inhibits the formation and recognition of shared values.

D. Legal Issues in Plea Bargaining
Questions exist concerning the voluntariness and sanctity of plea bargains. Many judges are now more open about admitting in court that they are aware of plea bargains struck in particular cases. Several Supreme Court cases have affirmed both defendants' rights in plea bargaining and the power of the prosecutor in plea bargains.

E. Criticisms of Plea Bargaining
The biggest criticism of plea bargaining focuses on due process violations and leniency in sentencing. Those concerned with due process believe that bargaining does not provide procedural fairness because defendants forfeit the constitutional rights designed to protect them. Critics concerned with leniency express concerns that offenders are "getting off" with sentences that are too lenient. Some are also worried that the plea bargaining process coerces innocent people into admitting crimes they did not commit.

V. TRIAL: THE EXCEPTIONAL CASE

Thanks to plea bargaining, judge and jury trials are unusual in the United States. They are usually reserved for more serious cases. The trial process is based on the adversarial system, a symbolic combat between prosecution and defense. Trials are also biased processes, because of vagaries in the criminal law and the fact that human error also enters into courtroom decisions. While defendants have the right to a jury trial, these are less common than a bench trial over which a judge presides.

A. Jury Trial

Juries provide important functions in the criminal justice system, including (1) preventing government oppression, (2) determining guilt, (3) representing the community, (4) serving as a buffer between the accused and the accuser, (5) promoting knowledge about the criminal justice system, and (6) symbolizing the rule of law.

B. The Trial Process

There are several steps in the trial process:

1. **Jury Selection**: Juries are theoretically supposed to consist of a cross-section of the community, but until the mid-twentieth century many states excluded women and members of minority groups. A jury pool is used to select members of the jury from the greater community.

   Voir dire is the process of questioning potential jurors to ensure a fair trial. Attorneys for both sides and the judge may question each juror about his or her background, knowledge of the case, or acquaintance with people involved in the case. If a juror says something to indicate that he or she may be unable to make a fair decision, then he or she may be challenged for cause.

   Attorneys can also make peremptory challenges, in which they can dismiss a juror without providing cause. Although the Supreme Court has said that peremptory challenges cannot be based on the race or gender of potential jurors, the Court also permits trial judges to accept flimsy excuses when it appears that race or gender is being improperly applied.

2. **Opening Statements** are made by attorneys. Lawyers use this opportunity to establish themselves with the jurors and to emphasize points they intend to make during the trial.

3. **Presentation of the Prosecution's Evidence**: The prosecution must prove the accused is guilty beyond a reasonable doubt. They may present real evidence, demonstrative evidence, testimony, direct evidence, or circumstantial evidence. The rules of evidence govern which pieces of evidence the judge will exclude or permit.

4. **Presentation of Defense's Evidence**: Evidence is usually presented to rebut the state's case, offer an alibi for the defendant, or to present an affirmative defense (such as self-defense or insanity). The defense also must consider whether or not the defendant will take the stand and thereby be subject to impeachment and cross-examination.

5. **Presentation of Rebuttal Witnesses**: The prosecution calls witnesses to rebut the defense's case.

6. **Closing Arguments by Each Side**: This is an opportunity for both prosecution and defense to tie the case together and to make impassioned, persuasive presentation to the judge or jury.

7. **Judge's Instructions to the Jury**: The judge instructs the jury on the manner in which the law bears on their decision. The judge may discuss the standard of proof (beyond a reasonable doubt), the necessity of the prosecution proving all of the elements of a crime, and the rights of the defendant. Judges will explain the charges and the possible verdicts.

8. **Decision by the Jury**: Jurors deliberate in private room after instructions from the judge. They may request that the judge reread to them portions of the instructions, and may ask for additional instructions or portions of the trial transcript. When a verdict is reached, it is read aloud to the courtroom. If the jury is unable to reach a verdict, the trial ends with a hung jury.

C. **Evaluating the Jury System**
Social relationships outside the courtroom tend to be reflected in the jury. Men, white jury members, and those with more education are generally more active in jury deliberations. It is important to note that juries may be more likely to make judgments based on personal characteristics about defendants than judges.

VI. APPEALS

Appeals are made when the defendant believes an error was made in his or her trial. Appeals from state court go through the state appeals system, but sometimes appeals go through the federal system if they involve a constitutional issue.

A. **Habeas Corpus**
This writ asks a judge to determine whether an individual is being property detained. A successful habeas corpus writ can result in a defendant being released from custody or order a new trial.

There has been a tremendous increase in habeas corpus petitions although only about 1% are successful—this causes an increase in caseloads for federal judges. There is no right to counsel for habeas corpus petitions, so most prisoners must attempt to present their own cases. They generally lack sufficient knowledge to identify and raise constitutional issues effectively.

Since the 1980s, the Supreme Court has made decisions imposing more difficult procedural requirements on prisoners seeking to file habeas corpus petitions. In 1996, Congress created further restrictions on petitions by passing a new statute affecting habeas corpus procedures.

B. **Evaluating the Appellate Process**

Some conservatives argue that appeals should be limited. Appeals can be regarded as a burden on the system and an impediment to swift punishment of convicted offenders. However, since 90% of accused persons plead guilty and relatively few of these people have any basis for appeal, the actual number of appeals (as a percentage of total cases) seems less significant.

Appeals can serve the function of correcting errors. Even if a defendant wins an appeal, there is no automatic release from prison. A successful appeal may simply lead to a new trial or provide the basis for a new plea bargain.

REVIEW OF KEY TERMS

Define each of the following:

appeal

arraignment

bail

bench trial

challenge for cause

circumstantial evidence

citation

demonstrative evidence

direct evidence

habeas corpus

jury

motion

percentage bail

peremptory challenge

preventive detention

real evidence

reasonable doubt

release on recognizance (ROR)

testimony

voir dire

Bordenkircher v. Hayes (1978)

Boykin v. Alabama **(1969)**

North Carolina v. Alford **(1970)**

Ricketts v. Adamson **(1987)**

Santobello v. New York **(1971)**

United States v. Salerno and Cafero **(1987)**

Williams v. Florida (1970)

SELF-TEST SECTION

KEY TERMS

Fill in the appropriate term for each statement:

1. _____ permits defense attorneys and prosecutors to exclude jurors without providing a reason.

2. _____ requires the jurors to draw inferences.

3. _____ creates the opportunity for reviews to determine whether trial judges made errors or constitutional rights were violated.

4. _____ results when bail is not set and a defendant remains in jail because he or she has been determined to be a danger to the community.

5. _____ is the process of questioning and selecting jurors.

6. Defendants can sometimes pay _____, which allows them to pay the remainder of bail when they appear for trial.

7. A trial overseen by a judge (with no jury present) is called a _____.

8. _____ provides the basis for incarcerated people to challenge the legal basis for their detention.

9. A _____ hears evidence, decides guilt or innocence, and represents the viewpoint of the community.

10. The Supreme Court decided in _____ that offenders can maintain his or her innocence while still pleading guilty to a lesser offense to reduce punishment.

11. Defense attorneys sometimes make _____ asking for evidence to be ruled inadmissible in trial.

12. _____ is not based on witness testimony but demonstrates that a crime has been committed.

13. _____ is to ensure that a defendant returns to court for subsequent proceedings.

14. The case of _____ assures that prosecutors keep their promises to offenders who plead guilty.

15. An offender who agrees to testify against a co-offender in exchange for a plea bargain must keep his side of the agreement, according to the case of _____.

16. According to _____, defendants must state in court that they are making their guilty plea voluntarily.

17. _____ is verbal evidence presented by witnesses.

18. In the case of _____, the Court ruled that prosecutors can threaten to charge defendants with serious punishment (if supported by evidence) if they refuse to plead guilty.

19. _____ permits, with the judge's approval, the exclusion of jurors who demonstrate a particular bias.

20. _____ is the standard of proof in criminal cases.

21. In _____, the Supreme Court decided that juries can have fewer than twelve members.

22. _____ is presented by the prosecutor and includes concrete objects, such as fingerprints and stolen property.

23. _____ includes eyewitness accounts of what happened.

24. _____ is the stage in the criminal justice process in which formal charges are read in court and a plea is entered.

25. In _____, the Supreme Court decided that preventive detention is not a violation of constitutional rights.

26. A _____ is a method of summoning defendants to return to court without using the system's resources for arrests and jailing.

27. _____ permits defendants to be freed from jail without paying bail and therefore reduces the harsh effects of bail upon the poor.

FILL-IN-THE-BLANK EXERCISE

During the process of **1.** _____, attorneys can use **2.** _____ to seek exclusion of potential jurors who make prejudicial statements before deciding strategically which remaining potential jurors to remove through the use of **3.** _____.

Prosecutors use many types of evidence to prove guilt beyond a reasonable doubt. The most well known types of evidence are considered **4.** _____ evidence (such as fingerprints, blood, holding stolen property), but there are several other kinds as well. Eyewitness accounts of crimes are considered **5.** _____ evidence, while evidence presented that causes the jury to make an inference about what occurred is called **6.** _____ evidence. Witnesses and experts can also provide **7.** _____ about the crime but this is not considered **8.** _____ evidence, which is presented to jurors to see and understand without testimony.

The **9.** _____ court examines arguments concerning errors that occurred during the trial. It may also consider **10.** _____ petitions from prisoners challenging the basis for their incarceration.

MULTIPLE CHOICE

8.1. Which of the following is true about the trial process?
   a) the selection of the jury occurs after the opening statements by the prosecution and the defense
   b) the defense presents evidence and witnesses before the prosecution
   c) the judge offers instructions to the jury after a decision is reached in a case
   d) the selection of jurors is never bias toward the defendant
   e) retired persons and homemakers are overrepresented on juries

8.2. The courtroom process of questioning prospective jurors in order to screen out those who might be incapable of being fair is called...
   a) *mala in se*
   b) habeas corpus
   c) voir dire
   d) ex post facto
   e) demonstrative evidence

8.3. In the elimination of jurors from the jury pool, what is the difference between a peremptory challenge and challenge for cause?
   a) peremptory challenges cannot be used in felony cases
   b) challenge for cause cannot be used in felony cases
   c) a judge must rule on a peremptory challenge, but attorneys control a challenge for cause
   d) a judge must rule on a challenge for cause, but attorneys generally control a peremptory challenge
   e) peremptory challenges and challenge for cause are the same

8.4. The prosecution must prove that a defendant is guilty beyond...
   a) probable cause
   b) all doubt
   c) reasonable doubt
   d) a preponderance of the evidence
   e) reasonable suspicion

8.5. In a trial, fingerprints submitted as evidence would be considered...
   a) circumstantial evidence
   b) reasonable evidence
   c) real evidence
   d) direct evidence
   e) probable evidence

8.6.   In a trial, eyewitness accounts submitted as evidence would be considered...
   a)   circumstantial evidence
   b)   reasonable evidence
   c)   real evidence
   d)   direct evidence
   e)   probable evidence

8.7.   In a trial, what type of evidence requires the jury to infer a fact from what a witness observed?
   a)   circumstantial evidence
   b)   reasonable evidence
   c)   real evidence
   d)   direct evidence
   e)   probable evidence

8.8.   Which of the following is true concerning Fifth Amendment rights?
   a)   defendants must take the stand and face cross examination
   b)   defendants do not have to testify against themselves, but a prosecutor can criticize a defendant for this strategy
   c)   defendants do not have to testify against themselves and a prosecutor cannot criticize a defendant for this strategy
   d)   defendants must take the stand, but the Fifth Amendment prevents cross-examination by the prosecution
   e)   all of the above are TRUE

8.9.   Juries with six members must reach ...
   a)   at least a two to four vote to convict
   b)   at least a three to three vote to convict
   c)   at least a four to two vote to convict
   d)   at least a five to one vote to convict
   e)   a unanimous vote to convict

8.10.   Social scientists who wish to study jury deliberations...
   a)   can observe or film after getting permission from the judge
   b)   can ask to become a member of the jury
   c)   are barred because jury deliberations are secret
   d)   must stay behind a two-way mirror
   e)   can watch the videos that the courts takes of all jury meetings

8.11.   According to social scientists, who is more likely to be active and influential during jury deliberations?
   a)   white women who are less educated
   b)   minority women who are less educated
   c)   white men who are less educated
   d)   minority men who are better educated
   e)   white men who are better educated

8.12. Who are the key participants in a plea bargain?
   a) bailiff and clerk
   b) probation officer and bail bondsperson
   c) prosecutor and defense attorney
   d) jury and the judge
   e) all of the above are key participants

8.13. Which of the following is NOT a function of a jury?
   a) safeguarding citizens against arbitrary law enforcement
   b) determining whether the accused is guilty
   c) representing the interests of the prosecutor
   d) educating citizens selected for jury duty about the criminal justice system
   e) symbolizing the rule of law

8.14. Which of the following is NOT a purpose of bail?
   a) to ensure that the defendant appears in court for trial
   b) to protect the community from further crimes that some defendants may commit while out on bail
   c) to punish the defendant
   d) all of the above are purposes of bail
   e) none of the above are purposes of bail

8.15. What is the strategy called when police file charges for selling a drug when they know they can probably convict only for possession?
   a) voir dire
   b) multiple-offense charging
   c) intimidation
   d) habeas corpus
   e) peremptory challenge

8.16. Which of the following is NOT true about bail bondspersons?
   a) they usually act in their own self-interest
   b) they usually have close relationships with police and correctional officials
   c) they slow the processing of cases
   d) they can cause problems when hunting for fugitives
   e) none of the above are TRUE

8.17. What is it called when the judge, the public, and sometimes even the defendant do not know for sure who got what from whom in exchange for what?
   a) bargain justice
   b) multiple-offense indictment
   c) implicit plea bargaining
   d) voir dire
   e) challenged for cause

8.18. Which of the following is a function of a jury?
   a) to prevent government oppression
   b) to determine whether the accused is guilty on the basis of the evidence presented.
   c) to represent diverse community interests
   d) to serve as a buffer between the accused and the accuser
   e) all of the above

8.19. Which of the following crimes would likely receive the highest amount of bail?
   a) Property
   b) Drug
   c) Public order
   d) Violent
   e) Vice

8.20. Who sets bail amounts for minor offenses?
   a) Prosecutors
   b) Judges
   c) Police
   d) Bondsmen
   e) Court clerks

8.21. What kind of offense is most likely to result in a citation?
   a) Robbing a bank
   b) Running a red light
   c) Sexually harassing a coworker
   d) Abusing a child
   e) Committing vandalism

8.22. The Bail Reform Act of 1984 authorized the following practice for federal cases:
   a) Preventive detention
   b) Plea bargaining
   c) Selective incapacitation
   d) Excessive bail
   e) Percentage bail

8.23. Most Americans arrested for felonies have their case heard in:
   a) Less than one week
   b) About three months
   c) Between six months and one year
   d) Between one year and five years
   e) Most wait longer than five years for trial

8.24. Guilty pleas can be entered even without formal bargaining (particularly if the evidence is strong). This is known as:
a) Exchange bargaining
b) Preventive detention
c) Explicit plea bargaining
d) Implicit plea bargaining
e) Barter bargaining

TRUE/FALSE

8.1. _____ Juries serve as a buffer between the accused and the accuser.

8.2. _____ Juries in the United States must always be comprised of twelve members.

8.3. _____ The prosecution presents evidence and witnesses before the defense presents its case.

8.4. _____ Juries typically represent all population groups, since most adults are registered voters.

8.5. _____ Peremptory challenges require that a justifiable reason be made for excluding a juror.

8.6. _____ Racial discrimination has been a problem in lawyers' use of peremptory challenges.

8.7. _____ Circumstantial evidence is usually sufficient to convict a defendant.

8.8. _____ Women tend to be more active participants in the jury room than men.

8.9. _____ Some research has indicated that jury trials are less likely to end in conviction than bench trials.

8.10. _____ Appeals are based on whether the defendant was actually innocent or guilty of the offense charged.

8.11. _____ Most appeals are unsuccessful.

8.12. _____ Bail is always set by a judge.

8.13. _____ The Eighth Amendment created the bail bondsperson as a key actor within the criminal justice system.

8.14. _____ A person cannot be denied bail.

8.15. _____ States that have abolished plea bargaining have been able to run just as efficiently without using it at all.

8.16. _____ Most habeas corpus petitions are unsuccessful.

8.17. _____ The Supreme Court has supported plea bargaining because it saves time and resources.

8.18. _____ Plea bargaining has always been discussed publicly at trial

8.19. _____ Plea bargaining reduces the time that people must spend in jail.

8.20. _____ Plea bargaining always occurs in a single meeting between prosecutor and defense attorney.

ANSWER KEY

Key Terms

1. peremptory challenge [p. 251, LO6]
2. circumstantial evidence [p. 252, LO7]
3. appeal [p. 255, LO7]
4. preventive detention [p. 239, LO2]
5. *voir dire* [p. 250, LO6]
6. percentage bail [p. 238, LO2]
7. Bench trial [p. 248, LO6]
8. *habeas corpus* [p. 256, LO7] jury [p. 248, LO5]
9. *North Carolina v. Alford* [p. 246, LO5]
10. motions [p. 234, LO6]
11. Demonstrative evidence [p. 251, LO7]
12. bail [p. 235, LO2]
13. *Santobello v. New York* [p. 242, LO4]
14. *Ricketts v. Adamson* [p. 246, LO4]
15. *Boykin v. Alabama* [p. 246, LO4]
16. testimony [p. 251, LO6]
17. *Bordenkircher v. Hayes* [p. 246, LO4]
18. challenge for cause [p. 251, LO6]
19. reasonable doubt [p. 253, LO6]
20. *Williams v. Florida* [p. 249, LO5]
21. real evidence [p. 251, LO7]
22. direct evidence [p. 252, LO6]
23. arraignment [p. 223, LO7]
24. *United States v. Salerno and Cafero* [p. 239, LO3]
25. citation [p. 238, LO2]
26. Release on recognizance (ROR) [p. 238, LO2]

Multiple Choice

8.1. E [p. 250, LO5]
8.2. C [p. 250, LO5]
8.3. D [p. 251, LO5]
8.4. C [p. 253, LO6]
8.5. C [p. 251, LO6]
8.6. D [p. 252, LO6]
8.7. A [p. 252, LO6]
8.8. C [p. 252, LO6]
8.9. E [p. 254, LO5]
8.10. C [p. 254, LO5]
8.11. E [p. 254, LO5]
8.12. C [p. 242, 243, LO4]
8.13. C [p. 249, LO5]
8.14. C [p. 235, 236, LO2]
8.15. B [p. 244, LO3]
8.16. C [p. 236, 237, LO2]
8.17. A [p. 246, LO4]
8.18. E [p. 249, LO5]
8.19. D [p. 242, LO3]
8.20. C [p. 235, LO2]
8.21. B [p. 238, LO1]
8.22. A [p. 239, LO3]
8.23. B [p. 240, LO3]
8.24. D [p. 246, LO4]

True/False

8.1. T [p. 249, LO5]
8.2. F [p. 250, 251, LO5]
8.3. T [p. 251, LO6]
8.4. F [p. 250, 251, LO5]
8.5. F [p. 251, LO5]
8.6. T [p. 251, LO5]
8.7. F [p. 251, LO6]
8.8. F [p. 254, LO5]
8.9. T [p. 254, LO5]
8.10. F [p. 255, LO7]
8.11. T [p. 255, LO7]
8.12. F [p. 235, LO3]
8.13. F [p. 235, LO2]
8.14. F [p. 235, 236, LO2]
8.15. F [p. 242, 243, LO4]
8.16. T [p. 256, LO7]
8.17. T [p. 242, 243, LO4]
8.18. F [p. 243, 244, LO4]
8.19. T [p. 242, LO4]
8.20. F [p. 242, LO4]

Fill-in-the-Blank

2. *voir dire* [p. 250, LO5]
3. challenges for cause [p. 251, LO6]
4. peremptory challenges [p. 251, LO6]
5. real [p. 251, LO6]
6. direct evidence [p. 252, LO7]
7. circumstantial [p. 252, LO7]
8. testimony [p. 251, LO7]
9. demonstrative evidence [p. 251, LO7]
10. appeals
11. habeas corpus

WORKSHEET 8.1: SETTING BAIL

If you were a judge, what would you set as an appropriate bail amount (if any) for each of the following defendants? You also have the option of NOT setting bail which, in effect, is an order for preventive detention. Explain each decision.

A woman stabs her husband and he dies. She claims that she has been a long-time victim of domestic violence and that she stabbed him in self-defense during an attack. She has three children, ages 5 to 12, and has lived in the community her entire life. Neighbors tell the police that the couple often had loud arguments, but they heard nothing the night of the incident.

_____

_____

_____

_____

_____

_____

A man kills his wife with a blow to the head. Police records show that home had been burglarized twice in the same month. The man claimed that his wife worked the midnight shift at a factory, but she came home early for some unknown reason. He awoke to the sound of someone entering his bedroom in the middle of the night. In a panic at the though of another burglary, he grabbed a lamp, threw it at the doorway, and hit her in the head. Neighbors tell the police that the couple often had loud arguments, but they heard nothing the night of the incident.

_____

_____

_____

_____

_____

_____

_____

A man steals four DVDs by sticking them into his pants and running out the door of a K-Mart store. It is the fourth time that he has been caught stealing from stores. Evidence indicates that he sells stolen items to support his drug habit. He is an unemployed transient who moves from town to town and sleeps wherever he can.

_____

_____

_____

_____

_____

The wife of the mayor hits and kills a bicyclist with her car. The incident occurred early in the morning and she claims that the glare on her windshield prevented her from seeing the cyclist, who was not wearing a helmet.

_____

_____

_____

_____

_____

_____

WORKSHEET 8.2: PLEA BARGAINING

Imagine that you are the prosecutor who has been responsible for investigating and prosecuting the case of a suspected serial killer. Over the span of a few years, eight hunters, fishermen, and joggers have been found dead in isolated areas of a three-county rural area. Each one had been shot by a sniper from a great distance. Two bits of evidence led you to arrest a suspect. First, among the many tips you received about possible suspects, one informant described the employee of a nearby city water department who owned many guns and frequently drove out into the country to shoot at random animals he encountered, including farmers' cows and pet dogs. Second, you knew that one of the victims was shot with a rifle that was made in Sweden and was not commonly available in local gun stores. You learned from a second informant that the city employee sold one of these unusual Swedish rifles to another gun enthusiast shortly after the time that a hunter was killed by a shot from such a rifle. You located the gun, and ballistics tests indicated a high probability that it was the weapon used in that particular murder. You charged the suspect with five of the eight murders and you scrambled to find evidence to link him with these and the remaining three murders. You have spoken publicly about seeking the death penalty. Now, after months of heavy publicity about the case, you announce that the defendant will plead guilty to one count of murder and be sentenced to life in prison. (These details are based on a real-life case that took place in Canton, Ohio).

When giving a guest lecture in a criminal justice course at a nearby university, a student asks you to explain how the plea bargain in this case can be viewed as a "good" or "fair" result in light of the number of victims and the fact that you could have pursued the death penalty. Whether or not you personally agree with the plea bargain, in your role as the prosecutor, how would you explain the benefits of the plea bargain with respect to various interested actors and constituents listed below?

Briefly explain if and how the plea bargain benefits the:

Prosecutor: _____

_____

_____

_____

Judge: _____

_____

_____

_____

_____

_____

Court system: _____

_____

_____

_____

_____

Defense attorney: _____

_____

_____

_____

_____

Defendant: _____

_____

_____

_____

_____

Society: _____

_____

_____

_____

Victims' families: _____

_____

_____

_____

_____

WORKSHEET 8.3: JURY SELECTION

Imagine that a thirty-year-old African-American woman is facing trial for the murder of her Hispanic husband. He was shot while standing in the doorway of the house soon after he returned home from work. There are no eyewitnesses. The murder weapon had the wife's fingerprints on it. On the advice of her lawyer, she never answered any questions from the police. Several defense witnesses will testify that the deceased husband used to beat his wife frequently.

1. If you are the prosecutor in this case, what is the demographic profile of your ideal juror? (e.g., age, race, education, occupation, gender, political party affiliation, religion, etc.) Why?

_____

_____

_____

2. If you are the defense attorney in this case, what is the demographic profile of your ideal juror? Why?

_____

_____

_____

3. If you were the prosecutor, what questions would you want to ask the potential jurors during *voir dire*? Why?

_____

_____

_____

_____

4. If you were the defense attorney, what questions would you want to ask the potential jurors during *voir dire*?

_____

_____

_____

_____

WORKSHEET 8.4: WHO IS THE IDEAL JUROR?

Lawyers often look for certain characteristics and attitudes in people when selecting and excluding potential jurors. Relevant characteristics may include a person's occupation, education, political party affiliation, and neighborhood of residence. If you were a defense attorney, how would you describe your ideal juror for each of the following cases? How would you describe the characteristics of the juror that you would most like to avoid? Explain

A civil rights lawsuit has been filed against the police by an African-American teenager who claims that the police broke his arm by knocking him off his bicycle when he failed to heed their command to stop. He says he did not hear the command because he was wearing headphones and listening to music at the time. The police claim that the youth looked like a burglary suspect and they thought he was attempting to flee.

Ideal juror: _____

_____

_____

Juror to avoid: _____

_____

_____

A popular multi- millionaire media figure who had built a business empire and television show based on gardening and home improvement tips is charged with violating federal laws by using inside information to sell stock for profit just before it was going to lose value. She claims that she sold the stock at that time for reasons other than inside information from her friends who ran the company in question.

Ideal juror: _____

_____

_____

Juror to avoid: _____

_____

_____

A domestic violence charge is made against a woman who is alleged to have struck her husband with a frying pan, thereby breaking his jaw. She says she was angry that he lost his entire paycheck gambling at the casino, but that she swung the frying pan to scare himBhe was only struck because he had been drinking and walked right into the arc of the swing. The husband admits that he lost his paycheck gambling, but claims that his wife is mentally unstable and wants her to be locked up for psychiatric treatment.

Ideal juror: _____

_____

_____

Juror to avoid: _____

_____

_____

WORKSHEET 8.5: JURY PROCESSES

There are many debates about changing the jury system. How would you address the following issues?

1. Should peremptory challenges be abolished? What would be the consequences of excluding potential jurors only for cause and not through attorneys' discretionary decisions?

_____

_____

_____

_____

_____

_____

2. Should juries have twelve members or should we use six-member juries for criminal cases? What are the consequences of using small juries?

_____

_____

_____

_____

_____

_____

3. Should guilty verdicts be unanimous? What would be the consequences of permitting people to be convicted of crimes by non-unanimous jury decisions?

_____

_____

_____

_____

_____

_____

PUNISHMENT AND SENTENCING

OUTLINE

- The Goals of Punishment
- Forms of the Criminal Sanction
- The Sentencing Process

CHAPTER 9
PUNISHMENT AND SENTENCING

LEARNING OBJECTIVES

After reading the material in this chapter, students should be able to:

1. Recognize the goals of punishment

2. Identify the types of sentences judges can impose

3. Understand what really happens in sentencing

4. Analyze whether the system treats wrongdoers equally

CHAPTER SUMMARY

The four major (and often conflicting) goals of criminal punishment in the United States are 1) retribution, 2) deterrence, 3) incapacitation, and 4) rehabilitation. Some jurisdictions are also currently experimenting with restoration as a new approach to punishment. These goals are carried out through a variety of punishments that range from probation, fines, and intermediate sanctions to incarceration and even death. The penal codes of different states establish varying guidelines as to the punishments that are permitted and whether sentences are indeterminate, determinate, or mandatory. Different approaches to sentencing reflect different assumptions about the goals of the criminal sanction. The philosophy of "good time," for example, allows correctional administrators to reduce the sentence of prisoners who live according to the rules and participate in various vocational, educational, and treatment programs. The death penalty is allowed as a form of punishment by the U.S. Supreme Court if the judge and jury are allowed to take into consideration mitigating and aggravating circumstances. The death penalty cannot be used by the states against juveniles, the mentally retarded, or the insane. Judges have considerable discretion in deciding sentence, and typically consider such factors as the seriousness of the crime, the offender's prior record, and mitigating and aggravating circumstances. The sentencing process is influenced by the administrative context of the courts, the attitudes and values of the judges, and the presentence report. Since the 1980s, sentencing guidelines have been formulated in federal courts and seventeen states as a way of reducing disparity among the sentences given offenders in similar situations. Severe or unjust punishments may result from racial discrimination or wrongful convictions.

CHAPTER OUTLINE

I. THE GOALS OF PUNISHMENT

Beliefs about appropriate punishments have differed over time and place. The American public has supported many different approaches to sentencing, depending on the social climate of the era and other factors.

A. Retribution—Deserved Punishment

Retribution is the concept that those who do wrong should be punished in proportion to the gravity of the offense or to the extent to which others have been made to suffer, a philosophy expressed in the Biblical injunction "an eye for an eye." Retribution is sometimes seen as an expression of the community's disapproval of crime. It is sometimes referred to as "just deserts" or "deserved punishment."

B. Deterrence

The concept of deterrence is based on the idea that criminals rationally weigh the pros and cons of offending before committing a crime. If the potential disadvantages of committing a particular crime are sufficiently strong, in theory, the rate at which that crime is committed should be reduced. There are two types of deterrence: general deterrence, i.e. keeping members of the population at large from committing a crime; and specific deterrence, i.e. keeping the individual being punished from committing crime in the future. Many question whether this philosophy has any effect on crime rates.

C. Incapacitation

The assumption of incapacitation is that a crime may be prevented if criminals are physically restrained (i.e., incarcerated). Prison is the typical mode of incapacitation, since offenders can be kept under control in them and are generally prevented from violating the rules of society. Capital punishment is the ultimate method of incapacitation. Selective incapacitation methods attempt to identify the most severe criminals and incarcerate them for long periods of time. Incapacitation has been criticized both for being unduly harsh and for being potentially both unjust and ineffective, in that predictions about who will be most likely to reoffend may be incorrect.

D. Rehabilitation

Philosophies of rehabilitation focus on treating and "curing" criminal offenders. They assume that techniques are available to identify and treat the causes of the offender's behavior. Because rehabilitation is oriented solely toward the offender, no relationship can be maintained between the severity of the punishment and the gravity of the crime. There is currently public support for rehabilitation, but the current political climate in the United States supports more punitive techniques.

E. <u>A New Approach to Punishment: Restorative Justice</u>

Recent developments in criminal justice have focused on restoration and the role of the victim. Using restorative justice philosophy, offenders are encouraged to return victims to the state they were prior to the crime. Monetary losses to the victim are restored, and victim/offender mediation is sometimes used to help victims feel safer.

II. FORMS OF THE CRIMINAL SANCTION

A. <u>Incarceration</u>

Incarceration is the most visible punishment used by the courts. It is generally believed to be a deterrent, but it is very expensive and does not usually serve to rehabilitate offenders. There are several different types of sentences that result in incarceration.

1. **Indeterminate sentences** allow correctional personnel to make decisions about when to release inmates. Judges sentence offenders to a range of months in prison, and the offender is released when the parole board determines they have served a sufficient amount of time.

2. **Determinate sentences** are set sentences that do not vary. Offenders are sentenced to a specific period of time and typically serve the entire sentence. Some states use presumptive sentences, in which the state legislature sets the expected sentence for specific crimes. These sentences reduce the discretion of the judge in setting sentences.

3. **Mandatory sentences** stipulate some minimum period of incarceration that must be served by persons convicted of selected crimes. No regard may be given to the circumstances of the offense or the background of the individual—the judge has no discretion and is not allowed to suspend the sentence. Mandatory prison terms are most often specified for violent crimes, drug violations, habitual offenders, or crimes where a firearm was used. Plea bargaining can undercut the intentions of the legislature by negotiating for a different charge.

4. **Sentence versus actual time served**: In all but four states, days are subtracted from prisoners' minimum or maximum term for "good time". This time is the equivalent of a credit and is meant to reflect good behavior in prison, or for participation in various types of vocational, educational, and treatment programs.

5. **Truth-in-Sentencing** is the requirement that offenders serve a substantial portion of their sentences before release on parole (usually 85% of their sentence) for a violent crime. This policy can increase imprisonment costs.

B. <u>Intermediate Sanctions</u>

Punishments such as fines, home confinement, intensive probation supervision, restitution and community service, boot camp, and forfeiture are among the sentencing forms that fall into this category. Such sentences have been increasingly employed in response to the expense and overcrowding of prisons, and it has been recommended that they be used in combination to sentence offenders.

C. Probation

This is the most frequently used criminal sanction. Probation is generally advocated as a way of rehabilitating offenders with less serious offenses or clean prior records. It is less expensive than prison and may avoid the embittering or "hardening" effect prison can have on young offenders. Shock probation is sometimes used to "shock" offenders into refraining from future criminal activity. Under this method, offenders receive a short jail period followed by a period of probation.

D. Death

Most other Western democracies have abolished the death penalty, but the United States continues to use it. The Supreme Court has decided the death penalty is not cruel and unusual punishment, although there was a moratorium on the death penalty in the U.S. from 1968 to 1976.

1. **The Death Penalty and the Constitution**: Several important Supreme Court cases have spoken to the constitutionality and implementation of the death penalty.

   Furman v. Georgia (1972): The Supreme Court ruled that the death penalty, as administered, constituted cruel and unusual punishment, thereby voiding the laws of thirty-nine states and the District of Columbia.

   Gregg v. Georgia (1976): The Court ruled that the death penalty was constitutional if judges weighed both mitigating and aggravating factors in sentencing decisions.

   McCleskey v. Kemp (1987): McCleskey's attorneys cited research that showed a disparity in the imposition of the death sentence in Georgia based on the race of the murder victim and, to a lesser extent, the race of the defendant. The death penalty was not found to be unconstitutional in this case.

   In *Atkins v. Virginia (2002),* Justice John Paul Stevens wrote for the majority in ruling that it was unconstitutional for states to execute the mentally retarded.

   Roper v. Simmons (2005): The Court finds that individuals who committed crimes as juveniles cannot be executed, since such an action violates the Eighth Amendment.

2. **Continuing Legal Issues**:
   a. *Execution of the Insane*: The U. S. Supreme Court has stated that states cannot execute the insane. However, there are problems with defining and identifying insanity. Controversy surrounds a 2003 Arkansas case that allows the state to force an inmate to take medication if it will make him/her "sane enough" to be executed.

b. *Effective Counsel*: Defendants charged with capital offenses have the right to effective counsel. Questions as to the adequacy of defense lawyers' efforts often surface. Some very public cases have provided evidence that some defense attorneys have literally fallen asleep during trial, and others have been incompetent.

c. *Death-Qualified Juries*: There is much debate about whether citizens opposed to the death penalty should be excluded from capital cases. Jurors opposed to the death penalty may currently be excluded, but some argue that these juries do not represent a cross-section of the community.

d. *Methods of Execution*: All capital punishment states (except Nebraska) use lethal injection as the preferred form of execution because it is more "humane" than other methods. However, critics of the death penalty have argued that even lethal injection can be extremely painful.

e. *Appeals*: The average length of time inmates sit on death row awaiting execution is about 11 years. During this time sentences are reviewed by the state courts and through the writ of habeas corpus by the federal courts. Innocent citizens are sometimes sentenced to death, and the appeals process makes it very difficult for them to obtain release. It is impossible to know how many innocent citizens are executed in the United States.

f. *International Law*: The United States has come under fire for sentencing foreign citizens to death without consulting their home countries. Several countries have filed complaints against the United States for violating the Vienna Convention.

4. **The Death Penalty: A Continuing Controversy**
While public support for the death penalty remains high, few offenders are actually executed each year. Several states have imposed moratoria on the death penalty, but there is much dissension over the issue.

III. THE SENTENCING PROCESS

Judges bear the responsibility for sentencing after conviction, whether the conviction was by judge, jury, or plea bargain. Initial definitions of punishments are defined by legislatures. There may be room under the law for judges to use discretion in shaping individual sentences.

A. **The Administrative Context of the Courts**
1. **Misdemeanor Courts: Assembly Line Justice**. Limited jurisdiction courts have limits on the punishments that can be meted out for specific offenses, usually a maximum of one year in jail. These courts handle over 90% of criminal cases for arraignment and preliminary hearing before referring case to a general jurisdiction trial court or for completion through dismissal or sentence.

Most lower courts are overloaded with work, and the time allotted for each case is minimal. Judicial decisions tend to be "mass-produced" by the combined efforts of actors who habitually work together. Most offenders in misdemeanor courts receive lenient sentences.

2. **Felony Courts**: In courts of general jurisdiction, sentencing is influenced by organizational considerations and community norms, including interactions and relationships between judges, prosecutors, and defense attorneys.

B. Attitudes and Values of Judges

Sentencing differences among judges can be ascribed to a number of factors. The individual characteristics of the judges, the blameworthiness of the offender, and other factors can affect judicial decisions.

C. The Presentence Report

The presentence report is based on the investigation of the probation officer. In some states, the probation officer makes an actual recommendation; in others, the probation officer merely provides information. Presentence reports can be based on hearsay. The presentence report helps to ease the strain of decision making on the judge and shifts some responsibility to the probation department.

D. Sentencing Guidelines

Guidelines have been established in the federal system as well as some state systems as a means of limiting the discretion of judges and reducing sentencing disparities for offenders convicted of the same offense.

Guidelines appear in a grid constructed on the basis of two scores: the seriousness of offense and the offender's history/prior record or other characteristics. The grid provides an offender score which indicates the sentencing range for the particular offender who commits a specific offense. Judges are expected to provide a written explanation if they depart from the guidelines/grid.

E. Who Gets the Harshest Punishment?

1. **Racial Disparities**. Some studies have shown that members of racial minorities and the poor are treated more harshly by the system. Other studies show no clear link between harshness of sentence and the offender's race or social status.

2. **Wrongful Convictions**: While much public concern is expressed over those who "beat the system" and go free, comparatively little attention is paid to those who are innocent, yet convicted. Each year several such cases of persons who were convicted but later found innocent come to national attention.

REVIEW OF KEY TERMS

<u>Define each of the following:</u>

determinate sentence

general deterrence

good time

incapacitation

indeterminate sentence

intermediate sanctions

mandatory sentence

presentence report

presumptive sentence

probation

rehabilitation

restorative justice

retribution

selective incapacitation

sentencing guidelines

shock probation

special deterrence

Atkins v. Virginia (2002)

Furman v. Georgia **(1972)**

Gregg v. Georgia (1976)

McCleskey v. Kemp (1987)

Roper v. Simmons (2005)

Witherspoon v. Illinois (1968)

SELF-TEST SECTION

KEY TERMS

Fill in the appropriate term for each statement:

1. _____ is the careful selection of offenders who will receive long prison sentences that will prevent them from committing additional crimes.

2. _____ is a term of incarceration based on a minimum and maximum amount of time; the actual amount to be served will be based on the judgment of the parole board.

3. _____ is punishment inflicted on criminals with the intent of discouraging them from committing any future crimes.

4. _____ is a sentence in which the offender is released after a short incarceration and placed in the community under supervision.

5. _____ aims to obtain justice for victims by "making them whole" and restoring their original state before the crime was committed.

6. _____ is a type of sentence determined by statutes which require that a certain penalty shall be imposed and executed upon certain convicted offenders.

7. _____ is a variety of punishments that are more restrictive than traditional probation but less stringent and costly than incarceration.

8. _____ is a punishment involving conditional release under supervision.

9. _____ is the underlying goal of punishment in which the offender is considered deserving of punishment and the punishment fits the seriousness of the crime.

10. _____ is the deprivation of the ability to commit crimes against society, usually through means of detention in prison.

11. _____ is a case in which the Supreme Court rejected a claim that systematic racial discrimination made the death penalty unconstitutional.

12. _____ is a sentence that fixes the term of imprisonment at a specified period of time.

13. _____ are a reform designed to reduce the disparities in sentences for people who have committed the same or similar crimes.

14. _____ is the goal of restoring a convicted offender to a constructive place in society.

15. _____ is the Supreme Court case that temporarily halted executions in the United States.

16. _____ is the punishment of criminals that is intended to serve as an example to the public and discourage others from committing crimes.

17. _____ is submitted by the probation officer to the judge.

18. Inmates can earn _____ _____ in prison, which subtracts time from their sentence.

19. The _____ _____ is that expected based on state statutes.

20. In the case of _____, the Supreme Court ruled that execution of the mentally ill was unconstitutional.

21. In the case of _____, the Supreme Court ruled that executing individuals who committed their crimes as juveniles was unconstitutional.

22. The issue of mitigating and aggravating factors regarding capital cases was the focus of the case of _____ .

23. In the controversial case of _____, the Supreme Court decided that jurors could be excluded from a jury pool if they feel so strongly about the death penalty that they might not be impartial.

FILL-IN-THE-BLANK EXERCISE

Among the purposes of punishment, 1.   deterrence and 2.   focus on the specific offender by, respectively, focusing the seriousness of the offense committed and seeking to turn the offender into a productive citizen. By contrast, 3.   deterrence and 4.   focus on society by, respectively, seeking to discourage others from crime and protecting society from acts by repeat offenders.

The underlying purpose of 5.   is to identify sentencing options that will save money while giving the offender a punishment more harsh than 6.   , in which the restrictions and supervision may not drastically change the offender's behavior while living in the community. More severe sentencing strategies are used in "three strikes" laws, or 7.   , which uses targeted sentencing to incarcerate offenders with the most serious criminal records.

8.   use a grid to help judges select the most appropriate sentences for offenders. The sentences recommended are also called the 9.   sentence.

MULTIPLE CHOICE

9.1.   The U. S. Supreme Court declared that the death penalty did not violate the Constitution through imposition in a racially discriminatory manner in the case of...
a) *Furman v. Georgia* (1972)
b) *Gregg v. Georgia* (1976)
c) *McCleskey v. Kemp* (1987)
d) *Payne v. Tennessee* (1991)
e) *Ford v. Wainwright* (1986)

9.2.   Which of the purposes of punishment do Americans think is most important in sentencing adults?
a) Incapacitation
b) Deterrence
c) Retribution
d) Rehabilitation
e) Restoration

9.3.   Punishments that are less severe and costly than prison, but more restrictive than traditional probation, are called...
a) indeterminate sentences
b) mandatory sentences
c) "good time" sentences
d) presumptive sentences
e) intermediate sanctions

9.4.   Which is the most frequently applied criminal sanction?
a) probation
b) the death penalty
c) life in prison
d) indeterminate sentences
e) presumptive sentences

9.5.   The U. S. Supreme Court declared that the death penalty is illegal in the case of the mentally retarded in the case of...
a) *Payne v. Tennessee* (1991)
b) *Ring v. Arizona* (2002)
c) *McCleskey v. Kemp* (1987)
d) *Stanford v. Kentucky* (1989)
e) *Atkins v. Virginia* (2002)

9.6. What is a "death qualified" jury?
a) A jury that hears a capital case
b) Juries in which all members are in favor of using the death penalty
c) Juries in which all members are convicted felons
d) Juries that convict capital offenders
e) Any jury hearing a felony case

9.7. According to the chart below, which of the following years had the largest gap between the number of offenders sentenced to death and the actual number of executions carried out?

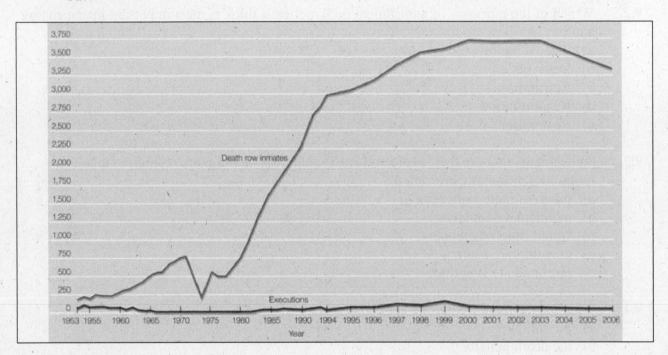

a) 2000
b) 1973
c) 1970
d) 1996
e) 2005

9.8. In what case did the Supreme Court rule that the Eighth Amendment prohibited the state from executing the insane?
a) *Furman v. Georgia* (1972)
b) *Gregg v. Georgia* (1976)
c) *McCleskey v. Kemp* (1987)
d) *Payne v. Tennessee* (1991)
e) *Atkins v. Virginia* (2002)

9.9. Focusing long sentences on "career criminals" is known as:
a) Selective incapacitation
b) Specific deterrence
c) General deterrence
d) Preventive detention
e) Intensive supervision probation

9.10. Shock probation is regular probation combined with periods of:
a) Parole
b) Community service
c) Drug testing
d) Incarceration
e) Therapy

9.11. This state has one of the greatest numbers of death row inmates:
a) California
b) Michigan
c) South Carolina
d) Illinois
e) Utah

9.12. This case tested new laws on the constitutionality of the death penalty in 1976:
a) *McCleskey v. Kemp*
b) *Furman v. Georgia*
c) *Gregg v. Georgia*
d) *Atkins v. Virginia*
e) *Roper v. Simmons*

9.13. Which of the following statements is false about incarceration?
a) It is the most visible punishment used by the criminal justice system
b) More than 60 percent of the people under correctional supervision are imprisoned
c) One purpose of incarceration is deterrence
d) Incarceration is expensive
e) After release, offenders can have trouble reintegrating to society

9.14. In what case did the U. S. Supreme Court hold that potential jurors who have general objections to the death penalty cannot be automatically excluded from jury service in capital cases?
a) *Witherspoon v. Illinois* (1968)
b) *Ring v. Arizona* (2002)
c) *McCleskey v. Kemp* (1987)
d) *Apprendi v. New Jersey* (2000)
e) *Atkins v. Virginia* (2002)

9.15. What is the average amount of time that a death row inmate is under the sentence of the death before the execution?
   a) one year
   b) six years
   c) eleven years
   d) twenty-one years
   e) six months

9.16. Which of the following factors influence the sentencing process?
   a) the administrative context of the courts
   b) the attitudes and values of judges
   c) the presentence report
   d) sentencing guidelines
   e) all of the above

9.17. What has the Supreme Court said about racial discrimination in the death penalty?
   a) If researchers can prove racial discrimination exists in imposition of the death penalty, it should be discontinued
   b) Defendants have to demonstrate racial bias occurred against them specifically to prove racial discrimination
   c) Findings from social science research cannot be presented at trial or appeal
   d) Racial discrimination is not as relevant as other forms of discrimination, such as that based on gender
   e) They have stated that there is no racial discrimination in application of the death penalty.

9.18. Which type of sentencing does not rely on a parole board for release decisions?
   a) Determinate sentencing
   b) Indeterminate sentencing
   c) Presumptive sentencing
   d) Mandatory sentencing
   e) Reintegrative sentencing

9.19. Which goal of punishment can be related to the biblical proverb, "An eye for an eye, a tooth for a tooth?"
   a) retribution
   b) deterrence
   c) incapacitation
   d) rehabilitation
   e) all of the above

9.20. Who is responsible for the presentence report?
    a) Probation officer
    b) Police
    c) Clerk
    d) Judge
    e) Prosecutor

9.21. Which of the following is TRUE about presentence reports?
    a) they are scientific
    b) they are not stereotypical
    c) they are largely determined by the present offense and the prior criminal record
    d) all of the above are true
    e) none of the above are true

9.22. If a person believes that techniques are available to identify and treat the causes of criminal behavior, then which goal of punishment would that person support?
    a) retribution
    b) deterrence
    c) incapacitation
    d) rehabilitation
    e) all of the above

9.23. Legislatures construct sentencing guidelines as a grid of two scores. What are the two scores?
    a) seriousness of the offense and criminal history
    b) race and age
    c) judges' attitudes and values
    d) age and status of employment
    e) community ties and family history

9.24. Which of the following is NOT a goal of punishment in the American system of criminal justice?
    a) retribution
    b) deterrence
    c) emancipation
    d) incapacitation
    e) rehabilitation

TRUE/FALSE

9.1. _____ Virtually all states and the federal government have some types of mandatory sentences.

9.2. _____ It is legal for states to execute the mentally retarded.

9.3. _____ "Good time" refers to the amount of a time that a judge allows a jury to deliberate a decision.

9.4. _____ The majority of industrialized democracies in the world use the death penalty as a form of punishment.

9.5. _____ Intermediate sanctions are punishments that are less severe and financially burdensome than prison.

9.6. _____ The most frequently employed criminal sanction is probation.

9.7. _____ Some doctors refuse to participate in the administration of the death penalty due to the precepts of the Hippocratic oath, which includes the promise to "do no harm".

9.8. _____ In recent years less attention has been paid to the concept of selective incapacitation, whereby offenders who repeat certain kinds of crimes are sentenced to long prison terms.

9.9. _____ Judges rarely give reasons for the punishments imposed at sentencing.

9.10. _____ Rehabilitation is focused upon the victim of a crime.

9.11. _____ Less than 30 percent of persons under correctional supervision are in prisons and jails.

9.12. _____ Truth-in-sentencing refers to laws that require offenders to serve a large proportion of their prison sentence before being released on parole.

9.13. _____ Most states do not use the death penalty as punishment in the United States.

9.14. _____ It is illegal to execute juvenile offenders in the United States.

9.15. _____ Offenders can have their prison sentence increased by earning good time for bad behavior.

9.16. _____ The United States is required to notify foreign governments if citizens from other countries have been sentenced to death in the U.S.

9.17. _____ Presentence reports are not scientific and can reflect stereotypes.

9.18. _____ Since the 1980s sentencing guidelines have been established in the federal courts and in all fifty states.

9.19. _____ Sentencing guidelines are constructed on the basis of past sentences.

ANSWER KEY

Key Terms

1. selective incapacitation [p. 265, LO2]
2. indeterminate sentence [p. 269, LO2]
3. specific deterrence [p. 264, LO1]
4. shock probation [p. 272, LO3]
5. restorative justice [p. 267, LO3]
6. mandatory sentence [p. 270, LO3]
7. intermediate sanctions [p. 272, LO3]
8. probation [p. 272, LO2]
9. retribution [p. 263, LO1]
10. incapacitation [p. 265, LO1]
11. *McCleskey v. Kemp* [p. 272, LO4]
12. determinate sentence [p. 269, LO2]
13. sentencing guidelines [p. 284, LO2]
14. rehabilitation [p. 266, LO1]
15. *Furman v. Georgia* [p. 274, LO4]
16. general deterrence [p. 264, LO1]
17. presentence report [p. 283, LO3]
18. good time [p. 270, LO4]
19. presumptive sentence [p. 269, LO3]
20. *Atkins v. Virginia* [p. 275, LO4]
21. *Roper v. Simmons* [p. 275, LO4]
22. *Gregg v. Georgia* [p. 274, LO4]
23. *Witherspoon v. Illinois* [p. 277, LO4]

Multiple Choice

9.1. C [p. 275, LO4]
9.2. C [p. 263, LO1]
9.3. E [p. 268, LO2]
9.4. A [p. 272, LO2]
9.5. E [p. 275, LO4]
9.6. B [p. 276, LO4]
9.7. A [p. 273, LO4]
9.8. E [p. 275, LO4]
9.9. A [p. 265, LO2]
9.10. D [p. 272, LO2]
9.11. A [p. 273, LO2]
9.12. C [p. 274, LO2]
9.13. B [p. 269,270,LO2]
9.14. A [p. 277, LO4]
9.15. C [p. 277, LO4]
9.16. E [p. 269, LO3]
9.17. B [p. 275, LO4]
9.18. A [p. 269, LO3]
9.19. C [p. 265, LO1]
9.20. A [p. 283, LO3]
9.21. C [p. 283, LO3]
9.22. D [p. 266, LO1]
9.23. A [p. 285, LO3]
9.24. C [p. 263, LO1]

True/False

9.1. T [p. 270, LO2]
9.2. F [p. 275, LO4]
9.3. F [p. 280, LO3]
9.4. F [p. 272, LO2]
9.5. T [p. 268, LO2]
9.6. T [p. 272, LO2]
9.7. T [p. 276, LO4]
9.8. F [p. 265, LO2]
9.9. F [p. 285, LO2]
9.10. F [p. 266, LO1]
9.11. T [p. 269, LO2]
9.12. T [p. 271, LO2]
9.13. F [p. 272,273, LO2]
9.14. T [p. 276, LO4]
9.15. F [p. 269, LO3]
9.16. T [p. 278, LO4]
9.17. T [p. 283, LO3]
9.18. F [p. 284, LO3]
9.19. T [p. 284, LO3]

Fill-in-the-Blank

1. specific [p. 264, LO1]
2. rehabilitation [p. 266, LO1]
3. general [p. 244, LO1]
4. incapacitation [p. 265, LO1]
5. intermediate sanctions [p. 268, LO2]
6. probation [p. 272, LO2]
7. selective incapacitation [p. 265, LO3]
8. sentencing guidelines [p. 284, LO3]
9. presumptive [p. 269, LO3]

WORKSHEET 9.1: PHILOSOPHIES OF PUNISHMENT

Describe how each of the following punishments corresponds (or is irrelevant) to each of the major goals of punishment: deterrence, incapacitation, rehabilitation, retribution, and restoration.

Ten-year prison sentence

Deterrence: _____

Incapacitation: _____

Rehabilitation: _____

Retribution: _____

Restoration: _____

Capital punishment

Deterrence: _____

Incapacitation: _____

Rehabilitation: _____

Retribution: _____

Restoration: _____

Probation: supervised release in the community under specified restrictions

Deterrence: _____

Incapacitation: _____

Rehabilitation: _____

Retribution: _____

Restoration: _____

Restitution: payments from the offender to the victim

Deterrence: _____

Incapacitation: _____

Rehabilitation: _____

Retribution: _____

Restoration: _____

Home confinement: required to stay at home wearing an electronic monitoring device

Deterrence: _____

Incapacitation: _____

Rehabilitation: _____

Retribution: _____

Restoration: _____

WORKSHEET 9.3: SENTENCING

Imagine that you are a judge deciding on sentences for individuals who have entered guilty pleas in the following situations. What sentence would you impose?

1. A nineteen-year-old high school dropout pleads guilty to burglary. He broke into a home and was caught carrying a VCR out the window when the homeowners awoke from the noise of someone in their living room. He has one previous felony conviction for burglary.

SENTENCE: _____

2. A college senior who was caught copying copyrighted computer software from a university computer system onto his own diskette without permission. The value of the software was $700. The student entered a guilty plea to a simple theft charge with an agreement that the prosecutor would recommend leniency. The student has been suspended from college for one year by the school's disciplinary board.

SENTENCE: _____

3. A man who recently completed a prison sentence for armed robbery killed a man during an argument at a bar. The defendant claimed that the victim owed him money so he went to the bar with a knife in order to scare the victim. A confrontation between the two developed into a fight and the victim was stabbed to death. The defendant entered a guilty plea to the charge of second-degree murder. He has served prior prison terms for two armed robbery convictions.

SENTENCE: _____

Now look at the Minnesota sentencing guidelines grid on page 281 of your textbook. What would be the sentence for each offender under the guidelines?

1. _____

2. _____

3. _____

Do you think the guidelines are too harsh, too lenient, or just right? Explain.

_____

_____

_____

WORKSHEET 10.4: THE DEATH PENALTY

How do you respond to the following arguments about the death penalty? Do you have enough knowledge to respond? If not, what additional knowledge would you need?

- The death penalty prevents murders by deterring people from killing others.

_____

_____

_____

_____

- The death penalty is applied in a discriminatory manner against poor people and members of racial minority groups.

_____

_____

_____

_____

- The death penalty is a necessary form of retribution because it is the only adequate way for society to express its revulsion about the most horrible murders to those responsible for such heinous crimes.

_____

_____

_____

_____

- The criminal justice system is incapable of ensuring fair application of the death penalty, with the result that many innocent people will inevitably be sent to death row.

_____

_____

_____

_____

224

CORRECTIONS

OUTLINE

- Development of Corrections
- Organization of Corrections in the United States
- The Law of Corrections
- Correctional Policy Trends

CHAPTER 10
CORRECTIONS

LEARNING OBJECTIVES

After reading the material in this chapter, students should be able to:

1. Understand how the American system of corrections has developed

2. Know the roles that the federal, state, and local governments play in corrections

3. Be familiar with the law of corrections and how it is applied to offenders and correctional professionals

4. Provide explanations as to why the prison population has more than quadrupled in the past forty years

CHAPTER SUMMARY

From the colonial days to the present, the methods of criminal punishment that are considered appropriate have varied significantly. The development of the penitentiary in the 19th century put an end to the traditional sanction of crime through corporal punishment. The Pennsylvania and New York penitentiary systems exemplified competing philosophies of corrections. In 1870, the Cincinnati Declaration of Principles advanced critical ideas about reform and rehabilitation for prisoners. The administration of corrections in the U. S. is decentralized and scattered across all levels of government. Jails are distinct from prisons, and are usually employed to hold persons awaiting trial and persons who have been sentenced for misdemeanors to terms of less than one year. U.S. prison populations have increased dramatically during the last ten years, alongside a great increase in the number of prison facilities and prison staff.

While prisoners lose many of their constitutional rights while incarcerated, the courts have upheld their freedom to practice their religion, as well due process rights, protection against cruel and unusual punishment, and equal protection under law. Community corrections involves the post-release monitoring of offenders through parole, which can be revoked if offenders fail to comply with conditions of release. The increasing number of people imprisoned in the U.S. has also generated an increased number of parolees, straining parole officer caseloads and making regular monitoring a difficult undertaking.

CHAPTER OUTLINE

The correctional system includes prisons, probation, parole, work camps, Salvation Army facilities, medical facilities, and other types of facilities. The U.S. correctional system is organized at multiple levels of government and administered by both public and private organizations, at a total cost of over $50 billion yearly.

I. DEVELOPMENT OF CORRECTIONS

A. The Invention of the Penitentiary

Prior to approximately 1800, the most commonly used methods of punishment in England and the U.S. were physical. Influenced by new ideas about human nature that arose during the Enlightenment, the emphasis of corrections shifted from corporal punishment to hard labor, with the idea of reforming criminals rather than simply inflicting pain. John Howard (sheriff of Bedfordshire, England) was an early proponent of the penitentiary, which provided a place for prisoners to work and reflect on their misdeeds. Prisoners were kept in solitary cells to allow time for reflection and penitence.

B. Reform in the United States

In the first decades of the nineteenth century, the creation of penitentiaries in Pennsylvania and New York attracted the attention of legislators in other states as well as Europe.

1. **The Pennsylvania System**: Philadelphia's Walnut Street Jail, built in 1790, was modeled on European penitentiaries. Inmates were kept in solitary confinement, one to each small, dark cell. No communications of any kind were allowed. The Pennsylvania system of separate confinement, based on the premise of rehabilitation, evolved from this beginning. Other states soon followed, building penitentiaries based on the Pennsylvania model. Critics of these early facilities charged that physical punishment was still sometimes used, and that the use of isolation was emotionally damaging to prisoners, who suffered mental breakdowns.

2. **The New York System**: New York's Auburn penitentiary opened in 1819. It employed the congregate system, in which prisoners were kept in individual cells at night but congregated in workshops during the day. However, inmates were forbidden to talk to one another or even to exchange glances while on the job or at meals.

   This system reflected some of the growing emphases of the Industrial Revolution. The men were to have the benefits of labor as well as meditation. They were to work to pay for a portion of their keep. Advocates of both the separate confinement and the congregate systems agreed that the prisoner must be isolated from society and placed in a disciplined routine. But by the middle of the nineteenth century, reformers had become disillusioned with the results of the penitentiary movement. There was no evidence these systems deterred or rehabilitated offenders.

3. **Prisons in the South and the West**: In the South, the lease system developed, allowing businesses in need of workers to negotiate with the state for the labor and care of prisoners. Prisoners were leased to firms that used them in milling, logging, cotton picking, mining, and railroad construction. Except in California, the prison ideologies of the East did not greatly influence penology in the West. Prior to statehood, prisoners were held in territorial facilities or federal military posts and prisons.

B. **Reformatory Movement**

Prisons quickly became overcrowded and understaffed by the middle of the 19th century. Discipline, brutality, and corruption were common, with New York's Sing Sing Prison among the most famous examples.

1. **Cincinnati, 1870**: In 1870 the newly formed National Prison Association (the predecessor of today's American Correctional Association) met in Cincinnati and issued a Declaration of Principles, which asserted that prisons should be operated in accordance with a philosophy of inmate change that would reward reformation with release.

2. **Elmira Reformatory**: Opened in 1876, the first reformatory (run by Zebulon Brockway) regarded education as the key to reform and rehabilitation. At Elmira, a "mark" system of classification was used in which prisoners earned their way up (or down) by following rules.

C. **Improving Prison Conditions for Women**

Elizabeth Gurney Fry led reform efforts in England after visiting London's Newgate Prison in 1813. Reform took longer in the United States, where recommended changes for female prisoners were sometimes thwarted by male leadership.

During this period, three principles guided prison reform: the separation of women prisoners from men; the provision of care in keeping with the needs of women; and the management of women's prisons by female staff.

D. **Rehabilitation Model**

In 1930s, attempts were made to implement fully what became known as the rehabilitation model of corrections. Backed by the newly prestigious social and behavioral sciences, penologists shifted the emphasis of the post-conviction sanction to treatment of criminals, whose social, intellectual, or biological deficiencies were seen as the causes of their illegal activities.

The medical model worked under the assumption that the causes of crime were biological or psychological in nature. Under this approach, correctional institutions were to be staffed with persons who could diagnose the causes of an individual's criminal behavior, prescribe a treatment program, and determine when a cure had been effected so that the offender could be released to the community.

The failure of these new techniques to stem crime, the changes in the characteristics of the prison population, and the misuse of the discretion required by the model caused rehabilitation to fall out of favor with the public by the 1970s, prompting another cycle of correctional reform.

E. Community Model

Community corrections is based on the assumption that the goal of the criminal justice system should be to reintegrate the offender into the community. This model arose from a sense of social disorder in turbulent 1960s and 1970s. It was argued that corrections should turn away from an emphasis upon psychological treatment to programs that would increase the opportunities for offenders to be successful citizens, e.g., vocational and educational programs. While the community model fell out of favor as the punitive philosophy reigned in the 1970s and 1980s, there has been a recent resurgence of interest in community corrections.

F. Crime Control Model

The popularity of the crime control model for punishing offenders dominated corrections in the late 1970's through the end of the century. This punitive model attacked rehabilitation philosophy as being too "lenient" on crime. Incarceration became the dominant form of punishment.

II. ORGANIZATION OF CORRECTIONS IN THE UNITED STATES

A. The Federal Corrections System

1. **Federal Bureau of Prisons**: The U.S. Bureau of Prisons was created by Congress in 1930. Facilities and inmates are classified in a security-level system ranging from Level 1 (the least secure) through Level 6 (the most secure). The federal prison population contains many inmates who have been convicted of white-collar crimes, although drug offenders are increasing, and fewer violent offenders than are found in most state institutions.

2. **Federal probation and parole supervision** for federal offenders are provided by the Division of Probation, a branch of the Administrative Office of the United States Courts. Officers are appointed by the federal judiciary and serve at the pleasure of the court. The Pretrial Services Act of 1982 required pretrial services to be established in each judicial district. Pretrial services officers must collect, verify, and report to the judge concerning information relevant to the pretrial release of defendants.

B. State Correctional Systems

Wide variation exists in the way correctional responsibilities are divided between the state and local governments. Every state has a centralized department of the executive branch that administers corrections, but the extent of these departments' responsibility for programs varies.

1. **Community Corrections**: Types of community corrections include probation, parole, and other intermediate sanctions. Probation and intermediate sanctions are typically handled by local and/or county jurisdictions, while parole is typically handled by the state.

2. **State Prison Systems**: Most state inmates are housed in very large "megaprisons" that are often antiquated and in need of repair. State correctional institutions are classified according to their level of security, which is usually maximum, medium, and minimum.

   Maximum security prisons (where 36% of state inmates are confined) are built like fortresses, surrounded by stone walls with guard towers and designed to prevent escape. Medium security prisons (which holding 48% of state inmates) resemble the maximum security prison in appearance, but are less rigid and tense, and have a greater emphasis on rehabilitative programs. Minimum security prisons (with 16% of state inmates) house the least violent offenders, principally white-collar criminals. The minimum security prison does not have the guard towers and walls usually associated with correctional institutions.

3. **State Institutions for Women**: Women only make up 6.9% of those incarcerated in the U.S., so there are few facilities designed solely for them. The low percentage of women incarcerated in part reflects the fact that women are less likely than men to commit violent crimes. Because there are few institutions for women, they usually find themselves far away from family, their children, and other mechanisms of social support.

C. Private Prisons
Private corporations have argued that they can run prisons more cheaply and efficiently than state governments. The largest providers of private correctional services are the Corrections Corporation of America and Wackenhut Corrections Corporation.

Critics argue that private corporations cut corners while attempting to maximize profits. Several high profile cases of inmate injury as well as facilities cutting back on staff and basic needs for inmates have led some to question the ability of corporations to provide adequate correctional services.

D. Jails: Detention and Short-Term Incarceration
Prisons are the holding facilities at the state and federal level which house inmates with sentences of one year or more. Jails are local facilities for people awaiting trial. They serve partly as a detention center for people awaiting trial, partly as a penal institution for sentenced misdemeanants, and partly as a holding facility for transients taken off the street.

1. **Who Is in Jail?:** There are an estimated 11 million jail admissions every year in the U.S., which breaks down to about 700,000 people in jail on any given day. Many people are held for less than twenty-four hours. Others may reside in jail as

sentenced inmates for up to one year, and a few may await their trials for more than a year. Most are young men of color.

2. **Managing Jails:** Problems with managing jails include:

   a. *Role of the Jail*: Jails are usually run by law enforcement agencies, mostly often the county sheriff. They hold accused offenders awaiting trial and convicted offenders serving terms of less than one year.

   b. *Inmate Characteristics*. The inmate population is made up of inmates of different races, ages, and economic backgrounds. These differences can cause problems for administrators and it can be difficult to keep order, especially in light of the transient nature of this population of offenders.

   c. *Fiscal Problems*. Jails can be a financial drain on the jurisdictions that administer them. Resources are often limited given overcrowding, and some jails do not have a strong focus on rehabilitative programming.

III. THE LAW OF CORRECTIONS

Until the 1960s, the courts, with few exceptions, took the position that the internal administration of prisons was an executive, not a judicial, function. Judges maintained a hands-off policy with regard to prisoner's rights. This changed in the 1960s with the prisoner's rights movement.

A. Constitutional Rights of Prisoners

In 1964, the Supreme Court ruled in *Cooper v. Pate* that prisoners may sue state officials over the conditions of their confinement such as brutality by guards, inadequate nutritional and medical care, theft of personal property, and the denial of basic rights. These changes had the effect of decreasing the custodians' power and the prisoners' isolation from the larger society.

The prisoner rights cases involved prison abuses: brutality and inhuman physical conditions. Gradually, however, prison litigation has focused more directly on the daily activities of the institution, especially on the administrative rules that regulate inmates' conduct.

1. **First Amendment**: Prisoner litigation has been most successful with respect to many of the restrictions of prison life. Barriers in access to reading materials, censorship of mail, and limits on some religious practices have been successfully challenged by prisoners in the courts. Generally, prisoners have freedom of speech in prisons. Freedom of religion has been a major part of prison litigation, and prisoners have been granted the right to worship.

2. **Fourth Amendment**: The Fourth Amendment prohibits unreasonable searches and seizures. However, the courts have not been active in extending these protections to prisoners. Withholding them has traditionally been viewed as reasonable in light of the institutions' needs for security and order.

3. **Eighth Amendment**: The Eighth Amendment's prohibition of cruel and unusual punishments leads to claims involving the failure of prison administrators to provide minimal conditions necessary for health, to furnish reasonable levels of medical care, and to protect inmates from assault by other prisoners. The "totality of conditions" may be such that life in the institution may itself constitute cruel and unusual punishment.

4. **Fourteenth Amendment:** The two clauses of the Fourteenth Amendment requiring procedural due process and equal protection are relevant to the question of prisoners' rights, and produced a great amount of litigation in the 1970s.

   a. *Due Process in Prison Discipline*: Administrative discretion in determining disciplinary procedures can usually be exercised within the prison walls without challenge. There are several certain procedural rights extended to inmates, but the Court also said that there is no right to counsel at a disciplinary hearing.

   b. *Equal Protection*: Institutional practices or conditions that discriminate against prisoners on the basis of race or religion have been held unconstitutional.

5. **Impact of the Prisoners' Rights Movement:** Conditions have improved for inmates since the prisoner's rights movement began. Law libraries and legal assistance are now generally available; communication with the outside is easier; religious practices are protected; inmate complaint procedures have been developed; and due process requirements are emphasized.

B. Law and Community Corrections

Offenders serving terms of probation or parole must abide by the specific conditions of their punishment, which usually interfere with an offender's constitutional rights. Offenders have the right to a preliminary and final hearing when probation or parole is revoked, but evidence usually not allowed in criminal trials can be used in revocation hearings.

C. Law and Correctional Personnel

Laws also define the relationship between inmates and personnel. Because prison guards are employees of the state, they are bound by certain regulations and can also be sued.

1. **Civil Service Laws**
   These laws regulate the hiring and firing of government employees. They also affect the organization and structure of labor unions and the work conditions of employees.

2. **Liability of Correctional Personnel**
   Under the civil service laws, inmates can sue correctional officials if they feel their civil rights have been violated.

IV. CORRECTIONAL POLICY TRENDS

A. <u>**Community Corrections**</u>
   The number of offenders on probation and parole has increased dramatically. This has occurred for a number of reasons, and there are significant implications for the future of community corrections.

   1. **Probation**: People on probation make up over 70 percent of the correctional population but resources, including both funding and personnel, have not risen accordingly.

   2. **Parole**: The number of persons on parole has also grown rapidly. Over one-half million felons are released from prison each year and allowed to live within a community under supervision. Many of these individuals have difficulty finding work and there are few programs to assist them. The average parolee has a 50/50 chance of returning to prison.

B. <u>**Incarceration**</u>
   Since 1973, the incarceration rate has quadrupled, but crime levels have stayed the same. This increase has not occurred "evenly" throughout the United States. Much of the increase is due to the southern region of the U.S. Why the increase in incarceration rates?

   1. **Increased Arrests and More Likely Incarceration:** Both the number of arrests and the probability of incarceration has increased in recent years.

   2. **Tougher Sentences**: A hardening of public attitudes toward criminals during the past decade has been reflected in longer sentences, in a smaller proportion of those convicted being granted probation, and in fewer being released at the time of the first parole hearing. In addition, the move toward determinate sentencing in many states means that many offenders are now spending more time in prison.

   3. **Prison Construction**: The increased rate of incarceration may be related to the creation of additional space in the nation's prisons. Again, public attitudes in favor of more punitive sentencing policies may have influenced legislators to build more prisons. If serious offenses are less common, judges will be inclined to use prison space for less harmful offenders.

   4. **War on Drugs**: The crusade against illegal narcotics has produced stiff mandatory sentences by federal government and states.

5. **State Politics**: The election of governors who campaign on platforms of "law and order" is associated with increases in prison populations, even in states with lower crime rates than neighboring states. Because of public attitudes, crime rates, and the expansion of prison space, incarceration rates are likely to remain high. A policy shift may occur if taxpayers begin to object to the high costs.

REVIEW OF KEY TERMS

Define each of the following:

community corrections

congregate system

contract labor system

corrections

crime control model of corrections

Enlightenment

hands-off policy

jails

lease system

mark system

medical model

penitentiary

prison

reformatory

rehabilitation model

separate confinement

Cooper v. Pate (1964)

Gagnon v. Scarpelli (1973)

Hudson v. Palmer (1984)

Mempa v. Rhay (1967)

Morrissey v. Brewer (1972)

Wolff v. McDonnell (1974)

SELF-TEST SECTION

KEY TERMS

Fill in the appropriate term for each statement:

1. Under the _____ , inmates' labor was sold to private employers and inmates made goods to be sold in the prison.

2. Increased use of incarceration and other strict punishments dominate the _____ .

3. The _____ is the policy that judges should not interfere with correctional management.

4. In _____ , the Supreme Court decided that prisoners may challenge the conditions of their confinement in court.

5. _____ was a philosophical movement that emphasized the individual, limitations on government, and rationalism.

6. The _____ assumes that offenders have biological or psychological irregularities and they need to be "cured" in order to stop offending.

7. According to _____ , prisoners have the right to procedural due process when decisions are made regarding the discipline of prisoners.

8. _____ is the body of programs, services, and organizations responsible for managing people who have committed crimes.

9. A _____ is a penitentiary system developed in New York in which prisoners worked together silently during the day before being held in isolation at night.

10. A _____ is an institution intended to isolate prisoners from society and from one another so that they could reflect on their misdeeds and repent.

11. The _____ involved leasing inmates to contractors, who gave prisoners food and clothing in exchange for their labor.

12. Offenders who are sentenced to one year or more of incarceration serve their sentence in a _____ .

13. According to the finding in _____ , prisoners do not have the same protections against search and seizure as non-incarcerated citizens.

14. _____ is a penitentiary system developed in Pennsylvania by the Quakers involving isolation in individual cells.

15. In the case of _____ , parolees are entitled to a hearing prior to revocation of probation.

16. A _____ is an institution for young offenders emphasizing training and reformation.

17. _____ is a model of corrections based on the assumption that the reintegration of the offender into society should be the goal of the criminal justice system.

18. The case of _____ determined that prisoners have the right to counsel at sentencing and revocation hearings.

19. When institutions use a _____ , offenders receive points for good behavior and negative points for bad behavior.

20. The _____ is a model based on behavioral and social sciences that emphasized treatment of criminals' deficiencies which caused them to commit crimes.

21. _____ are usually under the administration of local, elected law enforcement officials rather than corrections specialists.

22. The Supreme Court decided in _____ that in order for parole to be revoked, parolees are entitled to an official inquiry.

FILL-IN-THE-BLANK EXERCISE

The **1.** _____ led the reform movement, which led to the creation of **2.** _____ , the first institution to implement the **3.** _____ of **4.** _____ as a means to encourage offenders to repent.

5. _____ served as the warden of **6.** _____ , in which he tried to put into practice his ideas for gearing the length and nature of incarceration to the reform of prisoners. Because of the emphasis on indeterminate sentences, these nineteenth century practices shared a similarity with the so-called **7.** _____ or the **8.** _____ , which relied on science to determine when a prisoner had been cured.

9. _____ are short-term holding facilities that contain both **10.** _____ serving short sentences and **11.** _____ awaiting completion of their cases.

MULTIPLE CHOICE

10.1. Which of the following statements about "supermax" prisons is NOT true?
   a) Inmates spend up to 24 hours per day in their cells
   b) Inmates are shackled whenever they leave their cells
   c) Inmates cannot receive mail, phone calls or any contact with normal society
   d) These prisons typically house the "worst of the worst"
   e) Thirty-eight states currently use "supermax" facilities

10.2. The Enlightenment was the main intellectual force behind:
   a) the civil rights movement
   b) the women's rights movement
   c) the American Revolution
   d) the Crusades
   e) the Louisiana Purchase

10.3. The Penitentiary Act of 1779 called for the creation of:
   a) special facilities for women
   b) educational programs in prison
   c) special courts to hear cases regarding prisoner's rights
   d) rehabilitative programs
   e) houses of hard labor

10.4. Why was isolation an important part of the penitentiary?
   a) Reformers didn't like foul language being used in prison
   b) Reformers wanted inmates to have time to reflect upon their behavior
   c) Reformers wanted inmates to enter the monastery upon release
   d) Reformers didn't want the inmates to file lawsuits
   e) Reformers believed that inmates didn't need human companionship

10.5. How did prisons in New York in the mid-1800's attempt to cover expenses associated with running a prison?
   a) Contracting labor to private companies
   b) Selling prisoner's blood and organs
   c) Using inmates to provide legal services to other inmates
   d) Asking inmates for cash payments to run the prison
   e) Telling guards and staff they would have to accept cuts in pay

10.6. What has the Supreme Court decided regarding prisoner's rights under the First Amendment?
a) Prison officials can read inmate mail at any time, with no justification
b) Inmates should not be granted the permission to talk with individuals in "free" society
c) Muslim inmates may not practice their religion while incarcerated
d) Inmates may not communicate with inmates in other institutions
e) Inmates may not be served special meals in accordance with their religious practices

10.7. Which of the following is NOT an explanation given by the text for increasing rates of incarceration?
a) Increased arrests
b) Use of sentencing guidelines
c) Prison construction
d) The war on drugs
e) State politics

10.8. Prior to 1800, who did Americans copy in using physical punishment as the main criminal sanction?
a) Europeans
b) Japanese
c) Africans
d) Mexicans
e) Chinese

10.9. Under what conditions can prison administrators segregate prisoners by race?
a) When violence between races is demonstrably imminent
b) When administrators feel the need to punish prisoners
c) When inmates request it
d) When new inmates enter the facility
e) Administrators can segregate prisoners by race under any conditions they see fit

10.10. Which correctional model would be most likely to recommend psychological testing and classification for prisoners?
a) The reformatory model
b) The medical model
c) The community model
d) The crime control model
e) The penitentiary model

10.11. Jails are typically administered by:
a) Police departments
b) The district attorney's office
c) Judges
d) State correctional agencies
e) Private corporations

10.12. What was the first penitentiary created by the Pennsylvania legislature in 1790?
a) Philadelphia Jail Institute
b) Pittsburgh Prison House
c) Auburn House
d) Walnut Street Jail
e) Sing Sing Prison

10.13. To what issue does the term "totality of conditions" apply with regard to prisoners?
a) Denial of habeus corpus
b) Freedom of religion
c) Unreasonable search and seizure
d) Procedural due process
e) Cruel and unusual punishment

10.14. Which system rented prisoners to firms that used them in milling, logging, cotton picking, mining and railroad construction?
a) New York system
b) Pennsylvania system
c) lease system
d) Auburn system
e) loan system

10.15. The prison ideologies of the East did not greatly influence penology in the West, except for the state of…
a) Arizona
b) California
c) New Mexico
d) Oregon
e) Nevada

10.16. Which law passed by Congress restricted the employment of federal prisoners?
a) Federal Bureau of Prisons Act of 1930
b) Anticontract Law of 1887
c) Hatch Act of 1940
d) Pendleton Act of 1883
e) The Prisoners Services Act of 1982

10.17. What system based prisoner release on performance through voluntary labor, participation in educational and religious programs, and good behavior?
a) enlightenment system
b) congregate system
c) lease system
d) mark system
e) Walnut Jail system

10.18. The community model of corrections came about after which historical event?
a) The Vietnam War
b) September 11th, 2001
c) World War I
d) World War II
e) The Korean War

10.19. When did the reformatory system start to decline?
a) around the Civil War
b) around World War I
c) around World War II
d) around the Korean conflict
e) around the Vietnam conflict

10.20. When and where was the Women's Prison Association was formed?
a) 1804 in Boston
b) 1844 in New York
c) 1903 in Cleveland
d) 1925 in Kansas City
e) 1987 in Las Vegas

10.21. Private prisons are most commonly found in:
a) The Northeast
b) The Midwest
c) The South and West
d) New York
e) There are no private prisons in the U.S.

10.22. What was NOT addressed in the Cincinnati Declaration of Principles?
a) rewarding reformed prisoners with release
b) fixed sentences should be replaced with indeterminate sentences
c) the treatment of criminals through moral regeneration
d) the problems of female offenders
e) all of the above were addressed

10.23. According to the chart below, which correctional population has experienced the most growth since 1980?

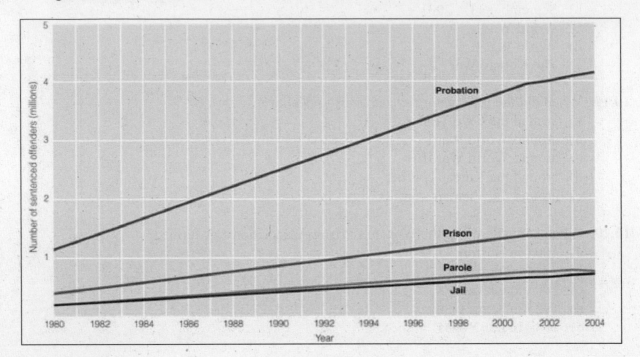

a) jail
b) parole
c) prison
d) probation
e) house arrest

10.24. The cell pictured below is most likely to be found in which type of facility?

    a) work farm
    b) group home
    c) super max prison
    d) minimum security prison
    e) local jail

10.25. In the late nineteenth century, which of the following principles guided female prison reform?
    a) the separation of women prisoners from men
    b) the provision of care in keeping with the needs of women
    c) the management of women's prisons by female staff
    d) all of the above
    e) none of the above

TRUE/FALSE

10.1. _____ The rate of incarceration in the U.S. in recent years has rivaled former Soviet nations.

10.2. _____ The Declaration of Principles did NOT deal with the problems of female offenders.

10.3. _____ Since the 1700s, women and men have been treated differently in prison.

10.4. _____ Group therapy became part of rehabilitation after World War II.

10.5. _____ From 1776 to 1826, the emphasis of corrections shifted to a belief that crime was a result of forces operating in the environment.

10.6. _____ The Enlightenment focused upon increasing the powers of government, group behavior, and irrationalism.

10.7. _____ The Crime Control Model emphasized incarceration as a way to solve the crime problem.

10.8. _____ The U. S. Bureau of Prisons was created by executive order in 1990.

10.9. _____ Community corrections focuses on reintegrating the offender into society.

10.10. _____ The Supreme Court has guaranteed parolees the right to counsel in revocation hearings.

10.11. _____ Women comprise roughly 35 percent of the incarcerated population.

10.12. _____ Privately run prisons do not exist anymore in the U. S.

10.13. _____ Private prisons provide better security than government-operated prisons.

10.14. _____ Private prisons are more expensive than government-operated prisons.

10.15. _____ Some believe the existence of a "prison-commercial complex" has increased the number of offenders who are sentenced to prison.

10.16. _____ The primary function of jails is to hold persons awaiting trial and persons who have been sentenced for misdemeanors to terms of less than one year.

10.17. _____ Most jails are operated at the county level.

ANSWER KEY

Key Terms

1. contract labor system [p. 297, LO1]
2. crime control model of corrections [p. 301, LO1]
3. hands-off policy [p. 309, LO3]
4. *Cooper v. Pate* [p. 310, LO3]
5. the Enlightenment [p. 294, LO1]
6. medical model [p. 300, LO1]
7. *Wolff v. McDonnell* [p. 312, LO1]
8. corrections [p. 294, LO1]
9. congregate system [p. 297, LO1]
10. penitentiary [p. 295, LO1]
11. lease system [p. 298, LO1]
12. prison [p. 307, LO2]
13. *Hudson v. Palmer* [p. 311, LO1]
14. separate confinement [p. 296, LO3]
15. *Morrissey v. Brewer* [p. 313, LO3]
16. reformatory [p. 299, LO1]
17. community corrections [p. 301, LO1]
18. *Mempa v. Rhay* [p. 313, LO3]
19. mark system [p. 299, LO3]
20. rehabilitation model [p. 300, LO1]
21. jails [p. 307, LO2]
22. *Gagnon v. Scarpelli* [p. 313, LO3]

Multiple Choice

10.1. C [p. 304, LO1]
10.2. C [p. 294, LO1]
10.3. E [p. 295, LO1]
10.4. B [p. 296, LO1]
10.5. A [p. 297, LO1]
10.6. D [p. 310, LO2]
10.7. B [p. 319, LO4]
10.8. A [p. 294, LO1]
10.9. A [p. 312, LO3]
10.10. B [p. 300, LO1]
10.11. A [p. 307, LO2]
10.12. D [p. 296, LO1]
10.13. E [p. 311, LO3]
10.14. C [p. 298, LO1]
10.15. B [p. 298, LO1]
10.16. B [p. 298, LO2]
10.17. D [p. 299, LO1]
10.18. A [p. 301, LO1]
10.19. B [p. 299, LO1]
10.20. B [p. 299, LO1]
10.21. C [p. 298, LO3]
10.22. D [p. 299, LO1]
10.23. D [p. 315, LO4]
10.24. D [p. 304, LO1]
10.25. D [p. 300, LO1]

True/False

10.1. F [p. 293, LO4]
10.2. T [p. 299, LO1]
10.3. F [p. 299, LO1]
10.4. T [p. 300, LO1]
10.5. T [p. 296, LO1]
10.6. F [p. 294, LO1]
10.7. T [p. 301, LO1]
10.8. F [p. 302, LO2]
10.9. T [p. 301, LO1]
10.10. T [p. 313, LO2]
10.11. F [p. 304, LO1]
10.12. F [p. 305, LO3]
10.13. F [p. 306, LO3]
10.14. F [p. 306, LO3]
10.15. T [p. 315, LO3]
10.16. T [p. 307, LO2]
10.17. T [p. 307, LO2]

Fill-in-the-Blank

1. Quakers [p. 295, LO1]
2. Walnut Street Jail [p. 296, LO1]
3. Pennsylvania system [p. 296,297, LO1]
4. separate confinement [p. 296, LO1]
5. Zebulon Brockway [p. 299, LO1]
6. Elmira Reformatory [p. 299, LO1]
7. medical model [p. 300, LO1]
8. rehabilitation model [p. 300, LO1]
9. jails [p. 307, LO2]
10. misdemeanants [p. 307, LO2]
11. pretrial detainees [p. 307, LO2]

WORKSHEET 10.1: HISTORY OF CORRECTIONS

Imagine that you are the head of a state department of corrections during several eras of American history. Describe each of the following approaches to corrections as you would implement them to make them work as well as they could. Then describe the drawbacks of each approach.

Separate confinement (Pennsylvania): _____

_____

_____

_____

_____

Drawbacks: _____

_____

_____

_____

_____

Congregate system (New York): _____

_____

_____

_____

_____

Drawbacks: _____

_____

_____

_____

_____

Rehabilitation Model: _____

_____

_____

_____

_____

Drawbacks: _____

_____

_____

_____

_____

Community Model: _____

_____

_____

_____

_____

Drawbacks: _____

_____

_____

_____

_____

WORKSHEET 10.2: STAGES OF CORRECTIONAL DEVELOPMENT

What do you see as the three most distinctive elements of the following important stages of corrections in the United States?

The Pennsylvania System

_____

_____

_____

The New York System (Auburn Prison)

_____

_____

_____

Rehabilitation Model

_____

_____

_____

Community Model

_____

_____

_____

Crime Control Model

_____

_____

_____

WORKSHEET 10.3: CAUSES OF RISING PRISON POPULATIONS

Describe each of the theories used to explain the increase in imprisonment of offenders.

Tougher sentencing: _____

_____

_____

_____

Increased arrests and more likely incarceration: _____

_____

_____

_____

_____

State
politics: _____

_____

_____

_____

_____

Construction: _____

_____

_____

_____

_____

War on drugs: _____

_____

_____

_____

_____

Which theory do you believe provides the best explanation? Explain why. _____

_____

_____

_____

_____

WORKSHEET 10.4: CONSTITUTIONAL RIGHTS OF PRISONERS

If we accept the fact that prisoners possess limited constitutional rights, how would you interpret the Constitution to define those rights? Are your interpretations based on a concern that prison officials might abuse their power and impose extra harms on prisoners beyond incarceration? Are they based on your feeling that prisoners should have the fewest and most narrowly defined rights possible? Explain what rights you believe the Constitution should provide under the following provisions as well as the reason for your interpretation.

First Amendment—Freedom of Speech

_____

_____

_____

_____

Fourth Amendment—Unreasonable Searches and Seizures

_____

_____

_____

_____

Eighth Amendment—Cruel and Unusual Punishments

_____

_____

_____

_____

Fourteenth Amendment—Equal Protection

_____

_____

_____

_____

COMMUNITY CORRECTIONS: PROBATION AND INTERMEDIATE SANCTIONS

OUTLINE

- Community Corrections: Assumptions
- Probation: Correction without Incarceration
- Intermediate Sanctions in the Community
- The Future of Community Corrections

CHAPTER 11
COMMUNITY CORRECTIONS:
PROBATION AND INTERMEDIATE SANCTIONS

LEARNING OBJECTIVES

After reading the material in this chapter, students should be able to:

1. Describe the philosophical assumptions that underlie community corrections

2. Explain how probation evolved and how probation sentences are implemented today

3. List the types of intermediate sanctions, and how they are administered

4. Discuss the key issues faced by community corrections at the beginning of the twenty-first century

CHAPTER SUMMARY

Community supervision through probation, intermediate sanctions, and parole are a growing part of the criminal justice system. Probation is imposed on more than half of offenders. Persons with this sentence live in the community according to conditions set by the judge and under the supervision of a probation officer. Intermediate sanctions are designed as punishments that are more restrictive than probation and less restrictive than prison. The range of intermediate sanctions allows judges to design sentences that incorporate one or more of the punishments and hopefully reduce recidivism (return to criminal activity). Some intermediate sanctions are implemented by courts (fines, restitution, forfeiture), while others take place in the community (home confinement, community service, day reporting centers, intensive supervision probation), or in a mixture of institutions and the community (boot camps).

CHAPTER OUTLINE

I. COMMUNITY CORRECTIONS: ASSUMPTIONS

The goal of community corrections is to build ties that can reintegrate the offender into the community. It assumes that the offender must change, but it also recognizes that factors within the community that might encourage criminal behavior (unemployment, for example) must change as well. Central to the community corrections approach is a belief in the "least restrictive alternative," the notion that the criminal sanction should be applied only to the minimum extent necessary to meet the community's need for protection, the gravity of the offense, and society's need for deserved punishment.

II. PROBATION: CORRECTION WITHOUT INCARCERATION

Probation is the conditional release of the offender into the community under supervision. It imposes conditions and retains the authority of the sentencing court to modify the conditions of sentence or to re-sentence the offender. Conditions may include drug tests, curfews, and orders to stay away from certain people or parts of town.

A. Origins and Evolution of Probation

Probation officers began with a casework model that dictated active involvement in the family, employment, free time, and religion of first-time and minor offenders. With the rising influence of psychology in the 1920s, the probation officer continued as a caseworker, but the emphasis moved to therapeutic counseling in the office rather than on assistance in the field.

During the 1960s, probation officers changed their strategies. Rather than counseling offenders in their offices, probation officers provided them with concrete social services, such as assistance with employment, housing, finances, and education. In the late 1970s the orientation of probation again changed. The goals of rehabilitation and reintegration gave way to an orientation widely referred to as risk control.

B. Organization of Probation

Probation may be viewed as a form of corrections, but in many states it is administered by the judiciary, usually with local control. Frequently, the locally elected county judges are the actors who are really in charge. However, judges usually know little about corrections and probation administration. Perhaps the strongest argument in favor of judicial control is that probation works best when there is a close relationship between the judge and the supervising officer. Some states have combined probation and parole in the same department, even though parolees are quite different than probationers—parolees need greater supervision and have significant adjustment problems when they leave prison.

C. Probation Services

Probation officers are expected to act as both police personnel and social workers. They prepare presentence reports for the courts and they supervise clients in order to keep them out of trouble and to assist them in the community. Most probation officers have backgrounds in social service and are partial to that role. In dangerous urban neighborhoods, direct supervision can be a dangerous task for the probation officer. In some urban areas, probationers are merely required to telephone or mail reports of their current residence and employment.

D. Revocation and Termination of Probation

Revocation of probation can result from a new arrest or conviction, or from failure to comply with a condition of probation. Since probation is usually granted in conjunction with a suspended jail or prison sentence, incarceration may follow revocation. Common reasons for revocation include failing a drug urinalysis test, failure to participate in treatment, failure to report to a probation officer (all technical violations), and rearrest for a new crime. Prison overcrowding and other factors have led to a current emphasis on avoiding incarceration except for flagrant and continual violation of the conditions of probation; thus most revocations occur because of a new arrest or conviction.

E. Assessing Probation

Critics argue that probation, especially in urban areas, does nothing. Probation does produce less recidivism than incarceration, but researchers now wonder if this effect is a direct result of supervision or an indirect result of people "growing out" of crime. Almost half of the nation's current probationers have been convicted on felony charges, which means they should be in prison but are not, largely owing to prison overcrowding. In addition, upwards of 75 percent of probationers are addicted to drugs or alcohol.

III. INTERMEDIATE SANCTIONS IN THE COMMUNITY

Intermediate sanctions may be viewed as a continuum—a range of punishments that vary in terms of level of intrusiveness and control. Probation plus a fine or community service may be appropriate for minor offenses, while six weeks of boot camp followed by intensive probation supervision may be the deserved punishment for someone who has been convicted of a more serious crime. Each individual intermediate sanction may be imposed singly or in tandem with others.

A. Intermediate Sanctions Administered Primarily by the Judiciary

1. **Fines** are routinely imposed today for a wide range of offenses. Recent studies have shown that the fine is used very widely as a criminal sanction and that probably well over $1 billion in fines are collected annually by courts across the country. Fines are rarely used as the *sole* punishment for crimes more serious than motor vehicle violations. Judges may shy away from using fines because of the risk that the affluent will be able to "buy" their way out of jail while the poor will have to serve time.

2. **Restitution** is repayment to a victim who has suffered some form of financial loss as a result of the offender's crime. It is only since the late 1970s that it has been institutionalized in many areas. It is usually carried out as one of the conditions of probation.

3. **Forfeiture** is seizure by the government of property derived from or used in criminal activity. Forfeiture proceedings can take both civil and criminal form. Using the civil law, property utilized in criminal activity (contraband, equipment to manufacture illegal drugs, automobiles) can be seized without a finding of guilt. Concerns have been raised about law enforcement self-interest in forfeiture, because the forfeited assets are often directed into the budget of the law enforcement agency initiating the action.

B. Intermediate Sanctions Administered in the Community

1. **Home Confinement**, also referred to as "house arrest," requires convicted offenders to spend all or part of their time in their own residence. They may be able to leave their residence for work, school, or treatment. This can be used as a sole sanction or

in combination with other penalties. Electronic devices that monitor offenders can either be passive (in which a probation officer must call in to check that the offender is home) or active (in which a continuous signal is sent by the device, which notifies the probation officer if the offender leaves the home).

2. **Community Service** is unpaid service to the public to overcome or compensate society for some of the harm caused by the crime. It can take a variety of forms, including work in a social service agency, cleaning parks, or assisting the poor. The sentence specifies the number of hours to be worked and usually requires supervision by a probation officer.

3. **Day reporting centers** employ a potpourri of common correctional methods. For example, in some centers, offenders are required to be in the facility for eight hours, or to report into the center for urine checks before going to work. Drug and alcohol treatment, literacy programs, and job searches may be carried out in the center.

4. **Intensive probation supervision (ISP)** is a way of using probation as an intermediate punishment. It is thought that daily contact between the probationer and officer may decrease rearrests and may permit offenders who might otherwise go to prison to be released into the community. Institutional diversion involves the selection of low-risk offenders who have been sentenced to prison to receive supervision in the community. Each officer has only twenty clients, and frequent face-to-face contacts are required. Because the intention is to place high-risk offenders who would normally be incarcerated in the community instead, it is expected that resources will be saved.

C. <u>Sanctions Administered in Institutions and Community</u>

Boot camps now operate in thirty states. They are all based on the belief that young offenders can be "shocked" out of their criminal ways if they undergo a physically rigorous, disciplined, and demanding regimen for a short period, usually three or four months, before being returned to the community for supervision. These programs are sometimes referred to as "shock incarceration." While boot camps have not been effective at decreasing recidivism, many point to the lack of aftercare programs to help transition offenders back into society.

D. <u>Implementing Intermediate Sanctions</u>

In many states there is competition as to which agency will receive additional funding to run the intermediate sanctions programs. Probation organizations argue that they know the field, have the experienced staff, and—given the additional resources—could do an excellent job.

A second issue concerns the type of offender given an intermediate sanction. One school of thought emphasizes the seriousness of the offense, the other concentrates on the problems of the offender. Some agencies want to accept into their intermediate sanctions program only those offenders who *will* succeed. Critics point out that this strategy leads to "creaming" (i.e., taking the cream of the crop), or taking the most promising offenders and leaving those with problems to traditional sanctions.

"Net widening" is the term used to describe a process in which a new sanction increases, rather than reduces, government control over offender's lives. This can occur when a judge imposes a *more* intrusive sanction than usual, rather than the *less* intrusive option.

IV. THE FUTURE OF COMMUNITY CORRECTIONS

In 1995, there were 3.7 million Americans under community supervision in 1995. By 2007, this figure had grown to almost 7.3 million. Despite its wide usage, community corrections often lacks public support, in part because it suffers from the idea that it is "soft on crime." When compared to those placed on probation in previous eras, today's offenders require greater supervision based on their crimes, prior records, and drug problems. Any probation organization requires sufficient resources to fulfill its responsibilities, particularly during an era of prison overcrowding, when the number of probationers is rapidly increasing. In order for organizations to receive the necessary community support, citizens must believe that the sanctions they provide are meaningful.

REVIEW OF KEY TERMS

Define each of the following:

boot camp

community service

day reporting centers

fine

forfeiture

home confinement

intensive probation supervision (ISP)

net widening

recidivism

restitution

technical violation

SELF-TEST SECTION

KEY TERMS

Fill in the appropriate term for each statement:

1. _____ is a sentence that uses electronic monitoring devices and restrictions on activities within the community.

2. _____ is the term for crimes that are committed after an offender has been punished.

3. _____ is compensation for an injury one has inflicted that must be paid to the victim.

4. If a probationer is incarcerated for failing to report to his/her probation officer, that offender has committed a _____.

5. _____ is a sentence requiring the offender to work on projects that benefit the town or city.

6. _____ occurs when intermediate sanctions end up giving the government increased control over citizens.

7. _____ is a place that probationers may be ordered to report to every day.

8. Assets of convicted offenders can be seized by the state under federal laws regarding _____.

9. _____ are sums of money to be paid to the state by a convicted person as a punishment for an offense.

10. _____ uses a military model to build discipline and self-esteem for young offenders.

11. Offenders sentenced to _____ are more closely monitored by probation officers, and there are usually strict conditions attached to successful completion of probation.

FILL-IN-THE-BLANK EXERCISE

Many intermediate sanctions can be applied in the context of **1.** _____ , because offenders who must provide labor under a sentence of **2.** _____ or are subject to electronic monitoring under a sentence of **3.** _____ are not sent away to prison. Although the officers who supervise **4.** _____ may make some efforts to fulfill the ideal of rehabilitation, many intermediate sanctions actually stem from prison overcrowding rather than from other underlying purposes.

With young offenders, judges may apply either **5.** _____ , which involve military-style discipline, or **6.** _____ , to give offenders an idea of what being deprived of their freedom is like. Like other forms of sanctions, these two do not necessarily prevent young offenders from becoming repeat offenders as adults.

MULTIPLE CHOICE

11.1. Which of the following is a reason that criminal justice experts tend to support the use of community corrections?
a) It is a harsh punishment
b) It is cheaper than incarceration
c) It serves to isolate offenders from the community
d) It does not assume guilt on the part of the offender
e) Offenders have no constitutional rights under a community corrections model

11.2. The public is generally not in favor of increased use of probation because:
a) It is too expensive
b) It contributes to prison overcrowding
c) It appears to be a "slap on the wrist"
d) Too many offenders charged with murder receive probation
e) The use of probation takes jobs away from non-criminal citizens

11.3. Which term describes the approach that seeks to minimize the probability than an offender will commit a new offense by making the punishment fit the crime?
a) recidivism
b) restorative justice
c) intensive supervision probation
d) mark system
e) risk management

11.4. What is meant by the term "stronger nets"?
a) Net widening increases the number of citizens under the control of the criminal justice system
b) Net widening transfers authority from one agency to another
c) Net widening releases inmates from prison earlier
d) Net widening augments the state's control over citizens
e) Net widening decreases state control

11.5. Which state developed the first statewide probation system in 1880?
a) Delaware
b) New Jersey
c) Pennsylvania
d) Massachusetts
e) New York

11.6. What is a common problem faced by graduates of boot camp programs?
a) The military structure causes laziness
b) Boot camp sentences are longer than regular prison sentences
c) They must return to the environment that caused problems for them initially
d) Boot camps are considered "schools for crime"
e) They are too young to find employment

11.7. According to research findings, why do ISP programs have higher rates of failure than regular probation?
a) Probation officers observe these offenders more closely and are more likely to find violations
b) ISP doesn't work very well
c) ISP is focused on violent offenders, who are most likely to reoffend
d) There are no opportunities for employment or skills training
e) Offenders are more likely to choose ISP over prison

11.8. Which of the following is true about probation?
a) Probation can only be revoked for a technical violation
b) Probation can only be revoked for committing a new crime
c) Probation has a higher rate of recidivism than incarceration
d) Probationers are usually the most serious offenders
e) Probationers have the right to a hearing before probation is revoked

11.9. Which laws established forfeiture as a valid sentence?
a) NIJ and BJS
b) DOJ and DHS
c) VAWA and CCD
d) FBI and INS
e) RICO and CCE

11.10. Which of the following terms best describes restitution?
a) Reparative
b) Retributive
c) Restrictive
d) Resumptive
e) Resurrective

11.11. Which of the following can be combined with probation?
a) fines
b) restitution
c) community service
d) all of the above
e) none of the above

11.12. A technical violation is:
   a) The commission of a new crime
   b) A recidivistic event
   c) Failure to meet the conditions of a sentence
   d) Usually imposed during home or electronic confinement
   e) Failure to pay a fine

11.13. In what case did the U. S. Supreme Court rule that the Eighth Amendment's ban on excessive fines requires that the seriousness of the offense be related to the property that is taken?
   a) *Austin v. United States* (1993)
   b) *Atkins v. Virginia* (2002)
   c) *Ring v. United States* (2002)
   d) *McCleskey v. Kemp* (1985)
   e) *Gregg v. Georgia* (1976)

11.14. Which constitutional right might be violated by electronic monitoring and home confinement?
   a) double jeopardy clause
   b) cruel and unusual punishment clause
   c) quartering of troops clause
   d) unreasonable search and seizure clause
   e) reserved powers clause

11.15. What is the national average caseload for probation officers?
   a) 150
   b) 60
   c) 30
   d) 15
   e) 5

11.16. During the 1960s, what shift occurred in probation?
   a) offenders were given probation less often
   b) offenders began to refuse probation and select incarceration
   c) offenders began to abuse probation
   d) offenders were given assistance with employment, housing, finances, and education
   e) offenders were given longer sentences of probation

11.17. In the late 1970s, how did the orientation of probation change?
   a) emphasis was placed upon rehabilitation
   b) efforts were made to minimize the probability that an offender would commit a new offense
   c) emphasis was placed upon reintegration into society
   d) efforts were made to eliminate probation
   e) probation did not change during the late 1970s

11.18. Which of the following is an example of an intermediate sanction administered primarily by the judiciary?
   a) home confinement
   b) day reporting centers
   c) forfeiture
   d) all of the above
   e) none of the above

11.19. Which of the following is an example of an intermediate sanction administered primarily inside institutions and followed by community supervision?
   a) boot camp
   b) day reporting centers
   c) forfeiture
   d) all of the above
   e) none of the above

11.20. Which of the following is an example of an intermediate sanction administered primarily in the community with a supervision component?
   a) home confinement
   b) fines
   c) forfeiture
   d) all of the above
   e) none of the above

11.21. Why don't American judges prefer to impose fines on offenders?
   a) judges do not have time to factor fines into the budget of the court
   b) money and justice should not become intertwined
   c) fines are usually embezzled by court officials
   d) fines are too light of a punishment for even minor offenses
   e) fines are difficult to collect from offenders who are predominately poor

11.22. A passive home confinement system…
   a) Responds only to inquiries from the probation officer
   b) Sends continuous signals and alerts the probation officer when the offender leaves his or her home
   c) Helps decrease net widening
   d) Is used in most prisons to prevent escape
   e) Is generally preferred over an active system

11.23. Which of the following is NOT a drawback of home confinement using electronic monitoring?
   a) failure to prevent crimes that occur in the home
   b) questionable constitutionality in terms of expectation of privacy
   c) high offender recidivism rates
   d) technical problems that may cause false reports
   e) the overall expense of a home confinement program

TRUE/FALSE

11.1. _____ The day fine has never been used in the United States.

11.2. _____ Before probation can be revoked, the offender is entitled to a preliminary hearing.

11.3. _____ The recidivism rate for offenders under community supervision is lower than those who are released from prison.

11.4. _____ Fines are used extensively in Europe as punishment.

11.5. _____ In regard to forfeiture laws, owners' property cannot be seized if they can demonstrate their innocence by a preponderance of evidence.

11.6. _____ Forfeited assets often go into the budget of the law enforcement agency taking the action.

11.7. _____ Because incarceration rates and probation caseloads are decreasing, intermediate sanctions probably will not play a major role in corrections during the first decade of the new century.

11.8. _____ Restitution is typically used when it is difficult to calculate damages from crime.

11.9. _____ Restitution was performed frequently in the Middle Ages, based on private arrangements between individuals.

11.10. _____ Intermediate sanctions can be thought of as a continuum of punishments.

11.11. _____ Few released prisoners are subject to conditional community supervision release.

11.12. _____ The size of a probation officer's caseload is often less important for preventing recidivism than the quality of supervision and assistance provided to probationers.

11.13. _____ Many judges order community service when an offender cannot pay a fine.

11.14. _____ There are few technical problems with electronic monitoring devices.

11.15. _____ The legislative branch is largely responsible for administering intermediate sanctions.

11.16. _____ Probation costs more than keeping an offender behind bars.

11.17. _____ A state probationer has a right to counsel at a revocation and sentencing hearing.

ANSWER KEY

Key Terms
1. home confinement [p.334,LO3]
2. recidivism [p.326, LO1]
3. restitution [p.333, LO1]
4. technical violation [p.330, LO3]
5. community service [p.335, LO3]
6. net widening [p.339, LO4]
7. day reporting centers [p.335, LO3]
8. forfeiture [p.333-334, LO3]
9   fines [p.333, LO3]
10. boot camp [p.337, LO3]
11. intensive supervision probation (ISP) [p.336, LO2]

Fill-in-the-Blank
1. community corrections [p.334, LO1]
2. community service [p.335, LO3]
3. home detention [p.335, LO3]
4. probation [p.328, LO2]
5. boot camp [p.337, LO3]
6. shock incarceration [p.337,LO3]

Multiple Choice
11.1. B [p.331, LO1]
11.2. C [p.327, LO2]
11.3. E [p.328, LO1]
11.4. D [p.339, LO1]
11.5. D [p.327, LO2]
11.6. C [p.338, LO3]
11.7. A [p.336, LO2]
11.8. E [p.330, LO2]
11.9. E [p.333, LO3]
11.10. A [p.333, LO1]
11.11. D [pgs. 334-335, LO2]
11.12. C [p330, LO4]
11.13. A [p.334, LO4]
11.14. D [p.335, LO4]
11.15. A [p.329, LO2]
11.16. D [p.328, LO2]
11.17. B [p.328, LO2]
11.18. C [p.332, LO3]
11.19. B [p.332, LO3]
11.20. A [p.332, LO3]
11.21. E [p.333, LO3]
11.22. A [p.335, LO3]
11.23. E [p.335, LO4]

True/False
11.1. F [p.333, LO3]
11.2. T [p.330, LO2]
11.3. F [p331, LO1]
11.4. T [p.333, LO3]
11.5. T [p.334-334, LO3]
11.6. T [p.334, LO3]
11.7. F [p.334-335, LO3]
11.8. F [p.336, LO3]
11.9. T [p.336, LO1]
11.10. T [p.332, LO1
11.11. F [p.327, LO1]
11.12. T [pgs. 329-330, LO2]
11.13. T [p.332, LO3]
11.14. F [p.335, LO4]
11.15. F [p.333-334, LO1]
11.16. F [p.331, LO2]
11.17 T [p.330, LO2]

WORKSHEET 11.1: PROBATION

If you were a judge, what kinds of offenders would you put on probation? What kinds of offenders would you *not* place on probation?

_____

_____

_____

_____

_____

If you were a probation officer, which aspect of your job would receive your strongest emphasis: surveillance/rule enforcement or social services/counseling to help reintegration? Why?

_____

_____

_____

_____

_____

If you were a judge, what conditions/restrictions would you impose on probationers? Why?

_____

_____

_____

_____

_____

WORKSHEET 11.2: EFFECTIVENESS OF INTERMEDIATE SANCTIONS

Take the following intermediate sanctions and list them in order of the sanctions that you believe are most effective (1 for most effective and 8 for least effective): fines, restitution, boot camps, intensive probation supervision, forfeiture, day reporting centers, community service, home confinement. Then describe its strengths and weaknesses with respect to the goals that should be accomplished.

1) _____ : _____
_____
_____
_____
_____

2) _____ : _____
_____
_____
_____
_____

3) _____ : _____
_____
_____
_____
_____

4) _____ : _____
_____
_____
_____
_____

5) _____ : _____

_____

_____

_____

6) _____ : _____

_____

_____

_____

7) _____ : _____

_____

_____

_____

8) _____ : _____

_____

_____

_____

WORKSHEET 11.3: PROS AND CONS OF INTERMEDIATE SANCTIONS

What do you see as the advantages and disadvantages of the following intermediate sanctions? Explain.

Boot camp: _____

_____

_____

_____

Home confinement / electronic monitoring: _____

_____

_____

_____

Restitution: _____

_____

_____

_____

Fines: _____

_____

_____

_____

Community service: _____

_____

_____

_____

WORKSHEET 11.4: THE COST OF SANCTIONS

Probation is often criticized for being ineffective. However, it is often a popular sanction for minor offenders because it is not as expensive as other sanctions. If you were the director of a corrections agency, how would you administer the following elements of probation to make this sanction as effective as possible? Explain what you would do with each item.

Supervision of probationers: _____

_____

_____

_____

Restrictions / conditions of probation: _____

_____

_____

_____

Technology: _____

_____

_____

_____

Education / employment counseling: _____

_____

_____

_____

275

INCARCERATION AND PRISON SOCIETY

OUTLINE

- The Modern Prison: Legacy of the Past
- Goals of Incarceration
- Prison Organization
- Governing a Society of Captives
- Correctional Officers: The Linchpin of Management
- Who is in Prison?
- The Convict World
- Women in Prison
- Prison Programs
- Violence in Prison

CHAPTER 12
INCARCERATION AND PRISON SOCIETY

LEARNING OBJECTIVES

After reading the material in this chapter, students should be able to:

1. Describe how contemporary institutions differ from the old-style "big-house" prisons

2. Understand the three models of incarceration that have predominated since the 1940's

3. Explain how a prison is organized

4. Know how a prison is governed

5. Understand the role of correctional officers in a prison

6. Explain the characteristics of the incarcerated population

7. Discuss what prison is like for men and for women

8. List some of the programs and services available to prisoners

9. Describe the nature of prison violence

CHAPTER SUMMARY

Since the 1940s, three models of incarceration have predominated in the United States: 1) the custodial model, which emphasizes the maintenance of security; 2) the rehabilitation model, which views security and housekeeping activities as mainly a framework for treatment efforts; and 3) the reintegration model, which recognizes that prisoners must be prepared for their return to society. The popular belief that the warden and officers have total power over the inmates is outdated and inaccurate. Good management through effective leadership can maintain the quality of prison life as measured by levels of order, amenities, and service. Because they are constantly in close contact with the prisoners, correctional officers are the real linchpins in the prison system. The effectiveness of the institution lies heavily on their shoulders. Since the 1960s, the prisoners' rights movement, through lawsuits in the federal courts, has brought many changes to the administration and conditions of American prisons.

In the United States, state and federal prisoners do not serve their time in isolation but are members of a subculture with their own traditions, norms, and leadership structure. Inmates deal with the stress of incarceration by assuming an adaptive role and lifestyle. Today, major problems in prison society include AIDS, an increase in elderly and mentally ill inmates, and inmates serving long terms. The state provides housing, food, and clothes for all inmates. To

278

meet the needs of prisoners for goods and services not provided by the state, an underground economy exists in the society of captives. Most prisoners are young men who have little education and come disproportionately from minority groups. Only a small portion of the inmate population is female. This is cited as the reason for the limited programs and services available to women prisoners. Social relationships among female inmates differ from those of their male counterparts. Women tend to form pseudo-families in prison and are less concerned about establishing authority over others. Many women experience the added stress of being responsible for their children on the outside. Educational, vocational, industrial, and treatment programs are available in prisons. Educational programs reduce the risk of an inmate committing a crime upon release from prison. Administrators also believe these programs are important for maintaining order. Prison violence is a major problem confronting administrators. The characteristics of the inmates and the recent rise of prison gangs contribute to this problem.

CHAPTER OUTLINE

I. THE MODERN PRISON: LEGACY OF THE PAST

Many people think of prisons in terms of the "big house"—a large, maximum security prison with tough inmates and tough guards. While there are many large prisons that fit this description, our current correctional institutions include a number of different types of facilities.

II. GOALS OF INCARCERATION

There are three models that predominate in correctional philosophy. The custodial model focuses on security, order and strict discipline in correctional facilities. The rehabilitation model instead focuses on treatment and educational programs in institutions. Finally, the reintegration model attempts to prepare inmates for their eventual return to society.

III. PRISON ORGANIZATION

Prison managers have the difficult task of managing a group of individuals who are being held against their will. Many different kinds of staff members are needed with skills in several different areas (custody, treatment, education, psychology, etc.). Similar to other agencies, their organization is hierarchical and divided by areas of responsibility.

IV. GOVERNING A SOCIETY OF CAPTIVES

Much of the public believes that prisons are operated in an authoritarian manner. Corrections officers presumably possess the power to give orders and have those orders obeyed. Keeping inmates safe, providing their basic needs, and enhancing their lives with training and education are all vital parts of managing prisons.

A. The Defects of Total Power

Simply issuing commands and enforcing them is an inefficient method of making inmates carry out complex tasks. Efficiency is further diminished by the realities of the usual high officer-to-inmate ratio and the potential danger of the situation. Thus correctional officers' ability to threaten the use of physical force is limited in practice.

B. Rewards and Punishments

Since prisoners receive most privileges at the outset, there is little that can be offered for exceptional behavior. Rewards may be in the form of privileges offered for obedience: "good time" allowances, choice job assignments, and favorable parole reports.

C. Gaining Cooperation: Exchange Relationships

Correctional officers obtain inmates' cooperation through the types of exchange relationships described in earlier chapters. Officers need the cooperation of the prisoners so that they will look good to their superiors, and the inmates depend on the guards to relax the rules or occasionally look the other way. Thus, guards exchange or "buy" compliance or obedience in some areas by tolerating violation of the rules elsewhere. Secret relationships that turn into manipulation of the guards by the prisoners may result in the smuggling of contraband or other illegal acts.

D. Inmate Leadership

Inmate leaders can serve as the essential communications link between the staff and inmates. Inmate leaders distribute benefits to other prisoners and thereby bolster their own influence within the prison. However, today's prison population is often divided according to the characteristics of race and ethnicity, gang affiliation, offense, and geographical origin, which may mean that there are multiple centers of power and no single set of leaders.

V. CORRECTIONAL OFFICERS: THE LINCHPIN OF MANAGEMENT

A. The Officer's Role

The officer functions as a member of a complex bureaucratic organization and thus is expected to deal with clients impersonally and to follow formally prescribed procedures. However, the officer must also address individual prisoners' personal problems. Not surprisingly, corrections officers often find it difficult to fulfill the varied and contradictory expectations generated by their role.

B. Recruitment of Officers

One of the primary incentives for becoming involved in correctional work is the security that civil service status provides. In addition, prisons offer better employment options than most other jobs available in the rural areas where most correctional facilities are located. Because correctional officers are recruited locally, most of them are rural and white, in contrast to the majority of prisoners, who come from urban areas and are either African American or Hispanic. It is increasingly possible for college graduates to achieve administrative positions without having to advance up through the ranks of the custodial force.

C. **Use of Force**

Corrections officers can generally use force in the following situations: self-defense, defense of a third party, to uphold prison rules, to prevent a crime, or to prevent escape. Each state department of corrections has detailed policies concerning the above contingencies.

VI. WHO IS IN PRISON?

Prison inmates are primarily repeat offenders convicted of violent crimes. Most prisoners are in their late twenties to early thirties, have less than a high school education, and are disproportionately members of minority groups.

A. **Elderly Prisoners**

Longer sentences produce increasing numbers of elderly prisoners who have special security and medical needs. The average annual cost to the institution of caring for elderly prisoners can be three times the cost for the average prisoner. Many elderly prisoners receive better medical care and nutrition than they would in the outside world because, if released, they would return to poor neighborhoods.

B. **Prisoners with HIV/AIDS**

The rate of HIV/AIDS among prisoners is five times higher than the general U.S. population. Prisoners who test positive create many challenges for preventing transmission of disease, housing infected prisoners, and medical care.

C. **Mentally Ill Prisoners**

Mass closings of mental hospitals has increased arrests and incarceration of mentally ill people. High percentages of inmates in some facilities are classified as mentally ill. Correctional facilities and workers are often poorly prepared to deal with mentally ill prisoners.

D. **Long-Term Prisoners**

More prisoners serve long sentences in the U.S. than in any other Western country. Long-term prisoners are less likely to cause disciplinary infractions, but they present administrators with challenges for maintaining livable conditions.

VII. THE CONVICT WORLD

Inmates in today's prisons do not serve their terms in isolation. They form a society with traditions, norms, and a leadership structure. The so-called inmate code refers to the values and norms that emerge within the prison social system and help to define the inmate's image of the model prisoner. The code also emphasizes the solidarity of all inmates against the staff. However, a single overriding inmate code does not exist in reality, and race has become a key variable dividing convict society.

A. Adaptive Roles

Newcomers entering prison must decide how to serve their time. Four categories have been used to describe the lifestyles of male inmates as they adapt to prison:

1. **"Doing time"** is the choice of those who try to maintain their links with and the perspective of the free world. They avoid trouble and form friendships with small groups of inmates.

2. **"Gleaning"** is taking advantage of prison programs. Usually inmates not committed to a life of crime.

3. **"Jailing"** is the style used by those who cut themselves off from the outside and try to construct a life within the prison. These are often "state-raised youth" who grew up in foster homes and juvenile detention centers.

4. The **"disorganized criminal"** includes those who are unable to develop role orientations to prison life; often afflicted with low intelligence or psychological problems.

B. The Prison Economy

Prisoners are limited as to what they may have in their cells. Restrictions are placed on what gifts may come into the institution, and money may not be in the inmate's possession. Officials have created a formal economic system in the form of a commissary or "store" in which inmates may, on a scheduled basis, purchase a limited number of items—toilet articles, tobacco, snacks, and other food items—in exchange for credits drawn from their "bank accounts," which are composed of money deposited on the inmate's entrance, gifts sent by relatives, and amounts earned in the low-paying prison industries.

An informal underground economy also exists in prisons and serves an important function for inmates. Many items taken for granted on the outside obtain a high value on the inside. These underground systems supply items to inmates that are not available at the prison commissary, or they are illegal. The standard medium of exchange in the prison economy is cigarettes. Because possession of coins or currency is prohibited and a barter system is somewhat restrictive, cigarettes often become a useful substitute. However, prison currency may change in the future, as more prisons consider banning smoking.

VIII. WOMEN IN PRISON

Women's prisons are smaller, security is less rigid, the relationships between inmates and staff are less structured, physical aggression seems less common, the underground economy is not well developed, and female prisoners appear to be even less committed to the convict code than men now are. Women serve shorter sentences, and there is perhaps more fluidity in the prison society as new members join and others leave.

Because of the small numbers of women's prisons, these inmates are typically held far from family and other social support groups. Female prisoners are typically young, poorly educated, are members of a minority group, and incarcerated for a serious offense.

A. The Subculture of Women's Prisons
Female inmates tend to form pseudo-families in which they adopt various roles—father, mother, daughter, sister—and interact as a unit. Esther Heffernan views these "play" families as a "direct, conscious substitution for the family relationships broken by imprisonment, or. . . the development of roles that perhaps were not fulfilled in the actual home environment."

B. Male versus Female Subcultures
The related concepts of adaptive roles, the inmate code, indigenous and imported values, the prison economy, and so on, have a similar explanatory value in both types of institution. A principal difference between male and female prison subcultures is in interpersonal relations.

Male prisoners act as individuals and their behavior is evaluated by the yardstick of the prison culture. Autonomy, self-sufficiency, and the ability to cope with one's problems are highly valued. In prisons for women, close ties seem to exist among small groups of inmates. These extended families may essentially provide emotional support and emphasize the sharing of resources. There are debates among researchers about whether these differences reflect biologically distinctive female qualities (e.g., nurturing, etc.), stem from different socialization of females or the particular characteristics of female prisons, or result from a combination of factors.

C. Issues in the Incarceration of Women
States have reacted to pressures for equal opportunity, by attempting to run women's prisons as they do prisons for men, with the same policies and procedures. Some believe that this comparison is incorrect given the differences in inmate subculture and the specific needs of women prisoners.

1. **Sexual Misconduct**: As the number of women in prison increases, so do accounts of sexual abuse by male guards. Several states have passed laws outlawing sexual relations between inmates and prison staff.

2. **Educational and Vocational Training Programs:** Some have criticized women's prisons for not having the same range of programming available as men's facilities, and for providing vocational programs (such as cosmetology or food service) that are both traditionally "feminine" and possess less earning potential.

3. **Medical services**: Women often have special or more serious medical problems than men. Pregnancies raise important issues: approximately 25% of incarcerated women were pregnant upon admission to prison or had given birth within the prior year.

4. **Mothers and Children:** The majority of incarcerated women leave children on the outside while they are serving their sentence. Many of these children are cared for by relatives or placed into foster care. Most incarcerated women cannot see their children on a regular basis because they are incarcerated long distances from their homes. Some lower-security facilities allow overnight visits with children, but most do not have such programs.

IX. PRISON PROGRAMS

Because the public has recently favored harsh treatment of criminals, legislators have reduced education and other programs in many states. Administrators must use institutional programs to manage the problem of time. They know that the more programs they are able to offer, the less likely it is that inmates' idleness and boredom will turn to hostility. Activity is the administrator's tool for controlling and stabilizing prison operations. Contemporary programs are educational, vocational, and treatment-based.

A. Classification of Prisoners
Determining the appropriate program for an individual prisoner is usually made through a classification process. Most states now have diagnostic and reception centers that are physically separated from the main prison facility. Unfortunately, classification decisions are often made on the basis of administrative needs rather than inmate needs

B. Educational Programs
Education programs are the most popular programs in prison. In many prisons, inmates who have not completed eighth grade are assigned full-time to a prison school. Many programs permit inmates to earn a high school equivalency diploma (GED). College-level programs are offered in some facilities, but legislation banning federal aid for prisoners has deterred many from taking college courses.

C. Vocational Education
Programs in modern facilities are designed to teach a variety of skills: plumbing, automobile mechanics, printing, computer programming. Unfortunately, due to poor planning some vocational programs seek to prepare inmates for careers on the outside that are actually closed to former felons, such as restaurant work (many states prohibit parolees from working where alcohol is sold).

D. Prison Industries
Traditionally, prisoners have been required to work at tasks that are necessary to maintain and run their own and other state facilities, such as food service, laundry, and building maintenance jobs. Prison farms also produce food for the institution in some states. Industry shops make furniture, repair office equipment, and fabricate items.

During the nineteenth century, factories were set up inside many prisons and inmates manufactured items that were sold on the open market. With the rise of the labor movement, however, state legislatures and Congress passed laws restricting the sale of prison-made goods so that they would not compete with those made by free workers. The

1980s saw initiatives promoted by the federal government efforts to encourage private-sector companies to set up "factories within fences" so as to use prison labor effectively.

E. Rehabilitative Programs
Reports in the mid-1970s cast doubt on the ability of treatment programs to stem recidivism and raised questions about the ethics of requiring inmates to participate in such programs in exchange for the promise of parole. In most correctional systems a range of psychological, behavioral, and social services is available to inmates. Nationally, very little money is spent for treatment services, and these programs reach only 5% of the inmate population.

F. Medical Services
Most prisons offer medical services through a full-time staff of nurses, augmented by part-time physicians under contract to the correctional system.

X. VIOLENCE IN PRISON
Prisoners are a natural environment for violence, given the type of people incarcerated there and the many deprivations and sources of tension.

A. Assaultive Behavior and Inmate Characteristics
1. **Age**: Young people, both inside and outside prison, are more prone to violence than their elders. Not only do young prisoners have greater physical strength, they lack those commitments to career and family that are thought to restrict antisocial behavior. The masculine code of machismo, which requires physical retaliation for even minor slurs or insults, increases violence in prisons where it is widely held.

2. **Attitudes**: Some believe there is a subculture of violence among certain economic, racial, and ethnic groups. Arguments are settled and decisions made by the fist rather than by verbal persuasion. These attitudes are brought into the prison as part of an inmate's heritage and experience growing up.

3. **Race**: Racist attitudes seem to be acceptable in most institutions and have become part of the convict code. Prison gangs are often organized along racial lines, which contributes to violence in prison.

B. Prisoner-Prisoner Violence
Most of the violence in prison is inmate-to-inmate. This leads many prisoners to avoid contact with other prisoners or request isolation.

1. **Prison Gangs**: Racial and ethnic gangs are now linked to acts of violence in many prison systems. In essence, the gang wars of the streets are often continued in prison. The "blood-in, blood-out" system means that inmates must stab an enemy to be admitted to a gang, and if they want to leave the gang they will risk their own lives. Rival gangs may be placed in different locations, or members of the same gang divided among separate facilities, to reduce violence.

2. **Protective Custody**: Some inmates are held in protective custody for their own safety. Unfortunately, they remain very isolated and spend most of their time in a cell.

C. Prisoner-Officer Violence

Violence against prison staff does not occur often, and is usually not random. Prisoners sometimes fashion weapons from regular items found in the prison. The threat of attack can contribute to anxiety among guards.

D. Officer-Prisoner Violence

Unauthorized physical violence by staff occurs against inmates in many institutions. Prisoners may have a hard time having their complaints taken seriously. Questions as to what constitutes *excessive* force in handling particular situations are usually difficult to resolve.

E. Decreasing Prison Violence

1. **The Effect of Architecture and Size**: The massive scale of some institutions provides opportunities for aggressive inmates to hide weapons, carry out private justice, and engage in other illicit activities free from supervision. Modern prisons are designed to increase officer safety and improve the living conditions of inmates.

2. **The Role of Management**: Effective management is key to reducing prison violence. Managers must understand the inmate social structure, the role of gangs, and the structure of the facility to keep prisons under control.

REVIEW OF KEY TERMS

Define each of the following:

classification

custodial model

inmate code

reintegration model

SELF-TEST SECTION

KEY TERMS

Fill in the appropriate term for each statement:

1. The _____ is the model of correctional institutions that emphasizes maintenance of the offender's ties to family and the community as a method of reform.

2. The _____ is the body of norms and beliefs shared by inmates in an institution.

3. The process of determining the correct placement for an inmate is known as _____.

4. _____ is the model of corrections that emphasizes security, discipline, and order.

FILL-IN-THE-BLANK EXERCISE

American prisons are typically organized using one of several different models. The
1. _____ model emphasizes security, discipline, and order. This is the most
commonly used model in the United States today. Prisons that focus on treatment follow the
2. _____ model, while prisons focused on teaching inmates how to function in
normal society upon release use the 3. _____ model. These two models are less
commonly found in American prisons, due to the focus on crime control exhibited during the
1980s and 1990s.

Wardens have to deal with changing prison populations, including the increasing numbers of
4. _____ prisoners, who are more likely to develop chronic illnesses while
incarcerated. Prisoners testing positive for 5. _____ are also problematic, as
administrators struggle with transmission of the disease in prison. Finally, inmates who are
6. _____ frequently do not receive adequate treatment or counseling in prisons.

Inmates find different methods of adapting to life in prison. Some try to improve themselves by
7. _____; that is, taking educational courses and job training. Others adapt to
prison (called 8. _____) by making friends and doing what they need to survive.
Many inmates who have served time in jail or prison in the past become comfortable while in
prison and cut themselves off from the outside world— a process known as
9. _____. Finally, the 10. _____ doesn't fit any particular
role and struggles through prison life. Many of these individuals develop emotional disorders or
even attempt suicide.

MULTIPLE CHOICE

12.1. Prison organizations are expected to fulfill goals related to...
a) keeping custody of the inmates
b) using and working the inmates
c) treating inmates
d) all of the above
e) none of the above

12.2. This model of incarceration is the least frequently used in American prisons:
a) The custodial model
b) The rehabilitation model
c) The reintegration model
d) The professional model
e) The psychological model

12.3. Which kind of inmate is least likely to pose a control problem for correctional administrators?
a) Long-term prisoners
b) Gang members
c) Mentally ill prisoners
d) Violent prisoners
e) Young prisoners

12.4. What is a sub-rosa relationship?
a) a homosexual relationship between prisoners
b) a secret relationship between a correctional officer and a prisoner
c) a violent relationship between a correctional officer and a prisoner
d) a violent relationship between prisoners
e) a friendly and open relationship between correctional officer and prisoner

12.5. Which of the following is TRUE about prisons?
a) prisons have multiple goals and separate lines of command
b) prison goals are characterized by simplicity and consensus
c) individual staff members are equipped to perform all functions
d) all of the above are TRUE
e) all of the above are FALSE

12.6. Which of the following is a situation when a correctional officer CANNOT use force?
a) self-defense
b) to defend a third person
c) when he/she has a right to be angry at an inmate
d) to prevent a crime
e) to prevent an escape

12.7. Which of the following is a common criticism of programming for women in prison?
a) There are too many opportunities for inmates
b) The programming tends to be conform to sexual stereotypes
c) The programming is not geared toward women
d) There are too few programs involving the 'womanly arts'
e) The programming tends to teach marketable job skills

12.8. What is the concept of male honor and sacredness of one's reputation as a man?
a) good time
b) machismo
c) inmate code
d) in the life
e) gleaning

12.9. What is the primary purpose of prisoner classification?
a) To send the prisoner to the appropriate security level institution
b) To make sure the prisoner is incarcerated with other gang members
c) To locate the prisoner close to family and friends for social support
d) To randomly assign inmates to facilities
e) To make management accountable for security violations

12.10. Vocational education programs are designed to:
a) Increase an inmate's level of education
b) Teach offenders a marketable job skill
c) Make money for prisons
d) Control inmates' drug and alcohol addictions
e) Provide medical treatment for inmates

12.11. The inmates' idea of the model prisoner is known as the:
a) Mix
b) Life
c) Code of conduct
d) Totality of conditions
e) Inmate code

12.12. Those inmates who take on the role of "jailing" would be most likely to:
a) Keep in contact with family and friends outside of prison
b) Be first-time offenders
c) Adapt quickly to prison life
d) Take advantage of rehabilitative and job-training programs
e) Serve their terms with the least amount of suffering and the greatest amount of comfort

12.13. Which of the following is NOT a factor that contributes to prison violence?
a) The physical design of prisons
b) Public opinion about sentencing
c) Placing violent prisoners near defenseless inmates
d) The availability of deadly weapons
e) Inadequate supervision by staff

12.14. Correctional institutions that follow the reintegration model are strongly linked with:
a) Police officers
b) Prosecutors
c) Community corrections
d) Defense attorneys
e) Judges

12.15. Which of the following is true regarding prison organization?
a) All staff perform similar functions
b) Staff members are not organized by function
c) The warden is the highest level of administration
d) The deputy warden is the highest level of administration
e) The deputy warden for custody is likely in charge of medical services

12.16. What is one reason why prisons have a difficult time recruiting correctional officers?
a) Correctional officers must have a college degree
b) Correctional facilities tend to be located in rural areas
c) Correctional facilities are rather unsecured
d) Correctional officers are paid too much
e) There are many opportunities for career advancement for corrections officers

12.17. Which of the following statements about inmates in state prisons is TRUE?
a) Most inmates in state prisons are female
b) Most inmates in state prisons have committed violent offenses
c) Most inmates in state prisons are over 55 years old
d) Most inmates in state prisons are Hispanic
e) Most inmates in state prisons have not graduated high school

12.18. As opposed to men's subculture in prisons, women's subculture is characterized by:
a) A black-market economy
b) Heterosexual relationships
c) Pseudofamilies
d) Aggression and fighting
e) Psychopathology

292

12.19. What is a common method used by prisons for dealing with the mentally ill?
a) Mandatory sterilization
b) Counseling and therapy
c) Electroshock treatment
d) Torture
e) Prisons do not provide treatment for mentally ill offenders

12.20. Some researchers have described female prisoners as wanting to avoid "the mix" while incarcerated. This refers to:
a) Behavior that can bring trouble with staff & other prisoners
b) Working in the kitchens
c) Behavior that can earn a prisoner "good time" credit toward release
d) Behavior that may earn an inmate a privileged positions in the facility
e) The gang lifestyle

12.21. Which of the following is FALSE regarding the difference between men's and women's prison subcultures?
a) Women's prisons are generally less violent than men's prisons
b) Women tend to respond more effectively to programming than male prisoners
c) A larger percentage of women than men are serving terms for drug offenses
d) Male inmates are more likely to get to know their guards, while female inmates are not
e) Women tend to segregate themselves by race while incarcerated

12.22. Inmates who adapt the role of the "disorganized criminal" while incarcerated tend to:
a) cut themselves off from the outside and construct a life in the prison
b) take advantage of prison programs
c) serve their terms with the least amount of suffering
d) become the supplier of illegal goods for fellow inmates
e) fail to adapt to any other role

12.23. There has been a significant increase in prisoners over the age of 55. What is likely responsible for this increase?
a) The use of alternatives to incarceration
b) The increased used of plea bargaining
c) Better crime detection methods, such as DNA analysis
d) Mandatory minimum sentences
e) More older people committing crime

12.24. What do inmates typically use as currency in prisons?
a) Cigarettes
b) Money
c) Drugs
d) Food
e) Sex

12.25. A prisoner who sees their time incarcerated as a "break" in their criminal career has taken the adaptive role of:
a) Doing time
b) Gleaning
c) Jailing
d) Acting as a disorganized criminal
e) Fish

TRUE/FALSE

12.1. _____ The custodial model emphasizes security and order.

12.2. _____ Prison managers can select their own clients.

12.3. _____ Prison managers must rely on clients to do most of the work in the daily operation of the institution.

12.4. _____ The most numerous employees in prisons are the custodial workers.

12.5. _____ The goals and lines of command often bring about clarity and consensus in the administration of prisons.

12.6. _____ Inmates typically have little to lose by misbehaving.

12.7. _____ Correctional officers are NOT allowed to rely on rewards and punishment to gain cooperation from prisoners.

12.8. _____ In most of today's institutions, prisoners are divided by race, ethnicity, age, and gang affiliation, so that no single leadership structure exists.

12.9. _____ In prisons today, most inmates and correctional officers are African-American.

12.10. _____ Over the past twenty five years, the correctional officer's role has changed greatly.

12.11. _____ Employment as a correctional officer is a glamorous and sought-after occupation.

12.12. _____ Correctional officers who are men are NOT allowed to work with female offenders.

12.13. _____ Few states have training programs for correctional officers.

12.14. _____ A correctional officer may use force to protect an inmate or another officer.

12.15. _____ The problem of sexual assault in prison gets too much attention from policy makers and the public.

12.16. _____ Violent behavior in prisons is related to the age of the inmates.

12.17. _____ Race has become a major divisive factor in today's prisons.

12.18. _____ Prisoners have no right against cruel and unusual punishment.

ANSWER KEY

Key Terms

1. reintegration model [p. 347, LO2]
2. inmate code [p. 357, LO7]
3. classification [p. 366, LO4]
4. custodial model [p. 346, LO1]

Fill-in-the-Blank

1. custodial model [p. 346, LO2]
2. rehabilitation model [p. 346, LO2]
3. reintegration model [p. 347, LO2]
4. elderly [p. 355, LO7]
5. HIV/AIDS [p. 355, LO7]
6. mentally ill [p. 355, LO7]
7. gleaning [p. 359, LO6]
8. doing time [p. 359, LO6]
9. jailing [p. 359, LO6]
10. disorganized criminal [p. 359, LO6]

Multiple Choice

12.1. D [p. 348, LO1]
12.2. B [p. 346, LO2]
12.3. A [p. 356,357, LO4]
12.4. B [p. 350, LO4]
12.5. A [p. 348, LO3]
12.6. C [p. 353, LO5]
12.7. B [p. 364, LO7]
12.8. B [p. 370, LO7]
12.9. A [p. 363, LO4]
12.10. B [p. 364,365, LO8]
12.11. E [p. 372, LO6]
12.12. C [p. 359, LO6]
12.13. B [p. 373, LO9]
12.14. C [p. 347, LO2]
12.15. C [p. 348, LO3]
12.16. B [p. 352, LO5]
12.17. B [p. 363, LO6]
12.18. C [p. 362, LO7]
12.19. B [p. 356, LO6]
12.20. A [p. 363, LO7]
12.21. E [p. 363, LO7]
12.22. E [p. 358,359, LO6]
12.23. D [p. 355, LO6]
12.24. A [p. 360, LO6]
12.25. A [p. 359, LO6]

True/False

12.1. T [p. 346, LO2]
12.2. F [p. 347, LO4]
12.3. T [p. 347, LO4]
12.4. T [p. 348, LO3]
12.5. F [p. 348, LO4]
12.6. T [p. 349, LO7]
12.7. F [p. 349, LO5]
12.8. T [p. 371, LO4]
12.9. F [p. 371, LO6]
12.10. T [p. 373, LO5]
12.11. F [p. 352, LO5]
12.12. F [p. 352, LO5]
12.13. F [p. 364, LO5]
12.14. T [p. 353, LO5]
12.15. F [p. 364, LO9]
12.16. T [p. 370, LO9]
12.17. T [p. 371, LO9]
12.18. F [p. 368,369, LO9]

WORKSHEET 12.1: PRISONS AND THEIR PURPOSES

If you were in charge of a state corrections department, how would you design your prisons? For each question, assume that the prisons have one primary purpose (listed below) and describe the physical design, policies, and programs that you would implement to help the institution advance the overriding goal.

1. Custodial Model: _____

_____

_____

_____

_____

_____

_____

2. Rehabilitation Model: _____

_____

_____

_____

_____

_____

_____

3. Reintegration Model: _____

_____

_____

_____

_____

_____

_____

WORKSHEET 12.2: PRISONERS' RIGHTS—YOU ARE THE JUDGE

Corrections officers at the main gate receive a report that a fight involving twelve prisoners has broken out in Cellblock C and that the corrections officers in Cellblock C are unable to break up the fight. Seven corrections officers run down the corridor from the main gate toward Cellblock C. As they round a corner, they practically run into inmate Joe Cottrell who is mopping and waxing the corridor floor. One officer grabs Cottrell by the shoulders and throws him aside while saying, "Get out of the way!" Cottrell falls into a wall, dislocates his shoulder, and later files a lawsuit against the officer by claiming that the rough treatment and resulting injury violated his Eighth Amendment right against cruel and unusual punishment. Were his Eighth Amendment rights violated? Explain.

_____

_____

_____

_____

_____

_____

A prison chapel is used every Sunday for Christian services. A small group of prisoners reserve the chapel for each Tuesday evening where they meet to study an ancient religion from Asia that they claim to follow. For two years, they use the chapel every Tuesday to meditate and discuss books about their religion, and they do not cause any trouble. Then, one year Christmas falls on a Wednesday, and the Asian religion group is told that they cannot have their meeting because the chapel is needed for a Christian Christmas eve service. They file a lawsuit claiming that their First Amendment right to free exercise of religion is being violated because they cannot use the chapel on Christmas Eve. Are their rights being violated? Explain.

_____

_____

_____

_____

_____

_____

WORKSHEET 12.3: EMERGING ISSUES IN CORRECTIONS

What should corrections departments do in response to the following emerging issues? Give reasons for your recommendations.

Elderly prisoners: _____

_____

_____

_____

_____

HIV/AIDS in prisons: _____

_____

_____

_____

_____

Mentally ill prisoners: _____

_____

_____

_____

_____

Long-term prisoners: _____

_____

_____

_____

_____

WORKSHEET 12.4: PRISON PROGRAMS AND SERVICES

If you were in charge of programs and services in a prison, how would you design the following? Should any of them be abolished? Explain

Weightlifting as recreation: _____

_____

_____

_____

_____

Job training: _____

_____

_____

_____

_____

Medical care: _____

_____

_____

_____

_____

Psychological counseling: _____

_____

_____

_____

_____

REENTRY INTO THE COMMUNITY

OUTLINE

- Prisoner Reentry
- Release and Supervision
- Release Mechanisms
- Parole Supervision in the Community
- The Future of Prisoner Reentry

CHAPTER 13
REENTRY INTO THE COMMUNITY

LEARNING OBJECTIVES

After reading the material in this chapter, students should be able to:

1. Understand what is meant by the "reentry problem"

2. Explain the origins of parole, and how it operates today

3. Identify the mechanisms for the release of felons to the community

4. Describe how ex-offenders are supervised in the community

5. Understand the problems that parolees face during their reentry

CHAPTER SUMMARY

Parolees are released from prison on the condition that they do not violate the law and they live according to rules designed to help them adjust to society and ensure that they do not return to crime. Parole officers are assigned to assist ex-inmates making the transition back into society, and to ensure that they follow the conditions of their release. The problem of prisoner reentry into society has become a major policy issue. Most inmates ultimately receive parole, but face a multitude of problems, such as finding employment and avoiding a return to the criminal life upon release. In addition, parolees who committed felonies cannot vote or hold office. Inmates must abide by certain conditions of release during their paroles. If they fail to abide by these conditions, their parole can be revoked and they can be returned to prison. Like probation officers, parole officers serve many functions that are relevant to both law enforcement and social services.

CHAPTER OUTLINE

I. PRISONER REENTRY

Many reentry issues have been generated by the widespread return of offenders to their communities after serving their prison terms. Unfortunately, a large percentage of them are expected to reoffend and return to prison. Because many prisons have reduced the number of program options available to prisoners, many do not leave with usable skills, further reducing their reasons to refrain from crime.

II. RELEASE AND SUPERVISION

When prisoners are released from incarceration, they are placed on parole. This period of time is used to monitor the offender as they are reintegrated into the community. The offender is still a responsibility of the government, but they have been given the privilege of release. In return, the offender agrees to abide by certain conditions of release.

A. The Origins of Parole
Tickets of leave were the first form of parole in the United States. Captain Alexander Maconochie was a key figure in developing parole, which began in Ireland. His system allowed inmates to complete their sentences early for good behavior, and they could reduce their level of incapacitation if they behaved well (from incarceration to chain gangs to limited freedom to ticket of leave to full release).

B. The Development of Parole in the United States
Parole developed about the same time as prison reforms took place in the United States, in the middle of the 19th century. Zebulon Brockway was one of the first administrators in the U.S. to begin using parole. In its early stages, members of the community agreed to monitor parolees. Eventually the job was given to professionals.

III. RELEASE MECHANISMS

Several states abolished parole in the 1970s, when the public began to believe the criminal justice system was too "soft on crime". Other states have kept the parole system, but have been reluctant to use it.

A. Discretionary Release
Parole boards can employ discretionary release when inmates are sentenced to indeterminate sentences. They can assess whether inmates are prepared to be released and "earn" parole.

B. Mandatory Release
Under this system, inmates must be released when they have served the entirety of their sentence (minus good time).

C. Other Conditional Release
Some states have developed methods to release inmates from prison prior to the end of their sentences by placing them in low-security facilities, such as halfway houses or home supervision.

D. Expiration Release
These offenders have served the maximum court sentence and are not eligible to remain in prison.

E. The Impact of Release Mechanisms

There are several options for correctional administrators who believe inmates are ready to be released, but have not served enough of their sentence according to the state. This discretion allows individualized decisions about when inmates are prepared to leave the prison. There is a great deal of variety in the percentage of the total sentence length served by each inmate. Critics of discretionary release believe it removes discretion from the appropriate criminal justice actor, the judge, who is the expert on sentencing and legal procedure.

IV. PAROLE SUPERVISION IN THE COMMUNITY

Offenders released from prison must abide by certain conditions of release. These conditions are meant to keep from associating with people who may be a bad influence on them. Most releasees face difficulties finding work, as they usually have little money and/or possessions when they leave prison. Many employers are reluctant to hire parolees given their backgrounds.

A. Community Programs following Release

There are several kinds of community programs available to parolees upon release. Unfortunately, most communities have neither a sufficient number of programs nor space in those programs for all releasees.

1. **Work and Educational Release:** In these programs, inmates are released from the correctional facility during the day to work or attend school. Critics content that it is wrong to provide job opportunities to convicts when there are non-criminal citizens in the public who may want them.

2. **Furloughs:** Furloughs allow inmates to leave the facility for short periods to visit family. This is thought to assist inmates with reintegration when the return home. This can be a good method to "test the waters" to see how inmates will react to release.

3. **Halfway Houses:** As non-secure facilities, halfway houses allow inmates to work and live in the community while still under supervision. The community can be reluctant to allow halfway houses into their area. These facilities have decreased in number with the more recent punitive focus of corrections.

B. Parole Officer: Cop or Social Worker?

1. **The Parole Officer as Cop:** The parole officer is responsible for keeping track of offenders and making sure they do not violate the conditions of their parole. If they find violations, they must report these just as a police officer reports crimes. Parole officers have some law enforcement powers in order to protect the community.

2. **The Parole Officers as Social Worker:** Parole officers also help parolees by directing them to services they need (finding jobs, restoring family ties). Some

believe that the roles of police officer and social worker are in conflict, and that parole officers should perform both.

C. <u>The Parole Bureaucracy</u>

Parole officers have smaller caseloads, but work with more serious offenders. As with probation officers, their caseloads sometimes become much larger than they can reasonably handle and they must prioritize which offenders deserve more of their time.

D. <u>Adjustments to Life outside Prison</u>

Inmates returning to the community can have great difficulty adjusting to an unstructured life. When combined with the loss of benefits that are available to non-criminal citizens (food stamps, access to public housing, student loans), the adjustment can be even more difficult.

Parolees face difficulties adjusting when their community is not receptive to their presence. Communities may fear, harass, and ostracize inmates post-release. The increased use of sex offender registries may also serve to stigmatize offenders to the point that they simply cannot integrate.

E. <u>Revocation of Parole</u>

A large percentage of parolees are sent back to prison for either violating the conditions of parole or committing a new crime. These parolees are entitled to a hearing prior to having their parole revoked.

V. THE FUTURE OF PRISONER REENTRY

Due to the increasing numbers of inmates leaving prison, there is an increased focus on the community for providing valuable reentry services. However, the public is not generally supportive of community programs, as the typical reaction to them is "Not in my backyard."

REVIEW OF KEY TERMS

Define each of the following:

conditions of release

discretionary release

expiration release

furlough

halfway house

mandatory release

other conditional release

parole

work and educational release

SELF-TEST SECTION

KEY TERMS

Fill in the appropriate term for each statement:

1. After leaving a prison, parolees must satisfy several _____ to avoid being reincarcerated.

2. _____ provides for release according to a time frame stipulated by a determinate sentence and/or parole guidelines.

3. _____ provide a mechanism for temporary release for a few days in order to visit family and prepare for release on parole.

4. _____ provides for release according to a decision by a parole board.

5. _____ _____ is the conditional release of an offender from incarceration but not from the legal custody of the state.

6. A _____ is an institution, usually located in an urban area, housing inmates soon to be released and designed to help reintegration into society.

7. Inmates who are released from a correctional facility to go to work or school during the day have received _____.

8. Inmates who are returned to the community through halfway houses, emergency release, and other methods have received __ _____.

9. Inmates who leave prison without having to serve parole have received an _____ release.

FILL-IN-THE-BLANK EXERCISE

Whether a prisoner receives **1.** _____, through a determinate sentence and parole guidelines, or a **2.** _____, through a decision by the **3.** _____, he or she immediately comes under the responsibility of the **4.** _____, who monitors the former prisoner for improper behavior and also provide social assistance.

MULTIPLE CHOICE

13.1.   Which of the following would most likely cause a revocation of parole?
a) failing a drug test
b) credit problems
c) parking ticket
d) marital problems
e) all of the above would cause a revocation of parole

13.2. Which of the following is likely NOT a valid condition of release
a) Finding employment
b) Getting married
c) Keeping away from criminal individuals
d) Abstain from drinking alcohol
e) Stay in the state of residence, unless granted permission to leave

13.3. What are the three concepts on which parole is granted?
a) Honesty, truth, and liberty
b) Life, liberty, and the pursuit of happiness
c) Faith, hope, and charity
d) Grace, contract, and custody
e) Care, contact, and supervision

13.4. The conditional release of a prisoner from incarceration to the community is called:
a) Probation
b) Custody
c) Detention
d) Parole
e) Booking

13.5. Which of the following were means of moving criminals out of prison?
a) Conditional pardon
b) Apprenticeship
c) Transportation
d) Tickets of leave
e) All of the above were used

13.6. This is the most commonly used method of returning offenders to the community:
a) Expirational release
b) Discretionary release
c) Other conditional release
d) Mandatory release
e) Escape

13.7. Mandatory release occurs when:
   a) An inmate has served their entire sentence
   b) The parole board has decided to release an inmate
   c) An inmate is placed on a work furlough
   d) An inmate is referred to a halfway house
   e) They have 'maxed out' on their time

13.8. What is one criticism of discretionary release?
   a) It shifts responsibility from the parole board to the judge
   b) It shifts responsibility from the police to the parole board
   c) It shifts responsibility from the judge to the police
   d) It shifts responsibility from the judge to the parole board
   e) It shifts responsibility to the inmate

13.9. According to this chart below, which crime has the largest gap between the sentence as imposed by the court and the sentence actually served?

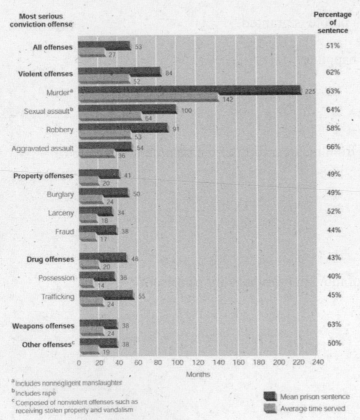

   a) Drug offenses
   b) Weapons offenses
   c) Murder
   d) Violent offenses
   e) Property offenses

13.10. Why are parolees usually denied work in restaurants?
a) There is too much contact with the public
b) Alcohol is served in restaurants
c) Most inmates do not have food service experience
d) Restaurants are open too late for parolees to work
e) Most parolees don't want work in restaurants

13.11. The largest group of unemployed people in the country is:
a) African-American, male, and under 30
b) African-American, female, and under 30
c) Caucasian, male, and over 55
d) Caucasian, female and over 55
e) Hispanic, male and under 30

13.12. The concept of grace refers to:
a) The offender agrees to abide by certain conditions in exchange for release
b) The government extends the privilege of release to the prisoner
c) The offender remains under the control of the justice system after release
d) The government agrees to provide an offer to supervise and control the offender
e) The offender understands it is likely he/she will reoffend and eventually end up in prison again

13.13. Which of the following keeps inmates from finding work?
a) Some jobs require union membership, which can prohibit convicts from joining
b) Carrying the label of a former convict
c) Many convicts cannot be licensed for particular careers
d) Many employers will not hire people who have served prison time
e) All of the above are reasons why parolees have trouble finding jobs

13.14. Inmates involved in work and educational programs...
a) Take courses or work during the day at the prison
b) Leave the prison during the day for work or school
c) Spend time training other inmates
d) Generally have a high recidivism rate
e) Get to stay at home on the weekends

13.15. Inmates can visit family members outside of the prison in:
a) Furlough programs
b) Work release programs
c) Educational programs
d) Parole programs
e) Halfway houses

13.16. What does the acronym "NIMBY" stand for?
   a) No, I'm Bored. You?
   b) Not In My Backyard
   c) No one Is Beyond the Law
   d) Nonsense is My Baseline Yardage
   e) No one is my baby, yo!

13.17. Which two roles do parole officers play?
   a) Police officer and teacher
   b) Police officer and social worker
   c) Social worker and judge
   d) Social worker and attorney
   e) Police officers and probation officer

13.18. Why is parole sometimes referred to as "invisible punishment"?
   a) Because parolees have their home phones tapped
   b) Because parolees are generally shunned by society
   c) Because parolees want to return to prison
   d) Because parolees have so many restrictions on their liberties
   e) Because many parolees end up back in prison

13.19. A parole officer who searches the home of a parolee is taking on the role of:
   a) Social worker
   b) Teacher
   c) Judge
   d) Cop
   e) Counselor

13.20. The first step in a parole revocation hearing focuses on:
   a) Whether there is reasonable doubt that the offender committed the offense
   b) The offender's ability to hold a job
   c) Whether the violation is severe enough to return the parolee to prison
   d) How frequently the offender meets with his/her parole officer
   e) Whether there is probable cause that the conditions of release have been violated

13.21. What is the most common reason for parole revocation?
   a) Failure to report for drug treatment
   b) Positive test for drug use
   c) Possession of drugs
   d) Distribution of drugs
   e) Arrest/conviction on a new offense

13.22. One consequence of the "get-tough" sentencing policies of the 1980's is:
   a) There is less need for reentry programs
   b) Reentry programs have decreased in effectiveness
   c) Fewer inmates are released from prison
   d) More prisoners are released from prison
   e) More rehabilitative programs are available after release

TRUE/FALSE

13.1. _____ Parole release does not impact other parts of the criminal justice system.

13.2. _____ Parolees face many problems when released from prison.

13.3. _____ Most inmates do not receive parole after release from prison.

13.4. _____ Discretionary release allows for individualized punishments.

13.5. _____ Upon release, inmates are usually provided with a temporary residence.

13.6. _____ Parole officers are given little power to restrict the parolee's life.

13.7. _____ Parole officers are granted law enforcement powers.

13.8. _____ Before parole is revoked, the offender is NOT entitled to a preliminary hearing.

13.9. _____ There are some inmates who "max out" on their time and do not require supervision in the community.

13.10. _____ Captain Alexander Maconochie developed a system of graduated release stages, the early forms of parole.

13.11. _____ The United States currently uses a nationwide sentencing and release policy.

13.12. _____ Parole officers typically have larger caseloads than probation officers.

13.13. _____ Sex offender registries and notification laws have resulted in the murder of several offenders released from prison.

13.14. _____ Discretionary release mitigates the harshness of sentencing policies.

13.15. _____ Most Americans think parolees who fail a drug test should not be returned to prison.

13.16. _____ Most inmates have access to reentry programs.

13.17. _____ Prison administrators do not like work release programs because they are usually expensive to manage.

13.18. _____ Some work release programs allow room and board to be deducted from inmate wages.

13.19. _____ Halfway houses are sometimes secure facilities in communities.

13.20. _____ Parole, which used to be focused on transitioning offenders back into society, is now more focused on surveillance and monitoring.

ANSWER KEY

Key Terms

1. conditions of release [p. 385, LO4]
2. mandatory release [p. 382, LO3]
3. furloughs [p. 386, LO3]
4. discretionary release [p. 381, LO3]
5. parole [p. 380, LO1]
6. halfway house [p. 387, LO3]
7. work and educational release [p. 386, LO3]
8. other conditional release[p. 382, LO3]
9. expiration release [p. 382, LO3]

Fill-in-the-Blank

1. mandatory release [p. 382, LO3]
2. discretionary release [p. 381, LO3]
3. parole board [p. 381, LO2]
4. parole officer [p. 388,389, LO3]

Multiple Choice

13.1. A [p. 391, LO2]
13.2. B [p. 385, LO2]
13.3. D [p. 380, LO2]
13.4. D [p. 380, LO2]
13.5. E [p. 380, LO2]
13.6. D [p. 382, LO2]
13.7. A [p. 382, LO2]
13.8. D [p. 383, LO2]
13.9. C [p. 384, LO2]
13.10. B [p. 385, LO4]
13.11. A [p. 385, LO4]
13.12. B [p. 380, LO3]
13.13. E [p. 385, LO4]
13.14. B [p. 386, LO2]
13.15. A [p. 386,387, LO2]
13.16. B [p. 388, LO4]
13.17. B [p. 388,389, LO2]
13.18. D [p. 389, LO2]
13.19. D [p. 388, LO4]
13.20. E [p. 390, LO4]
13.21. E [p. 391, LO4]
13.22. D [p. 392, LO4]

True/False

13.1. F [p. 382, LO1]
13.2. T [p. 385, LO4]
13.3. F [p. 385, LO2]
13.4. T [p. 381, LO3]
13.5. F [p. 387,388, LO3]
13.6. F [p. 387,388, LO4]
13.7. T [p. 388, LO4]
13.8. F [p. 390, LO4]
13.9. T [p. 382, LO4]
13.10. T [p. 380, LO2]
13.11. F [p. 381, LO2]
13.12. F [p. 389, LO2]
13.13. T [p. 390, LO2]
13.14. T [p. 382, LO3]
13.15. F [p. 390, LO5]
13.16. F [p. 386, LO5]
13.17. F [p. 386, LO3]
13.18. T [p. 386, LO3]
13.19. T [p. 387, LO3]
13.20. T [p. 388, LO5]

WORKSHEET 13.1: THE PAROLE BOARD

You are a member of a parole board. The prisoner appearing before you has had perfect behavior throughout her ten years in prison, including tutoring other prisoners to help them learn to read and organizing a large Bible study group. To what extent do you consider the following factors in your decision about whether to grant release on parole?

The state is facing a budget crisis and the corrections department must cut its budget by 10 percent.

_____

_____

_____

_____

The offender was convicted of a violent murder—while under the influence of drugs, she killed a sleeping stranger inside his tent at a campground by hitting him in the head with a baseball bat.

_____

_____

_____

_____

The family of the victim opposes any release on parole.

_____

_____

_____

_____

The prisoner has been diagnosed with breast cancer that requires expensive treatment at prison expense, and she is likely to die within two years.

_____

_____

_____

_____

WORKSHEET 13.2: THE ROLE OF THE PAROLE OFFICER

Describe the different visions of the parole officer's role below, then offer your own view of the ideal role that should be served by the parole officer.

Parole officer as social worker: _____

_____

_____

_____

_____

_____

Parole officer as cop: _____

_____

_____

_____

_____

_____

_____

The ideal role of the parole officer (in your view): _____

_____

_____

_____

_____

_____

_____

_____

TECHNOLOGY AND CRIMINAL JUSTICE

OUTLINE

- Technological Development and Criminal Justice
- Crime and Technology
- Policing and New Technology
- Technology in Courts and Corrections
- Current Questions and Challenges for the Future

CHAPTER 14
TECHNOLOGY AND CRIMINAL JUSTICE

LEARNING OBJECTIVES

After reading the material in this chapter, students should understand:

1. Understand how adaption and belief in science may affect the use of technology

2. Recognize the many aspects of cybercrime and counterfeiting

3. Analyze the role of communications, computers, and databases in policing

4. Describe developments and problems in DNA testing and new weapons technologies

5. Understand the use of technology in courts and corrections

6. Recognize continuing questions about the effects of technology on civil liberties

CHAPTER SUMMARY

New technology can be employed by criminals as well as by criminal justice officials. Criminal justice officials and the public must be wary of automatically assuming that new scientific developments will achieve their intended goals or avoid undesirable consequences. Cybercrime includes identity theft, internet child pornography, hackers' theft of trade secrets and destruction of computer networks. Counterfeiting extends beyond currency and consumer goods to include dangerous and worthless fake prescription drugs. Calls for service to police have expanded from 911 numbers to 311 and 211 for other non-emergency purposes. Computers in patrol cars have expanded police officers' access to information. Police also use computers in crime mapping, gunshot detection systems, and investigation of cybercrimes. Databases permit the collection and matching of information concerning fingerprints, DNA, tattoos, criminal records, and other useful information. DNA testing permits the identification of the source of biological material with a high degree of certainty. Some crime labs have been careless and unethical in testifying about DNA results and some prosecutors have opposed DNA testing that might benefit criminal defendants. New less-lethal weapons such as Tasers, pepperballs, and other projectiles are increasingly used by police. Less-lethal weapons have been involved in incidents that led to the death of individuals against whom the police used these weapons. Courts use technology in computerized recordkeeping and presentation of evidence. There are risks of problems from jurors' perceptions about forensic science and use of technology during trials. Corrections officials use technology for security purposes and for monitoring offenders in the community. The expanded use of technology by government raises questions about the protection of Americans' rights.

CHAPTER OUTLINE

I. TECHNOLOGICAL DEVELOPMENT AND CRIMINAL JUSTICE

Technology affects criminal justice just as it affects other areas of human activity. In our field, though, there is a clash between those who would seek to profit (e.g., theft) or cause harm (e.g., murder) by breaking society's laws and those who seek to stop, identify, apprehend, process, and punish criminals. New developments that benefit one side in this competition, whether lawbreaker or law enforcer, will lead to adjustments and adaptations by the other. That said, the pressure to find new and better devices to combat crime can lead to excessive faith in effectiveness of technology, with a risk of attendant problems if people are not careful and cautious about examining the consequences of new technology.

A. Competition and Adaptation

Just as weaponry has advanced throughout time, so have protective devices. Both affect the preservation of persons and property, which is one of the fundamental goals of criminal justice. In relation, technological developments that impact opportunities for crime have led to criminals developing adaptive strategies for overcoming these barriers.

B. Science and the Presumption Progress

In criminal justice, there is a need to guard against automatic acceptance of new technologies as providing beneficial improvements over older techniques and devices. Similarly, even when the benefits of new technologies are apparent, there is a need to consider whether there are also undesirable risks and consequences that were not fully examined or known when the technology was first put into use.

II. CRIME AND TECHNOLOGY

Computers and other technologies have created opportunities to commit new kinds of crimes, such as cyber crime and counterfeiting.

A. Cyber Crime

Cyber crimes involve the use of computers and the Internet to commit acts against people, property, public order, or morality. Cyber criminals use computers to steal information, resources, or funds. These thefts can be aimed at simply stealing money or they can involve the theft of companies' trade secrets, chemical formulas, and other information that could be quite valuable to competing businesses. Others use computers for malicious, destructive acts, such as releasing internet viruses and "worms" to harm computer systems. They may also take innocent victims' computers and issue remote commands to those computer to assist in crimes, such as the dissemination of child pornography. Some forms have historically remained a salient problem – such as piracy of movies, music, and software – while others have only recently grown in frequency and prevalence – such as cyber-

321

bullying between teenagers. One of the fastest growing trends is identity theft, which involves the use other people's credit card numbers and social security numbers to secure fraudulent loans and steal money and merchandise.

Efforts to create and enforce effective laws that will address such activities have been hampered by the international nature of cybercrime. Agencies in various countries are seeking to improve their ability to cooperate and share information. Differences in legal principles and social values also impact the effectiveness of pursuing cybercrime. Since the events of September 11, many countries' law enforcement agencies have increased their communication and cooperation in order to thwart terrorist activities. As these countries cooperate in investigating and monitoring the financial transactions of groups that employ terror tactics, it seems likely that they will also improve their capacity to discover and pursue cybercriminals.

B. Counterfeiting

Traditional counterfeiting involves the creation of fake currency that can be used to purchase items, deposit into banks, and otherwise let criminals make financial gains from passing worthless paper into the economic system. Continued improvements in computer and printing technology permitted counterfeiters to produce fake currency of better and better quality.

This said, currency is not the only product susceptible to counterfeiting through the use of available production technologies. For example, legitimate businesses lose billions of dollars in potential sales each year when consumers purchase illegally copied, "pirated" Hollywood movie DVDs and counterfeit luxury products, and prescription drugs – which not only has financial costs, but human costs as well.

III. POLICING AND NEW TECHNOLOGY

Policing has long made use of technological developments – from automobiles, to radios, to bulletproof vests, to polygraphs. New tools and devices are continually being implemented to assist law enforcement in their mandate.

A. <u>Communications and Computer Technology</u>

New cell phone and computer technology has altered both citizens' communications with dispatchers and police officers' reliance on their central headquarters. In addition, the use of computers and databases has enhanced the ability of law enforcement officers to investigate many kinds of crimes.

1. **Communications**: In many places, the number of calls to 911 emergency operators increased significantly as the spread of cell phones made it easier for people to make reports as incidents arose. Although 911 systems can automatically trace the location of calls made from landlines, many cities are struggling to upgrade their 911 systems so that they can trace wireless calls to the vicinity of nearest cell phone tower.

2. **Computers**: Computers are also used more frequently in criminal investigation, especially to catch individuals engaging in cyber crime (such as identity theft or soliciting young people for sex online). Furthermore, they are essential tools in law enforcement agencies for crime analysis and crime mapping. Through the use of Geographic Information System (GIS) technology and software, police departments can analyze hot spots, crime trends, and other crime patterns with a level of previously unavailable sophistication and precision. Computers are also now being regularly used inside patrol cars. They enable instant electronic communication that permits the radio airwaves to be reserved for emergency calls rather than for requests to check license numbers and other routine matters. Computer programs permit officers to type information about traffic violations, crime suspects, and investigations directly into central computers without filling out numerous, separate forms by hand. Officers can also gain quick access to information about automobile license plates and pending warrants, and newer systems pull electronic mug shots and even display live video from crime scenes. Two other new technologies are gaining traction. First, "smart cars" are currently being evaluated in some police departments. These vehicles contain a camera that can scan license plates at high speed and then the car's computer tells the officers if the car was stolen or if the owner of the vehicle is wanted. The camera computer system can process 8,000 license plates during a 10-hour shift, whereas an officer could manually process only about 100 license plates during the same time. Second, a new tool being developed helps police in the task of detecting gunshots, quickly analyzing their location, and instantly communicating the information to police without reliance on human witnesses to dial the phone and guess where a shooting took place. About 90% of all large police agencies have computers in patrol cars, with smaller police departments less likely to use computers.

3. **Databases**: Finally, computer technology permits law enforcement officials to gather, store, and analyze data. In minutes, or even seconds, computers can sort through data with the effectiveness that spares a user from spending hours combing through papers stored in a filing cabinet. Databases have been used to archive and process millions of sets of fingerprints, ballistic evidence, and DNA.

B. DNA Analysis

Scientific advances have enabled police and prosecutors to place greater reliance on **DNA analysis**. This technique identifies people through their distinctive gene patterns (also called genotypic features). DNA, or deoxyribonnucleic acid, is the basic compononent of all chromosomes; all the cells in an individual s body, including those in skin, blood, organs, and semen, contain the same unique DNA. The characteristics of certain segments of DNA vary from person to person and thus form a genetic fingerprint. Although fingerprint evidence is still used, advances in DNA technology have greatly reduced any reliance on the less-precise testing of blood and hair evidence as the sole means of identifying suspects.

1. **DNA Databases:** The Combined DNA Index System (CODIS) contains DNA samples from a large number of individuals, including federal prisoners and even noncitizens detained in the U.S. While many state and local jurisdictions have begun collecting DNA samples from offenders, budgetary limitations have kept many of these samples from being analyzed in a timely manner. Some are advocating the expansion of DNA to include the family of suspects, to attempt to identify offenders through family members.

2. **Issues and Problems with DNA Analysis**: DNA testing is emerging as an increasingly important tool in criminal cases, but this technology is quite expensive and samples can take long amounts of time to test, with the result that many U.S. laboratories now have a substantial backlog. Serious errors made in crime labs demonstrate that DNA identification is not foolproof, and has resulted in the release of many innocent people from prison and death row.

C. Surveillance and Identification

Police have begun using surveillance cameras in many ways. American cities increasingly use surveillance cameras at intersections to monitor and ticket people who run red lights or exceed speed limits, although quality problems affecting the video and photographs can limit the effectiveness of these efforts. Some cities are moving forward with plans for the widespread use of surveillance cameras in public places, to help fight crime as well as improve the ability to identify and prevent potential acts of terrorism. Face- and iris-recognition technology, along with devices that detect heat, sweat, or microexpressions increasingly are being used to find and identify criminals.

Critics complain that constant surveillance by government intrudes on the privacy of innocent, unsuspecting citizens and that there is insufficient evidence that this surveillance leads to reduced crime rates. Supporters argue that apart from the benefits of increased identification and recording of wrongdoing, cameras can help to protect rights and hold police accountable when used in different surveillance contexts. For example, some states now mandate the videotaping of police interrogations for murder cases and other serious crimes. When police know that their actions are being recorded, they are less likely to engage in questionable behavior that may violate suspects' rights. Similarly, video cameras in police cars and surveillance cameras on buildings have caught officers engaged in crimes or using excessive force.

D. Weapons Technology

Police departments have given greater attention to less-lethal weapons, largely due to the fallout stemming from unintentional or unjustified injury or death stemming from the actions of officers. Less-lethal weapons include pepper spray, pepper balls, and air-fired beanbags or nets that intend to incapacitate a suspect without inflicting serious injuries. Police are trying to develop alternative less-lethal weapons following needless citizen injury and lawsuits against officers and departments. Emerging technologies include weapons that blast heat, flashes of light, and even radiation are also being tested and evaluated. Tasers – devices with prongs that send an incapacitating electric jolt of 50,000 volts into people on contact - are popular across approximately 12,000 agencies in the United States. However, the use of Tasers is surrounded in controversy as allegations have been made about their possible contribution in hundreds of deaths.

IV. TECHNOLOGY IN COURTS AND CORRECTIONS

A. Courts

1. Electronic File Management

Many courts have moved toward electronic file management systems in which records are digitized and made available as computer files. Such systems typically also use electronic filing systems in which attorneys file motions and other documents via email rather than as traditional paper documents. Additionally, computers can also help to increase efficiency in judges' calculation of possible sentencing options.

2. Presentation of Evidence in Court

The presentation of evidence in court is changing through the introduction of new technology. Previously, lawyers presenting documents and objects as evidence often needed to carry them in front of jurors or have jurors pass them through the jury box. This meant that jurors often got only a fleeting glimpse of specific pieces of evidence. Now many courthouses are developing electronic courtrooms, using presentation technologies that have long been used in business meetings. These mechanisms include projection screens or multiple monitors that permit jurors to simultaneously study documents and photographs. Contemporary attorneys have attempted to use computer technology to advance an image of their version of events. Much like realistic video games, similar realism has now been developed in computer-generated re-creations of crime scenes.

3. Juror Misuse of Technology During Trials

Problems also arise through jurors' use of technology. For instance, the use of such devices as iPhones and Blackberries has even enabled some jurors to contravene judicial instruction and do their own research on a case during a lunch break in the middle of the attorneys' arguments. Problems have also arisen as jurors use blogs and Twitter to post announcements about the progress of a case or about jury deliberations. There is evidence that some jurors even send out messages by cellphone during breaks in the trial. Another potential impact of technology on jury trials is the so-called "CSI effect," which argues that forensic science-based television dramas raise jurors' expectations about the use of scientific evidence in criminal cases and thereby reduce the likelihood of "guilty" verdicts in trials that rely solely on witness testimony and other forms of non-scientific evidence.

B. Corrections

Many of the technologies previously discussed for policing and courts also have applications in corrections. Computerized recordkeeping and state-wide databases can reduce the burden of maintaining, storing, and transporting paper files on each prisoner. Instead, officials throughout the state can access records instantly via computer, and some of these are publicly-accessible.

In corrections institutions, technology enhances safety and security through the use of such developments as electronically controlled cell doors and locks, motion sensors, surveillance cameras, and small radios attached to the shirts of corrections officers. It should be noted that surveillance cameras are not always universally popular with corrections officers because they can also reveal whether officers are doing their jobs conscientiously and properly. Finally, the tasks of transporting and monitoring those under correctional supervision has also benefited from technological advances such as GPS - which enhance the safety of officers and society.

V. CURRENT QUESTIONS AND CHALLENGES FOR THE FUTURE

Technological changes have affected nearly every agency and process within the criminal justice system. The desire for efficiency and effectiveness will lead to continued efforts to create new technologies and refine existing technologies to assist law enforcement, courts, and corrections in their tasks. More powerful computing capabilities, more effective surveillance cameras and body scanners, expanded use of GPS devices, new iterations of less-lethal weapons, and an expansion of surveillance and monitoring technologies are all being introduced and implemented with high promise. However, technological developments produce risks, questions, and consequences beyond increased efficiency in carrying out tasks. While preventing crime and controlling criminals using new technology are noteworthy goals, there exist equally important concerns about their impact on the civil rights and liberties of individual Americans as they increase the scope of governmental social control. The attendant issues must be examined through systematic study of their pros and cons.

REVIEW OF KEY TERMS

Define each of the following:

DNA analysis

Geographic Information System (GIS)

Kyllo v. United States (2001)

Less-lethal weapons

Electronic file management

CSI effect

SELF-TEST SECTION

KEY TERMS

Fill in the appropriate term for each statement:

1. _____ technology has advanced in the United States from daggers and swords to firearms and then later to multishot pistols that could be concealed.

2. New devices designed specifically to protect property or to assist police officers will generate _____ behavior by would-be lawbreakers.

3. In 2001, the state of _____ declared that execution by electric chair mposed unconstitutional "cruel and unusual punishment" on condemned offenders.

4. _____ use computers to steal information, resources, or funds. These thefts can be aimed at simply stealing money or they can involve the theft of companies' trade secrets, chemical formulas, and other valuable information.

5. As evidenced by the fact that some laws in the United States intended to punish people involved in online pornography have been struck down for violating First Amendement rights, differences in _____ principles and _____ values impact our ability to pursue cybercrime.

6. Traditional counterfeiting involves the creation of _____ that can be used for illegal profit.

7. Counterfeit goods are also known as _____ products.

8. The proliferation of Internet pharmacies has led to a growth in counterfeit _____ available without a legal prescription.

9. _____ is a technique that identifies people through their distinctive gene patterns (also called genotypic features).

10. Through computers inside _____, officers can also gain quick access to information about automobile license plates and pending warrants.

11. Through the use of _____ technology and software, law enforcement can analyze the locations and frequencies of specific crimes, such as burglary, or the nature of calls for service in various neighborhoods, and thereby deploy their personnel effectively and plan targeted crime-prevention programs.

12. _____ are the patterned residue of natural skin secretions or contaminating materials such as ink, blood, or dirt that were present on the fingertips at the time of their contact with the objects.

13. Scandals involving ethics and the _____ of DNA scientists and technicians confound the proper use of DNA testing in solving cases.

14. American cities increasingly use _____ cameras at intersections to monitor and ticket people who run red lights or exceed speed limits.

15. Critics complain that constant surveillance by the government intrudes on the _____ of innocent, unsuspecting citizens and that there is insufficient evidence that this surveillance leads to reduced crime rates.

16. _____ may detect faint blushing in the faces of suspects who answer untruthfully when questioned by law enforcement.

17. Nightsticks, pepper spray, beanbags, and rubber bullets are examples of _____ weapons, which can be used to incapacitate or control people without causing serious injuries or deaths.

18. The _____ is a weapon with prongs that sends an incapacitating electric jolt of 50,000 volts into people on contact.

19. Many courts have moved toward _____ systems in which records are digitized and made available as computer files.

20. Many jurors violate court rules when they use the _____ to research a case on which they are currently sitting.

21. _____ databases permit crime victims to keep track of when specific offenders gain release on parole and help employers to do background checks on job applicants.

FILL-IN-THE-BLANK EXERCISE

1. _____ are those who use computers and the Internet to commit law violations against people, property, public order, or morality. These include, but are not limited to piracy, identity theft, the creation of worms and viruses, and the creation and dissemination of child pornography. **2.** _____, which involves the creation of fake currency that can be used for illegal profit, is also a growing problem due to advances in copying and printing technologies. To be sure, this problem is not solely restricted to currency, and can involve DVDs, designer clothing and handbags, and even medication.

Technology increasingly used by law enforcement include **3.** _____ hardware and software, which allows for the identification of hot spots and crime trends. In addition, **4.** _____ that store data on fingerprints and DNA evidence are being employed frequently by criminal justice officials to process and analyze immense amounts of information in an efficient manner.

Some are concerned that expansion in some of these areas, can infringe the **5.** _____ of innocent citizens. Innovative methods of surveillance may also limit personal liberties and freedoms, as increasing numbers of citizens are monitored daily as they walk, drive, and generally move around public areas.

As weapons technology becomes increasingly sophisticated, police departments must alter their existing policies (or add new ones) regarding the appropriate use of **6.** _____ weapons. Courthouses are developing **7.** _____ courtrooms, implementing presentation technologies such as projection screens or multiple monitors that permit jurors to study evidence in a more detailed manner. Corrections personnel are focused on **8.** _____ as their top priority, and use technology resources to enhance their ability to surveil and control offenders.

MULTIPLE CHOICE

14.1.   According to James Byrne, advances in technology have resulted in new:
a) opportunities for crime
b) forms of criminality
c) techniques for committing crime
d) categories of offenders and victims
e) all of the above

14.2.   Most states have moved away from the use of the electric chair as the primary method of execution, and towards _____
a) firing squad
b) hanging
c) gas chamber
d) lethal injection
e) none of the above

14.3.   Cyber criminals use _____ to steal information, resources, or funds.
a) cars
b) robbery
c) computers
d) individuals
e) social skills

14.4.   _____ is a relatively new phenomenon among youth involving the misuse of computers and cell phones to harass others, and suggestions are being made to criminalize the act.
a) identity theft
b) virus writing
c) hacking
d) phishing
e) cyber bullying

14.5.   Perpetrators of _____ use other people's credit card numbers and social security numbers to secure fraudulent loans and steal money and merchandise.
a) identity theft
b) counterfeiting
c) child pornography
d) embezzlement
e) piracy

14.6. Counterfeiting not only constitutes theft by permitting criminals to exchange fake bills for actual products and services; it also harms our _____ by placing into circulation bills that have no monetary value.
a) society
b) moral fabric
c) criminal justice system
d) economy
e) political system

14.7. DNA analysis identifies people through their distinctive _____.
a) personality makeup
b) bone structure
c) blood type
d) fingerprints
e) gene patterns

14.8. Using in-vehicle computers, police officers potentially can have access to:
a) mug shots
b) driving records
c) criminal histories
d) fingerprints
e) all of the above

14.9. Police use databases to store and process data on:
a) fingerprints
b) DNA samples
c) ballistics
d) arrest recorde
e) all of the above

14.10. Surveillance cameras and recognition technology are being used to identify:
a) traffic law violators
b) suspicious activity
c) perpetrators of crimes
d) police brutality
e) all of the above

14.11. An example of a less-lethal weapon would include:
a) firearm
b) knife
c) pepper spray
d) none of the above
e) all of the above

14.12. May courthouses are seeking to reduce their dependency on paperwork and hard-copy case files through the use of _____.
a) electronic file management
b) the Internet
c) cell phone technology
d) GIS systems
e) surveillance cameras

14.13. The "_____" is a widely discussed but unproved belief that television dramas revolving around forensic science raise jurors' expectations about the use of scientific evidence in criminal cases and thereby reduce the likelihood of "guilty" verdicts in trials that rely solely on witness testimony and other forms of nonscientific evidence.
a) Hawthorne effect
b) placebo effect
c) CSI effect
d) DNA effect
e) media effect

14.14. In correctional institutions, technology enhances safety and security through the use of:
a) electronically controlled cell doors and locks
b) motion sensors
c) surveillance cameras
d) small radios attached to correctional officers
e) all of the above

TRUE/FALSE

14.1. _____ Technological developments always help criminal justice officials.

14.2. _____ Accurate counts are readily available on how many cyber crimes occur and how much money is lost through identity theft, auction fraud, investment fraud, and other forms of financial computer crime.

14.3. _____ Counterfeiting is a criminal act involving only currency, and no other products or goods.

14.4. _____ The counterfeiting of currency is largely due to the advancement and availability of copying and printing technologies.

14.5. _____ Fingerprint evidence processes have been scientifically verified, and are a much better method of identifying perpetrators of crimes than DNA evidence.

14.6. _____ Among state law enforcement departments with more than 100 sworn officers, over half use in-vehicle computers.

14.7. _____ GIS technology allows police departments to deploy resources efficiently, based on the identification of crime patterns and trends.

14.8. _____ Surveillance cameras can be useful in protecting civil rights of citizens and holding police accountable for their actions.

14.9. _____ Tasers are a popularly-assigned, though controversial, form of less-lethal technology.

14.10. _____ Computer software has been developed to make the sentencing decisions of judges easier.

14.11. _____ Problems arise when judges investigate the facts of a case on their own, which leads to mistrials and a waste of prosecutorial and defense team resources.

14.12. _____ OTIS (Offender Tracking Information Systems) databases permit crime victims to keep track of when specific offenders gain release on parole, and can also help employers to do background checks on job applicants.

14.13. _____ Recently, local jails have been saving money by charging fees to nonviolent offenders who choose to pay for electronic monitoring and home confinement, rather than imposing expenses on the county for food and supervision by serving their misdemeanor sentences in jail.

ANSWER KEY

Key Terms
1. Weapons [p. 399, LO1]
2. Adaptive System [p. 399, LO1]
3. Georgia [p. 401, LO1]
4. Cybercriminals [p. 402, LO2]
5. Legal, social [p. 404, LO3]
6. Fake currency [p. 404, LO3]
7. Pirated [p. 405, LO3]
8. Medication [p. 407, LO3]
9. DNA analysis [p. 407, LO4]
10. Patrol cars [p. 409, LO3]
11. GIS [p. 410, LO3]
12. Latent fingerprints [p. 412, LO3]
13. Competence [p. 415 , LO3]
14. Surveillance [p. 417, LO3]
15. Privacy [p. 418, LO3]
16. Thermal-imaging cameras [p. 420, LO4]
17. Less-lethal [p. 421, LO4]
18. Taser [p. 422, LO4]
19. Electronic file management [p. 423, LO5]
20. Internet [p. 425, LO3]
21. OTIS [p. 427, LO5]

Multiple Choice
14.1. E [p. 400, LO1]
14.2. D [p. 401, LO1]
14.3. C [p. 402, LO2]
14.4. E [p. 402, LO2]
14.5. A [p. 402, LO2]
14.6. D [p. 404, LO2]
14.7. E [p. 407, LO4]
14.8. E [p. 409, LO3]
14.9. E [p. 411-413, LO3]
14.10. E [p. 417-418, LO3]
14.11. C [p. 422, LO4]
14.12. A [p. 423, LO5]
14.13. C [p. 426, LO4]
14.14. E [p. 427, LO5]

True/False
14.1. F [p. 399, LO1]
14.2. F [p. 403, LO2]
14.3. F [p. 404, LO2]
14.4. T [p. 405, LO2]
14.5. F [p. 408, LO4]
14.6. T [p. 409, LO3]
14.7. T [p. 411, LO3]
14.8. T [p. 418, LO3]
14.9. T [p. 422, LO4]
14.10 T [p. 423, LO5]
14.11. F [p. 425, LO5]
14.12. T [p. 427, LO5]
14.13. T [p. 428, LO5]

Fill-in-the-Blank
1. Cybercrime [p. 402, LO2]
2. Counterfeiting [p. 405, LO2]
3. GIS [p. 410, LO3]
4. Databases [p. 411, LO3]
5. Civil liberties [p. 418, LO1]
6. Less-lethal [p. 421, LO4]
7. Electronic [p. 423, LO5]
8. Security [p. 427, LO5]

WORKSHEET 14.1: CREATING A DNA DATABASE

There is a great amount of debate over who should have to provide DNA samples for inclusion in databases such as CODIS. These databases can be used when crimes have been committed to identify offenders quickly and speed the investigation process. In your opinion, which of the following groups do you think should be required to provide DNA samples for inclusion in CODIS? For each group, explain why you think (or don't think) these people should have to provide DNA samples.

An offender convicted of murder and sexual assault: _____

_____

_____

_____

An offender convicted of illegally trading stocks: _____

_____

_____

_____

The family of a man suspected of killing his wife: _____

_____

_____

_____

A police officer brought up on charges of police brutality: _____

_____

_____

_____

Someone apply for a federal job: _____

_____

_____

WORKSHEET 14.2: ETHICS IN THE COLLECTION OF DNA EVIDENCE

In a case from Buffalo, New York in 2007, police officers secretly following a suspect collected saliva from the sidewalk after he had spit on the ground. This was then compared with DNA evidence from the scene of an old murder law enforcement believed the suspect had committed. The suspect was then charged with rape and murder in one of Buffalo's oldest unsolved cases.

Investigate whether this action is legally appropriate, and discuss why or why not. Also determine if law enforcement and proescutors should be bound by ethical considerations in their actions, and whether this specific action crosses a line.

WORKSHEET 14.3: TECHNOLOGY AND WARRANTLESS SEARCHES

Sophisticated technologies allow law enforcement to search more thoroughly than in the past. Some are concerned that there are search technologies that violate citizen's right to privacy and perhaps even violate the presumption of innocence. For each type of technology below, explain whether you agree or disagree with the use of the technology and why you feel that way.

1. Using metal detectors at high schools to find students carrying weapons to school.

_____

_____

_____

_____

2. Using helicopters with thermal cameras to look for homes in which illegal drugs are manufactured.

_____

_____

_____

_____

3. Using backscatter x-ray devices at airports, in which travelers appear to be naked on the officer's screen.

_____

_____

_____

_____

4. Using computers to scan library records to search for people who check out books related to terrorist activities.

_____

_____

_____

_____

WORKSHEET 14.4: PRIVACY MOVIE ANALYSIS

Choose a film with a strong surveillance theme. Generally, the director will not highlight the privacy implications. Write an essay, beginning with your definition of privacy, that makes explicit the privacy implications of the story and identifies the surveillance paradigm of the director. Movies must be available on rental video. Relevant films include, but are not limited to:

- 1984 (Director, Michael Radford)
- Attica (Director, Cinda Firestone)
- Brazil (Director, Terry Gilliam)
- Enemy of the State (Director, Tony Scott)
- Family Viewing (Director, Atom Egoyen)
- Fortress (Director, Stuart Gordon)
- Listen (Director, Gavin Wilding)
- Lost Highway (Director, David Lynch)
- Minority Report (Director, Steven Spielberg)
- Panic Room (Director, David Fincher)
- Sliver (Director, Phillip Noyce)
- Snake Eyes (Director, Brian DePalma)
- Surveillance (Director, Jennifer Chambers Lynch)
- The Conversation (Director, Francis Ford Coppola)
- The End of Violence (Director, Wim Wenders)
- The Net (Director, Irwin Winkler)
- The Truman Show (Director, Peter Weir)
- THX1138 (Director, George Lucas)
- Until the End of the World (Director, Wim Wenders)

Write a two-page paper on the privacy implications that may or may not be presented overtly and covertly in the film. Usually, there are many potential and actual breaches of personal privacy, civil liberties, and other freedoms that we currently take for granted. Explain whether you think the benefits of security and surveillance outweigh the expectation or need for privacy, or if you think that personal privacy must be preserved at all costs.

JUVENILE JUSTICE

OUTLINE

- Youth Crime in the United States
- The Development of Juvenile Justice
- The Juvenile Justice System
- The Juvenile Justice Process
- Problems and Perspectives

CHAPTER 15
JUVENILE JUSTICE

LEARNING OBJECTIVES

After reading the material in this chapter, students should understand:

1. Recognize the extent of youth crime in the United States

2. Understand how the juvenile justice system developed and the assumptions on which it was based

3. Identify what determines the jurisdiction of the juvenile justice system

4. Understand how does the juvenile justice system operates

5. Analyze some of the problems facing the American system of juvenile justice

CHAPTER SUMMARY

This chapter explores the extent and nature of juvenile crime in the United States by providing a variety of statistics regarding juvenile crime. It also traces the history of the juvenile justice system from the colonial era to the modern era by dividing it into five distinct periods 1) the Puritan period, 2) the Reform period, 3) the Juvenile Court period, 4) the Juvenile Rights period and 5) the Crime Control period. The development of juvenile courts in the United States is examined, as are the specific rulings by the U. S. Supreme Court that established constitutional protections for juveniles in the 1960s, as well as the movement to get tough on juveniles that has developed since the 1980s. Finally, the problems that the juvenile justice system faces today are presented alongside coverage of continuing controversies, such as whether juveniles, under specific circumstances, should be tried as adults.

CHAPTER OUTLINE

I. YOUTH CRIME IN THE UNITED STATES

Youth crime in the U.S. peaked between the mid-1980s and early 1990s. Possible reasons for this increase include a large birth cohort that led to a larger population of crime-prone young men, as well as the increased prevalence of crack cocaine and the rise of youth gangs.

II. THE DEVELOPMENT OF JUVENILE JUSTICE

Like the trends in punishment of adult offenders, juvenile justice trends have swung from rehabilitation to punitiveness. The doctrine of *parens patriae* (the state as parent) has evolved to provide the theoretical foundation for dealing with juvenile offenders in the United States. The history of juvenile justice in the United States can be divided into five major historical periods.

A. The Puritan Period (1646-1824)

In general, society relied on the family unit to discipline youths who committed crime. If the family was unable or unwilling to do, the state stepped in. Puritans viewed delinquent children as evil, often comparing their rebellion against family or social authority to that of Satan against God.

B. The Refuge Period (1824-1899)

In this period of increasing governmental responsibility, the state assumed that parents were unable to discipline their children. Institutions, designed to function as both prisons and schools, were created for children who committed crime.

C. The Juvenile Court Period (1900-1959)

The "child savers" sough to save children from a life of crime. They believed children could be reformed, and promoted a separate juvenile court system founded on the idea of *parens patriae*. This early juvenile court forms the basis of the modern juvenile courts, in which records are kept sealed and children are protected. In addition, the terminology for offenders was changed from "criminal" to "delinquent" to imply that children could be rehabilitated more easily than adults.

D. The Juvenile Rights Period (1960-1979)

The early juvenile justice system was very powerful, and juveniles were not always accorded the same rights as adults. At the same time the rights guaranteed to adult offenders were being affirmed and expanded, the United States Supreme Court made several similar rulings with regards to juvenile offenders.

In *In re Gault* (1967), the Court decided that juveniles were entitled to due process rights, including procedural rights, including notice of charges, right to counsel, right to confront and cross-examine witnesses, and privilege against compelled self-incrimination.

In the case of *In re Winship* (1970) the Court held that proof must be established "beyond a reasonable doubt" before a juvenile may be classified as a delinquent for committing an act that would be a crime if it were committed by an adult.

The Supreme Court held in *McKeiver v. Pennsylvania* (1971) that juveniles do not have a constitutional right to trial by jury.

In *Breed v. Jones* (1975) the Court extended the protection against double jeopardy to juveniles by requiring that before a case is adjudicated in juvenile court, a hearing must be held to determine if it should be transferred to the adult court.

In 1974, Congress passed the Juvenile Justice and Delinquency Prevention Act, which included provisions for the deinstitutionalization of status offenders (truants, runaways, etc.).

E. The Crime Control Period (1980-Present)
The more recent punitive stance seen in the criminal justice system in general has spread to the juvenile court. Decisions such as *Schall v. Martin* (1984) determined that juveniles could be held in detention prior to trial if they threaten the safety of the community. This punitive philosophy has also resulted in more juveniles being tried as adults.

III. THE JUVENILE JUSTICE SYSTEM

A. Age of Clients
The upper age limit for a juvenile varies from sixteen to eighteen. In 49 states, judges have the ability to transfer some juveniles to adult court.

B. Categories of Cases Under Juvenile Court Jurisdiction
Four types of cases enter the juvenile justice system: delinquent children, Persons in Need of Supervision (PINS), neglected children, and dependent children. Most cases referred to juvenile court are delinquency cases.

IV. THE JUVENILE JUSTICE PROCESS

The prevention of delinquency is the system's justification for intervening in the lives of juveniles who are involved in either status or criminal offenses. It is still assumed that the juvenile proceedings are to be conducted in a non-adversarial environment, and that the court should be a place where the judge, social workers, clinicians, and probation officers work together to diagnose the child's problem and select a rehabilitative program to attack this problem.

A. Police Interface
Many police departments have special units to deal with youthful offenders. Most complaints against juveniles are brought by the police, although parents, school officials and others can refer juveniles to the juvenile court. Police officers have a lot of discretion when deciding how to handle juvenile offenders.

B. Intake Screening at the Court
Rather than arrest, juveniles are referred to juvenile court through the filing of a petition (intake). About half of all cases are disposed of at this stage through diversion.

C. Pretrial Procedures
For cases in which a formal hearing is warranted, a detention hearing may be held if the court wishes to detail the juvenile prior to trial. Almost 20% of all cases referred to formal hearing involve detention of the accused.

D. <u>Transfer to Adult Court</u>

In serious cases, judges may choose to waive juveniles to adult court. Some juvenile courts are not allowed by law to hear cases involving murder, rape, and armed robbery— these cases must be tried in adult court. One result of the increased use of waiver is that juveniles are being sent to adult prisons more frequently.

E. <u>Adjudication</u>

Adjudication is the equivalent of the trial stage in juvenile court proceedings. The Supreme Court has extended constitutional rights to juveniles at this stage, but the rights of the accused are not always respected in juvenile court. Adjudication is a closed process, so as to protect the privacy of the accused.

F. <u>Disposition</u>

If a juvenile is found delinquent, the juvenile receives a disposition (punishment). Most offenders are found delinquent at adjudication, since the less serious cases are typically filtered out early in the process. While the preferred method of sentencing is usually indeterminate sentencing, the trend toward punitiveness in corrections has called for more stringent sentencing practices.

G. <u>Corrections</u>

The different perspective of the juvenile court results in differences in the correctional models of the adult and juvenile systems. One goal of the juvenile justice system is avoid unnecessary incarceration, as many believe this will harm juveniles more than it will help them. Noninstitutional programs can help with rehabilitation as well as keep them in the family unit.

1. **Probation**: The most common method of handling juvenile offenders is to place them on probation. Juvenile probation has been more satisfactorily funded than adult probation, and hence officers have much smaller caseloads. Because juvenile offenders have a higher rehabilitation rate than their adult counterparts, a career in juvenile probation can be more enjoyable than on in adult probation.

2. **Intermediate Sanctions**: As with the adult system, intermediate sanctions are sometimes used for juveniles. These programs are meant to keep juveniles from incarceration, which might increase their delinquent behavior.

3. **Custodial Care**: Facilities to hold juvenile offenders can be categorized as secure or nonsecure. Most secure facilities are small, and managing these facilities can be quite challenging. As with the adult system, African American youth are over-represented in secure facilities.

4. **Institutional Programs**: The emphasis on rehabilitation present in the juvenile court has resulted in a number of programs for juveniles, focused on counseling, education, vocational training, and some psychological counseling programs.

5. **Aftercare**: This is similar to adult parole, in which juveniles are monitored and provided assistance with their transition back into non-custodial care.

6. **Community Treatment**: Treatment in community-based facilities has greatly expanded during the past decade. Foster homes developed as a means for implementing a policy of limited intervention into juvenile lives, hoping to keep a child with a family if his or her own family is not available or a negative influence on the child. Group homes are also used to place juvenile offenders.

V. PROBLEMS AND PERSPECTIVES

The juvenile court is an extremely complex organization, with a variety of goals. It must deal with both criminal youth and neglected youth, and strike a balance between treatment and punishment—much more so than in the adult court. The push toward more punitive treatment of adult offenders has also been reflected in the juvenile court, and it is unclear how this will affect juvenile offenders.

REVIEW OF KEY TERMS

Define each of the following:

aftercare

delinquent

dependent child

detention hearing

diversion

neglected child

parens patriae

PINS

status offense

waive

Breed v. Jones (1975)

In re Gault (1967)

In re Winship (1970)

McKeiver v. Pennsylvania (1971)

Schall v. Martin (1984)

SELF-TEST SECTION

Fill in the appropriate term for each statement:

1. In the case of _____, the Supreme Court decided that juveniles have the right to counsel, to confront their accusers and have adequate notice of charges.

2. _____ is a term used to refer to juveniles who have not committed a crime, but are in need of attention for some reason.

3. The juvenile equivalent of parole is called _____.

4. Juveniles can be held in detention prior to trial, according to the findings in the case of _____.

5. _____ is the concept of the state as the guardian and protector of juveniles and other citizens who cannot protect themselves.

6. A _____ is a child who has committed a criminal or status offense.

7. _____ is the process of discretionary decisions that move children away from the system's most punitive consequences.

8. The standard of proof required in juvenile proceedings (beyond a reasonable doubt) was specified in _____.

9. Juveniles cannot be transferred directly to adult court without a hearing, according to _____.

10. _____ is any act committed by a juvenile that would not be a crime if it were committed by an adult but that is considered unacceptable for a juvenile.

11. Prior to being held awaiting trial, juveniles must have a _____.

12. In the case of _____, the Court found that juveniles do not have the right to trial by jury.

13. Judges sometimes choose to _____ juveniles to the adult court system.

14. A _____ is a child whose parents are unable to give proper care.

15. A _____ is a child who is not receiving proper care because of parental inaction.

FILL-IN-THE-BLANK EXERCISE

Unlike the **1.** _____, who sought to develop rehabilitation for juveniles during the
Progressive era, contemporary critics of juvenile justice who believe that sentences are not tough
enough have ushered in a new era, the **2.** _____, which represents a change
from the preceding era, the **3.** _____, in which the focus was on judicial
decisions, such as the fundamental due process case of **4.** _____, to
provide constitutional protections for children who had broken the law.

When a child is declared to be **5.** _____, he or she may be sent to a residential setting
with other juveniles, such as a community-based **6.** _____, which is among the
treatment settings left after the **7.** _____ movement affected how the government
places and treats various troubled populations.

MULTIPLE CHOICE

15.1. The standard of proof used in a juvenile court is:
   a) Reasonable suspicion
   b) Probable cause
   c) Preponderance of the evidence
   d) Clear and convincing evidence
   e) Proof beyond a reasonable doubt

15.2. Which of the following is applicable to juveniles but not to adults?
   a) right to counsel
   b) right against unreasonable searches and seizures
   c) privilege against self-incrimination
   d) right to treatment
   e) none of the above are applicable to adults

15.3. What is one possible explanation for the "epidemic" of juvenile crime in the mid-1980's in the United States?
   a) The increased use of marijuana in public schools
   b) Children living in single-parent homes
   c) Increasing numbers of immigrants in the U.S.
   d) The drug trade
   e) Lack of adequate education

15.4. According to the following chart, what is the most common offense for which juveniles are arrested in the United States?

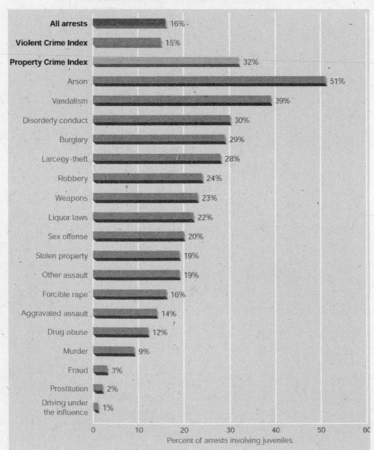

   a) vandalism
   b) arson
   c) burglary
   d) sex offenses
   e) fraud

15.5. Operation Cease Fire is a program in Boston, Massachusetts designed to:
a) Reduce drug use among juveniles
b) Enforce mandatory curfews
c) Fight truancy
d) Avoid status offenses
e) Reduce street gang gun violence

15.6. The juvenile court is guided by the concept of:
a) *parens patriae*
b) *mens rea*
c) *actus rea*
d) *voir dire*
e) *persona non grata*

15.7. During the Puritan period, the overriding belief of delinquent children was that:
a) Children could be reformed
b) Children should be left to their parents for discipline without interference of the law
c) Children were evil
d) Repeat offenders were the biggest problem
e) Immigration caused delinquency among youth

15.8. In what case did the Court declare that juveniles have the right to counsel, to confront and examine accusers, and to have adequate notice of charges when there is the possibility of confinement as a punishment?
a) *Fare v. Michael C.* (1979)
b) *McKeiver v. Pennsylvania* (1971)
c) *Schall v. Martin* (1984)
d) *In re Gault* (1967)
e) *Breed v. Jones* (1975)

15.9. Which of the following is NOT applicable to juveniles in most states?
a) right to counsel
b) right to treatment
c) right to a trial by jury
d) right against unreasonable searches and seizures
e) privilege against self-incrimination

15.10. What legislation was the earliest attempt by a colony to deal with problem children?
a) Georgia Juvenile Delinquent Act
b) Massachusetts Stubborn Child Law
c) New York Troubled Child Act
d) Illinois Juvenile Court Act
e) Virginia Child Protection Act

15.11. Which of the following best describes the House of Refuge?
a) One-half prison and one-half nursing home
b) One-half school and one-house nursing home
c) One-half prison and one-half school
d) School
e) Prison

15.12. Which of the following acts included provisions for taking status offenders out of corrections institutions?
a) Juvenile and Status Act
b) Massachusetts Stubborn Child Law
c) Delaware Troubled Child Act
d) Illinois Juvenile Court Act
e) Juvenile Justice and Delinquency Prevention Act

15.13. The Refuge Period focused its attention on:
a) evil children
b) immigrant children
c) reformism
d) serious crime by repeat offenders
e) juvenile rights

15.14. The "child savers" were influenced by:
a) A belief that deviance could be treated
b) Immigration policy
c) The Enlightenment
d) World War II
e) The Vietnam Era

15.15. Which state created the first juvenile court in America?
a) Illinois
b) Michigan
c) New Jersey
d) Ohio
e) Massachusetts

15.16. In most states, the upper age limit for jurisdiction of the juvenile court is:
a) 15
b) 16
c) 17
d) 18
e) 19

15.17. What is the difference between a neglected and a dependent child?
   a) A neglected child has committed a crime; a dependent child has no parent or guardian
   b) A neglected child has no parent or guardian; a dependent child is receiving inadequate care from his/her parents
   c) A neglected child is receiving inadequate care from his/her parents; a dependent child is also delinquent
   d) A neglected child is receiving inadequate care from his/her parents; a dependent child has no parent or guardian
   e) A neglected child is a PIN; a dependent child is not.

15.18. What does the acronym PINS stand for?
   a) A person in need of supplies
   b) A person in need of supervision
   c) A prostitute in need of services
   d) A person in suspended animation
   e) A penalty in *nolo suspendere*

15.19. Which of the following is a status offense?
   a) Vandalism
   b) Shoplifting
   c) Running away
   d) Forgery
   e) Assault

15.20. The juvenile court is designed to be:
   a) Nonadversarial
   b) Punitive
   c) Economic
   d) Adversarial
   e) Triangular

15.21. This Supreme Court case determined that juveniles do not have the right to trial by jury:
   a) *In re Winship*
   b) *In re Gault*
   c) *Breed v. Jones*
   d) *McKeiver v. Pennsylvania*
   e) *Eddings v. Oklahoma*

15.22. Which term in the juvenile court is the adult court equivalent of "trial"?
   a) Diversion
   b) Detention
   c) Waiver
   d) Adjudication
   e) Disposition

15.23. Which sentences is most often used for convicted juvenile offenders?
a) Probation and release to parent
b) Intermediate Sanctions
c) Custodial care
d) Community Treatment
e) House of Refuge

15.24. What is the sentencing philosophy most often used in teen courts?
a) Punitiveness
b) Deterrence
c) Restorative justice
d) Addiction treatment
e) Just deserts

15.25. The juvenile equivalent of parole is:
a) Probation
b) Discretion
c) Diversion
d) Referral
e) Aftercare

TRUE/FALSE

15.1. _____ Youth gangs are a dangerous presence in most American cities.

15.2. _____ In *Schall v. Martin*, the Supreme Court ruled that juvenile suspects cannot be subjected to preventive detention.

15.3. _____ It is legal in some states to waive juveniles to adult court as young as 10 years old.

15.4. _____ Most juveniles taken into police custody handle the cases in the department and release the juvenile soon after.

15.5. _____ The concept of *parens patriae* refers to the juvenile court acting as parent to delinquent children.

15.6. _____ Even with reforms made during the Refuge Period, juveniles could still be arrested, tried, and imprisoned.

15.7. _____ Juveniles were given the right to an attorney during the Juvenile Court period.

15.8. _____ As of 2005, offenders cannot be executed for crimes they committed as juveniles.

15.9. _____ The "Child savers" were lower-class reformers who fought to "save" children from the state.

15.10. _____ A juvenile under the age of fifteen is harshly punished for a crime in Norway.

15.11. _____ The terminology used in the juvenile justice system reflected the underlying belief that these children could be "cured" and returned to society as law-abiding citizens.

15.12. _____ The U. S. Supreme Court began to afford constitutional protections to juveniles in the 1960s.

15.13. _____ Delinquent children have committed acts that would be considered crimes if committed by adults.

15.14. _____ Murder is a status offense for a juvenile.

15.15. _____ While the public currently takes a punitive stance toward adult offenders, this philosophy has not been reflected in the juvenile court.

15.16. _____ One predominant goal of juvenile corrections is to avoid unnecessary incarceration.

ANSWER KEY

Key Terms

6. *In re Gault* [p. 440, LO2]
7. PINS [p. 445, LO3]
8. aftercare [p. 457, LO4]
9. *Schall v. Martin* [p. 441, LO2]
10. *parens patriae* [p. 437, LO2]
11. delinquent [p. 445, LO1]
12. diversion [p. 448, LO2]
    In re Winship [p. 440, LO2]
    Breed v. Jones [p. 440, LO2]
15. status offense [p. 440, LO2]
16. detention hearing [p. 449, LO4]
17. *McKeiver v. Pennsylvania* [p. 440, LO2]
18. waive [p. 442, LO3]
19. dependent child [p. 446, LO3]
20. neglected child [p. 446, LO3]

Fill-in-the-Blank

1. "child saver" [p. 439, LO2]
2. Crime Control Period [p. 441,442, LO2]
3. Juvenile Rights priod [p. 442,443, LO2]
4. In re Gault [p. 440, LO2]
5. delinquent [p. 445, LO3]
6. group home [p. 457, LO4]
7. deinstitutionalization [p. 475, LO5]

Multiple Choice

15.1. E [p. 440, LO2]
15.2. D [p. 452, LO2]
15.3. D [p. 456,457, LO1]
15.4. B [p. 435, LO1]
15.5. D [p. 436, LO4]
15.6. A [p. 437, LO2]
15.7. C [p. 437, LO2]
15.8. D [p. 440, LO2]
15.9. C [p. 452, LO4]
15.10. B [p. 437,438 LO2]
15.11. C [p. 438, LO2]
15.12. E [p. 438, LO2]
15.13. B [p. 438, LO2]
15.14. A [p. 439, LO2]
15.15. A [p. 439, LO2]
15.16. D [p. 444, LO3]
15.17. D [p. 446, LO3]
15.18. B [p. 445, LO3]
15.19. C [p. 440, LO1]
15.20. A [p. 446, LO2]
15.21. D [p. 440, LO4]
15.22. D [p. 451, LO4]
15.23. A [p. 448, 449, LO4]
15.24. C [p. 449, LO2]
15.25. E [p. 457, LO4]

True/False

15.1. T [p. 453, LO1]
15.2. F [p. 441, LO2]
15.3. T [p. 442, LO3]
15.4. F [p. 452, LO4]
15.5. T [p. 437, LO2]
15.6. T [p. 438,439, LO2]
15.7. F [p. 439,440, LO2]
15.8. T [p. 442, LO2]
15.9. F [p. 439, LO2]
15.10. F [p. 444, LO2]
15.11. T [p. 440, LO2]
15.12. T [p. 440,441, LO2]
15.13. T [p. 445, LO2]
15.14. F [p. 440, LO4]
15.15. F [p.443, LO2]
15.16. T [p. 453, LO2]

WORKSHEET 15.1: THE HISTORY OF JUVENILE JUSTICE

For each era listed below, assume the role of the listed official. Describe how much discretionary authority you have to determine which children will be drawn into the system and what will be done with them. Briefly describe what you would decide to do with such children during that era.

THE REFUGE PERIOD (1824-1889). Police officer: _____

_____

_____

_____

_____

_____

_____

_____

_____

THE JUVENILE COURT PERIOD (1899-1960). Juvenile court judge: _____

_____

_____

_____

_____

_____

_____

_____

_____

_____

JUVENILE RIGHTS PERIOD (1960-19800). Social worker: _____

_____

_____

_____

_____

_____

_____

_____

_____

CRIME CONTROL PERIOD (1980-present). Prosecutor: _____

_____

_____

_____

_____

_____

_____

_____

_____

_____

WORKSHEET 15.2: TREATMENT OF DELINQUENTS

Assume each of the following occupational roles. In each role, formulate a recommendation for what should happen to a fourteen-year-old boy whose seventeen-year-old companion killed a man while the two of them attempted to steal a bicycle. Justify your reasons in each case.

Social worker: _____

_____

_____

_____

_____

State legislator: _____

_____

_____

_____

_____

Director of group home for delinquents: _____

_____

_____

_____

_____

Juvenile court judge: _____

_____

_____

_____

_____

WORKSHEET 15.3: THE TRANSFER OF JUVENILES TO ADULT COURT

The transfer of juveniles into adult courts has become a controversial issue. Imagine that you are a legislator who must design a law to determine which juveniles may be eligible for transfer. How would you address the following issues? Explain each response.

The age of eligibility for transfer to adult court.

_____

_____

_____

_____

_____

_____

The kind of crimes for which offenders are eligible for transfer to adult court.

_____

_____

_____

_____

_____

_____

The process used to determine which juveniles will be transferred.

_____

_____

_____

_____

_____

_____